A SEARCH FOR THE
HISTORICAL JESUS

Other Works by the Author

Buddhist Kashmir (1973)
British Policy (1976)
Ladahk Moonland (1975)
Hindu Kashmir (1977)
History of Ladakh (1970)
Gilgit (1978)
Heritage of Kashmir (1980)
Kashmir Misgovernment (1980)
The Abode of Shiva (1987)
Freedom Struggle in Kashmir (1988)
The Fifth Gospel (1988) with Dahan Levi

A Search for the Historical Jesus

Professor
FIDA M. HASSNAIN

Gateway Books, Bath

First published in 1994 by
GATEWAY BOOKS
The Hollies, Wellow,
Bath BA2 8QJ, U.K.
Copyright © Fida M. Hassnain 1994

Distributed in the U.S.A. by
ATRIUM PUBLISHERS GROUP
11270 Clayton Creek Road,
Lower Lake, CA95457

Cover picture: "Remember" by Nicholas Roerich
(courtesy Nicholas Roerich Museum, New York)

Cover design by Studio B
Maps by Palden Jenkins
Text set in Bembo $10^1/_2$ on $12^1/_2$ by
MetraDisc of Castleton, Rochdale
Printed and bound by
Redwood Books of Trowbridge
Colour section printed by
Star Print of Ramsey

British Library Cataloguing-in Publication Data:
A catalogue record for this book is
available from the British Library

ISBN 0 946551 99 5

Contents

Introduction

The quest for the historical Jesus Christ is a very important one, not just for Christians. I am one of those who have joined this quest. My interest in the life of Jesus Christ was aroused by chance, under rather unusual circumstances.

As Director of Archives in Jammu and Kashmir State, I was ordered, in the 1960s, to proceed to Leh, the capital of the former kingdom of Ladakh, to examine historical records and maps relevant to the border dispute between China and India. I had visited Ladakh earlier, and had established the first State Archive Repository there. But my new assignment led me to make many more journeys to the region, and during one such visit I came by chance upon a document relating to Jesus Christ. This was the event which aroused my curiosity and led me to embark on a quest for the historical Jesus.

Many in the West might question my credentials, because I happen to live in the East, and I am a Muslim. It is certainly not my intention to undermine the faith of any Christian. But I am able to show, from evidence I have found concerning the 'Lost Years' of Jesus, that in his lifetime he had a mission in virtually *the whole of the known world*, not just in Palestine. His message, according to what I seek to demonstrate in this book, was intended for people of *all* faiths, not just for the three sects of Pharisees, Sadducees and Essenes, who lived in Palestine in his time, nor only for later Christians.

People in the West might find it difficult to acknowledge that Jesus was born, brought up and educated in Asia, and is revered by Islamic and Buddhist people as well as Christians. During the past two thousand years, the Christian Church of the West has monopolised Jesus Christ, and he has become an integral part of the psyche of the people of the West. This, I would suggest, is based on a profound misconception: in my view *he belonged to the whole world*. It seems to me that the reason why our efforts to achieve human reconciliation have failed is that such efforts have been political and secular, and in religious terms doctrinal and sectarian.

There are still wide rifts and misunderstandings in spiritual terms between followers of the great religions.

It was by chance that I was drawn into the quest for the historical Jesus. It is the belief of Muslims such as myself that Jesus is a prophet of God, together with other prophets. Hence, my respect and reverence for him is great. From this viewpoint, the Christian Church has taken it upon itself to hijack Jesus Christ. I am a Sufi, and we see no separation between one person and another. We love God and we respect all His creations regardless of creed, colour or caste. We adhere to a religion of the heart.

I should perhaps give you a little background on my own story. I was born in Srinagar in Kashmir to parents who were schoolteachers. My father belonged to the Shakhi Khokars of Sialkot, who were a branch of the old hill tribe of Kassites. My mother was a direct descendent of Imam Husain, a grandson of Muhammad, the Prophet of Islam. I was trained in the *Holy Quran* by an Imam, came to know the Christian *Bible* and later studied under various Buddhist teachers.

As head of Oriental Research in Kashmir for 20 years, and later as Director of Archives, Archaeology and Museums in Jammu and Kashmir State, I made comparative studies of the major religions. While I am a Sufi or Islamic mystic, in real terms I feel that I have escaped many of the limitations of subscribing to but one faith. In latter years, I have travelled widely in Europe and Asia lecturing on philosophy, history and mysticism – on themes of reconciliation close to my heart.

Unfortunately, followers of religions have become so sectarian. If you are a Catholic, you cannot be a Protestant. Similarly, if you are a Christian you cannot be a Buddhist. For a Sufi every human being is a replica of God. We believe He is not concerned with differences in religion, and to Him the religions of Buddha, of Moses, of Jesus and of Muhammad become one at a higher level.

Western peoples had a new look at Islam during the Gulf War of 1990-91. It came as a surprise to many that 10% of the population of Iraq is Christian. People assume that the Middle East is entirely Islamic. In fact a thousand years ago Muslims constituted a minority, though they did form the ruling castes. At the time of the introduction of Islam, there existed many religious communities, including Jews, Christians, Sabians, Pagans, Zoroastrians and

Magians.

Out of these, Judaism, Christianity and Islam *all* trace their heritage back to Abraham. Islam was seen as the culmination of the monotheistic tradition of these three faiths. There were substantial Jewish and Christian communities in the region, living in harmony with their Islamic rulers. They provided many skilled craftsmen, doctors and merchants.

Early Islam was particularly tolerant of Christianity. The medieval European Crusades to 'liberate the Holy Land', followed by later invasive excesses, brought to an end some of the earlier tolerance of the Muslim rulers. Christianity became the most militant and least tolerant of the modern religions, and the repercussions of some of these actions are being felt 800 years later.

The *Holy Quran* specifically mentions twenty-eight prophets: four are Arab, one Greek, three came from the New Testament of the Bible, and the remainder from the Old Testament; the last was Muhammad. Divine revelation was granted to Moses in the Jewish *Torah*, to David in the *Psalms*, to Jesus in the *Gospels* and to Muhammad in the *Quran*. All of them preached salvation through the recognition that God is One. Muslims are expected to accept and believe all of these scriptures, for they are the Word of God, and, in the Muslim view, they corroborate each other. The last Word of God, the *Holy Quran*, attests to the revelations of the other scriptures, clarifies all previous uncertainties and brings man to perfect Truth.

My research has shown that there are common threads of origin between the great revelations. It is no accident that some of Christ's teaching has something in common with Buddhism. It is my earnest hope that a greater awareness among Christians of the essential common ground of the *People of the Book* (Jews, Christians and Muslims) on the one hand, and of Buddhism on the other may bring about a renaissance of faith throughout humankind. I would wish therefore that this book might be seen as a humble effort towards reconciliation between faiths, which must be found if true harmony is to come to earth.

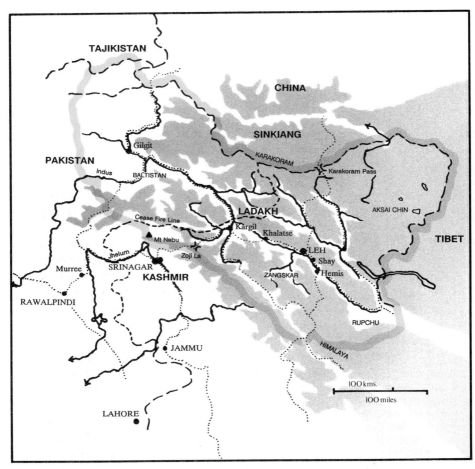

Kashmir and Ladakh – uneasily shared between India, Pakistan and China.
The ancient princely state of Ladakh perches at the edge of the Tibetan
plateau, between the enormous Himalayan and Karakoram ranges

1

Kashmir and the Hebrews

Kashmir

Kashmir is a country which I have found became an abode of Jesus Christ during his last days. Let me tell you about this valley which is known as 'Paradise on Earth'.

The valley of Kashmir is part of the Jammu, Kashmir and Ladakh State in the north of the Indian sub-continent, in the lap of the Himalayas. The state lies in the heart of Asia, surrounded by Pakistan and Afghanistan, the Central Asian Republics of Tadjikistan and Kazakhstan, Western China (Kashgaria, Tibet and Yarkand) and India.

Kashmir is cradled in a high, beautifully fertile valley, blessed with a Mediterranean-like climate. It has been called 'The Garden of Eden'. These qualities and the vibrant energies of the valley have attracted people over thousands of years, and made of it a melting-pot of races.

Surrounded by lofty snow-covered mountains, Kashmir is an enchanting land of forests, fruits, flowers and fields. The main river is now known as the *Jehlum*, while in the past it was called *Beth* or *Veth* or *Vitesta*. Its springs and streams, gushing pure water, are full of fish. It has green forests, flowers, herbs and plants, with countless birds and animals. The whole valley is patched with green rice fields and fruit gardens of apple, plum, cherry and apricot. Jami, the Persian Sufi poet, speaks of Kashmir as the land of wonderful fairies, fit to be called Paradise on Earth. To some it is the Switzerland of the East. The description of the

1

Land of Promise, given in the Old Testament, fits the natural beauty of the valley of Kashmir.

This is where I grew up and was educated and where I now live, although the continued hostilities between Muslims and Hindus over the future of Kashmir have made this very difficult and distressing.

It is important to understand the historical background to this documentation of Jesus in India. This area of north-west India has been the cradle of some of the earliest civilisations. The earliest reference to Kashmir is contained in the *Annals of the Early Han Dynasty* of China, which dates back to 220 AD. We also find Kashmir mentioned in the Greek classics of Ptolemy, Dionysios, Hekatoaios and Herodotos. Further, Kashmir and its people are described in the Arabic works of al Masudi, al Qizwini, al Idrisi and al Beruni.

The Kassites

The etymology of the name *Kashmir* has perplexed scholars, who have given different versions of its origin. Kashmiris call their country *Kasheer* and their language as *Koshur*. It was Babar, the founder of the Mughal dynasty in India, who first pointed out in his memoirs that the etymology of the valley is derived from the *Kash* or *Cush* tribe, also designated as *Kassites*. Cush is mentioned as the grandson of Noah in *Genesis*, whose tribe is known as *Kasshu* in Babylonia, *Cossaei* in Persia, *Kasha* in the Himalayas and *Kush* in Egypt. As the vowels are lacking in ancient works, the designations *Kash, Kush, Kish* and *Kosh* were written in the same way.

But the one thing stands out: wherever this tribe went, it named rivers, mountains and towns after the name of its ancestors. In about 1780 BC, the Kassites established themselves in Babylonia. Prior to this, they had fully established a dynasty in Egypt, which they named as *Kash* in their writings. From Babylonia, they proceeded towards Iran, where they founded the towns of Kashan, and Kashmar (near Nishapur). In central Asia, they founded towns such as Kashmore near Merv, Kash near Bokhara, Kashband and Kashania near Samarkand and the celebrated Kashgar. When they moved into Afghanistan, they founded settlements at Kashil, Kashak and Kashu. While the Hindu-Kush mountains are named after them, they also founded a settlement in the south of these mountains, named Kashmor. The valley of the river Chinab was named by them as Kashtawar and the valley of the river Jehlum as Kasheer, now known as Kashmir[1].

The Dispersion of the Jews

At this point, we need to look at a factor in Kashmiri history which is of central relevance to the main theme of this book. It has been forgotten how wide the Jewish diaspora was in ancient times, into Asia, amongst other places, long before the advent of Jesus. This must be what drew Jesus in his travels to the East.

The Jewish people are a very distinctive people. They have developed an identity as a group, with related physical features, common traditions, language and religion that has lasted longer than any other group in history, and this despite the fact that, more than any other people, they have been persecuted and enslaved. The Jews have been stateless for some 1,900 years, and have become used to developing their skills and wits as guests of other nations.

Their roots go back probably to the third millennium BC, when a tribe from Armenia migrated into Mesopotamia and Palestine and became known as the *Habiru* by the local Canaanites. The Old Testament of the Bible chronicles much of the history of the Jewish people.

Jacob had twelve sons, by his wives and concubines, and from them were derived the twelve tribes of Israel, known to history as the *Children of Israel*, and in the East as *Bani Israel*. They achieved a new identity under Moses, who united them into one nation, and gave them a structured religion after the shape of the Ten Commandments[2], and the calling of 'the Chosen of God'. After Moses was gone, they fought amongst themselves, with the result that Joshua partitioned them into two groups, and settled them in the land of Palestine. The 'League of the Twelve Tribes' was formed around 1200 BC. The Hebrews were united and achieved prosperity and peace as a nation by King David around 970 BC, but by

926 BC this kingdom broke into two, Israel and Judah.

Ever since then, the volatility of Palestine brought unrest and conquest, and finally dispersion, and nationhood eluded the Jews for nineteen centuries. First there was internecine fighting between the twelve tribes, then fierce conquest by Assyria around 721 BC – many Israelites were taken to Mesopotamia. In the sixth century BC there were many persecutions of Jews. Some escaped to Syria and the north, but there followed the conquest of the land by Nebuchadnezzar (597 BC) and the Jewish captivity in Babylon. Cyrus the Great of Persia became a hero for the Jews when he conquered Babylon and let them go. Though many returned to Palestine, a substantial number stayed or moved to Persia, where there was a relatively happy blending of Judaic and Zoroastran thought. Others, who were scattered to wide-flung lands, intermingled and lost their identity.

A conservative reaction among the priests in Palestine forbade modernism and many Jews were forced to give up Persian wives and ways. Some of the Israelites who had emigrated to Persia were skilled in many arts, and they are thought to have migrated further eastwards towards Afghanistan, Bactria and North-west India. The two tribes remaining in Palestine were those of Judah and Israel. What became of the ten lost tribes has been a mystery. It became a mission of succeeding Hebrew prophets to search them out and bring them back or connect them to the homeland.

Some Afghan tribes trace their ancestry to the Hebrew prophets and others claim their descent from the tribe of *Kish* or *Kush*. Kush was said to be the son of Ham and the grandson of Noah. One of the oldest people known to have settled in Kashmir are known as the Kassites, whose origins are shrouded in mystery. These Kassite tribes have also been called Semites, who migrated into North-west India from the West. Several of the Hebrew prophets are said to have graves along the southern Silk Road to the East.

Afghanistan has always been the meeting-place of many trade routes. The word *Afghan* derives from the Armenian word *Aghvan*, meaning 'mountaineers'. This establishes an ethnological connection between the Afghans and the Syrian captives of Armenia[3]. Afghans belong to Caucasoid or Mediterranean stock, but there is a predominance of Armenoid amongst them.

Some Afghani tribes trace their genealogy to the Hebrew prophets, and carry these cognomen to this day: prominent tribes of this kind are the Ammon-zye, Amma-zye, Davood-zye, Abrahim-zye, Shemoo-zye, Yusuf-zye, Ayub-zye, Haroon-zye, Issa-khel, Ishaq-khel, Sulaiman-khel, Yahya-khel, Yaqoob-khel,, Yunus-khel and Zakaria-khel. The words *zye* and *khel* stand for 'clan' and 'tribe'. All the above-mentioned tribes and clans carry their ancestral line right back to Jacob. They were converted to Islam in 633 by Khalid-ibn-al-Walid.

It is interesting to note that the tomb of Ezekiel is in Herat, and Samuel is buried on the side of the road leading to Khorasan from Hamdan. Another Hebrew prophet is buried at Rangbarang, near Bajoor in Afghanistan[4].

Bani Israel in Kashmir

Recent researches have revealed remnants of *Beni Israel* in Kashmir, Nagaland, Bombay, Cochin, Kerala and Tamil Nadu[5]. In Kerala, the Jews are divided into the White and Black sects. They do not mix, looking down on each other, each claiming to be the original followers of Judaism.

The legend of Hebrews being drawn to the East is very ancient. Although Western scholars maintain that the circumstances under which the prophet Moses died are shrouded in mystery, there is a lot of evidence that he came to Kashmir in his last days. He was ordered by God to leave Sinai and die on the Hill of Nabo: "Go thee unto Mount Nabo and die, but thou shalt not go unto the land which I give to the children of Israel".

And Moses went up from the plains of Moab unto the mountain of Nebo to the top of Pisgah, which is opposite Jericho. And the Lord showed him all the land... And the Lord said to him, "This is the land of which I swore to Abraham, to Isaac and to Jacob, 'I will give it to your descendants'. I have let you see it with your eyes, but you shall not go over there". So Moses the servant of the Lord died there in the land of Moab, according to the word of the Lord, and he buried him in the

The Monastery at Aish-Mugan in Kashmir in which is preserved the rod of Moses an Shofar *(Franz Sache)*

valley of the land of Moab opposite Beth-peor, but no man knows the place of his burial to this day.[6]

While it is implied from this that Moses died in a neighbouring land to the east of Jericho, I would suggest that this Biblical statement was made without geographical accuracy. Most scholars who have tried to locate the site of his grave have admitted failure, suggesting that the five place-names mentioned must have become lost during the last 3,000 years[7]. Yet five places mentioned in connection with this land are found in Kashmir: Bethpoer (*Bandipor*, though earlier called *Bethpor* or *Vethpor*), Hesbub, Pisgah (*Pish* or *Pishga*), Mount Nabu (*Nebo-bal*) and the valley of Moab (*Mowu*).

The tomb of Moses is identified by some to be in Kashmir, and is tended traditionally by people who have Jewish physical features. It was mentioned in Persian works[8] that the *Qbar-i-Moosa*, or Grave of Moses, was on the top of Nebo-baal in Bethpor. I

6

visited the place twice and interviewed its caretaker, Wali Reshi. He informed me that near the tomb of Sanga-Bibi, a hermitess, there is the grave of *Hazrat Mosa* or Moses, between two deodar trees. It is recorded in old histories of Kashmir that he came to this place and died here. His grave is a much revered shrine in the Hill of Nabu; it is called the shrine of the 'Prophet of the Book', and is visited today by many Kashmiri devotees, who believe Moses came to Kashmir to preach the word of God.

Abdul Qadir, a historian, in his *Hashmat-i-Kashmir*, records that *Hazrat Mosa* is buried at *Booth*, on the Hill of Nebo in Bandipor[9]. George Moore, who conducted exhaustive research on the Lost Tribes[10], is of the opinion that Moses came to Kashmir to preach because he had failed among the Children of Israel. I am more of the opinion that while Canaan was the holy land of the Semites, the Valley of Kashmir might be also a Promised Land.

There are two sacred relics associated with Moses in Kashmir. One is known as *Assa-i-Mosa*, or the Staff of Moses, and the second, *Ka Ka Pal*, or the Stone of Moses. At Aish-Muqam in Kashmir, there is the tomb of Zain Rishi, on an elevated spur of a hill. Amongst other sacred relics the Staff, *Assa-i-Mosa* is preserved there. This wooden staff is exposed to the public at times of calamity, like floods or epidemics. As some scholars have associated Aish Muqam with *Issa* or Jesus, they are of the opinion that this staff belonged to Jesus. It is also mentioned in a Persian work, the *Rishi Namah*, or 'The Book pertaining to the Tombs of Rishis' (saints), that *Issa* visited here.

The other relic is the *Ka Ka Pal* or the Stone of Moses, lying in the compound of the Shiva Temple at Bijbehara in Kashmir. I made numerous visits to see graves marked with Hebrew inscriptions mentioned by some scholars. I located the east-west oriented graves but saw no inscriptions. Also, I wanted to test the legend connected with the *Ka Ka Pal*, that it is apparently raised off the ground by eleven fingers. The custodian collected eleven people, asking each of us to place one finger on the stone, and to recite the words "*Ka Ka Ka*". We did as he told us, and to our surprise, the stone was raised three feet off the ground. To test this, we tried ten fingers, but the stone did not rise. This oval stone is about 40 kilos

The stone of Moses at Bijbehara, Kashmir. This miraculous stone is raised by the touch of eleven fingers of eleven people repeating the mantra "Ka-ka" eleven times *(Holger Kersten)*

in weight. *Kah* means 'eleven' in Kashmiri. *Kaka* means 'honoured person', and may refer to Moses.

In the Old Testament, we are told of a heavenly stone which was set up by Jacob, on to which he poured oil[11]. In Kashmir, a stone pillar known as a *Lingam* is anointed daily by the Hindu Pandits. In Canaan, the calf, the bull and the serpent were worshipped by some, and in every Hindu Pandit temple in Kashmir, we find the sacred stone pillar carved with images of the calf, cow, bull and serpent. While the Jews blew the *Shofar*, a curved horn, the Kashmiri Pandits blow a *Shank*, which is a curved horn, both at the climax of ceremonies. Also, the dress of Pandit ladies is similar to that worn in Palestine in earlier times. I am of the opinion that Kashmiri Pandits are descendants of ancient Jews.

It is recognised that the Kashmiris prepare their graves in the manner of the Jewish tombs. They are called *Mosai graves*, and aligned from east to west. Coffins today are of the same design as Jewish ones. Mourning for the dead is fixed at forty days, as in

Palestine. The Jews and the Kashmiris have some similar food habits, such as the eating of smoked fish, and using oil only for cooking. Both peoples will only cook meat if the animal has been bled by the cutting of the jugular veins, while invoking the name of God at the time of slaughter. Note the Hebrew name for this, *Kosher*, and the Kashmiri name for the country, *Kasheer*. Many rites of birth, marriage and death are similar between the two also. The required period of purification is the same, and *levirate* marriages are common to both communities.

There is an abundance of material to show Kashmiri people's ethnological connections with the Semites. Josephus Flavius speaks of an immense multitude of Jews who migrated to Persia, Afghanistan and north India[12]. According to another scholar, "the physical and ethnic character which so sharply marks off the Kashmiris from the surrounding races has always struck observant visitors to the valley, and they have been universally connected with the Jews"[13].

Al Beruni wrote in 1048 that the Kashmiris do not allow anyone other than Jews to enter their country[14]. The Jesuit Father, Catrou, in his *History of the Moghul Empire* of 1708, makes a categorical statement that the Kashmiris are descendants of the Jews. In order to save themselves from the invasions of Alexander the Great, some Jewish tribes reached Kashmir and Tibet, bringing their religious relics with them[15]. Claudius found an ancient copy of *Torah* in Kashmir[16].

My own researches about the Kashmiris have covered wide fields of anthropology and ethnography. I found many place names in Kashmir which have been mentioned in the Old Testament:

Kashmiri	*Biblical name*	
Asham	Ashema	*2 Kings*, 17, 30
Achabal	Ashbal	*Genesis*, 46, 21
Amairah	Amairah	*I Chronicles*, 23, 19
Bethpore	Bethpoer	*Deuteronomy*, 34, 1
Babal	Babel	*Genesis*, 10, 10
Doru	Dor	*I Kings*, 4, 11

Ludu	Lud	*I Chronicles*, 1, 17
Keran	Cheran	*I Chronicles*, 1, 41
Mamre	Mamre	*Genesis*, 18, 1
Moab	Moab	*Judges*, 3, 12
Pishga	Pisgah	*Deuteronomy*, 3, 27

The Gujjars of Kashmir, who are Muslims, say they are descended from Israel. They dress and wear their hair in the Jewish manner. The paddle used by Kashmiri boatmen, in the shape of a heart, is found only in Palestine and Kashmir. The Kashmiri boatmen call themselves the descendants of Noah. In the architecture of older buildings, the outside staircase leads always from the west, which is not the case with ancient Hindu, Muslim or Buddhist houses.

During my travels, I found a compact community in Gutlibagh, Gandarbal, who claimed that they were *Beni Israel*. They migrated from Afghanistan. The chief of this community told me that they descend from Jacob[17]. Today the Kashmiri language contains 30% Persian, 25% Arabic and 45% words from Sanskrit and other languages, including 9% from Hebrew. A few examples are (Hebrew first): *Ajal* = Ajal (death); *Am* = Am (death); *Ab* = Bab (father); *Awn* = Aun (blind); *Baal* = Bal (spring); *Brrah* = Bar (door); *Hoon* = Hoon (dog); *Tair* = Tur (cold); *Shaul* = Shaal (fox); and *Sahar* = Sehar (dawn).

There is reason to believe that a Jewish tradition lived on in Kashmir, later to draw Jesus to the region. But before we examine this, there is more historical background to consider.

Greeks and Kushans

This area of North-west India has been the cradle of some of the earliest civilisations. The Indus valley culture centred on Mohenjo-Daro and Harappa survived for a thousand years until 1550 BC. This was followed by the Rig-Vedic Aryans, who gradually spread over northern India, giving a cultural unification that was ready to receive Alexander the Great.

In the 6th century BC, Cyrus the Great founded a great Persian empire which included Palestine, Syria, Elam, Babylonia, Afghanistan, Baluchistan and Gandhara. Cyrus allowed the Jews,

A Greek king. 1st century North-west India *(Archeol. Survey of India)*

after their forty years' captivity in Babylonia, to return to Palestine. At that time the valley of Kashmir formed a part of Gandhara, which was variously under the influence of Bactrians, Scythians and Parthians. Alexander the Great marched his armies into India right up to the river Jehlum in about 326 BC.

After his departure, many small states ruled by Greeks arose in the north-western regions of India. Demetrius became the king of a vast region, which included Kashmir. Among the Greek rulers of Kashmir, mention may be made of Apollodotos, Menander, Nikephoros and Azez. It was through this influence that the cultural traditions of Greece, Rome, Byzantium and Persia travelled into Kashmir – this can be traced in the archaeological style of the Sun Temple of Martand.

The Yueh-chi tribes of Kansu, China moved west and south and occupied the northern regions of India during the second century BC. They founded the Kushan Empire in North-west India and Turkestan, which included Kashmir. It was Kanishka,

11

the great Kushan king, who convened the Fourth Buddhist Council in the valley in 87 AD. Henceforth, Kashmir became the fountainhead of Mahayana Buddhism, which was spread by Kashmiri missionaries in central Asia, China and South-east Asia. During this period Kashmir became a focus of Asiatic civilisation and was connected with the renowned Silk Road – the great trans-Asian highway linking Rome with China.

Modern history

Hinduism asserted its dominant position over Buddhism in Kashmir in the 7th century. It was Sri Harsha (r.1089-1101) who showed leanings towards Islam by inviting Muslims to settle in his kingdom. But it fell upon Gyalpo Rinchina (1320-1323) to bring Islam to the masses by his voluntary conversion, along with his Buddhist followers. The rule of the local Muslim kings over Kashmir and adjacent regions continued up to the 16th century. After this, the Kashmiris were conquered and reconquered by Mughals, Afghans, Sikhs and Dogras, between 1586 and 1947.

After the Second World War, the British decided to leave India by dividing it into the dominions of Pakistan and India. Pakistan made an attempt to annex the State of Jammu & Kashmir, and the Maharajah sought military help from India. The net result was a war between India and Pakistan in 1949, which terminated by a cease-fire agreement under the United Nations. This agreement left Gilgit, Baltistan, the Islamic parts of Ladakh, and Mirpur and Muzzafarabad in the control of Pakistan.

---

(1) *Encyclopaedia of India*, Rima, New Delhi, 1992, vol XI (Part 2). p1.

(2) *Deuteronomy*, chapter 5.

(3) Holditch, Thomas, *The Gates of India*, Macmillan, London, 1910, pp49-50.

(4) Khan, Roshan, *Tazkirah* or *History of the Afghans*, (in Urdu), Karachi, 1982, p74.

(5) Benjamin, Yehoshua, *Mystery of the Lost Tribes*, New Delhi, 1989, p19. Benjamin, J Israel, *The Jews of India*, New Delhi, 1982.

(6) *Deuteronomy*, 34, 1-6.

(7) Faber-Kaiser, Andreas, *Jesus Died in Kashmir*, Gordon & Cremonesi, London, 1977, p120.

(8) Khwaja Muhammad Azam Deedamari, *Tarikh-i-Azami* (in Persian), Muhammadi Press, Lahore, 1747, p84. Pandit Hargopal Koul Khasta, *Guldasta-i-Kashmir*, (in Persian), Arya Press, Lahore, 1833, p17.

(9) Abdul Qadir, *Hashmat-i-Kashmir*, Persian MS no 42, Royal Asiatic Society of Bengal, Calcutta, f7.

(10) Moore, George, *The Lost Tribes*, Longman Green, London, 1861.

(11) *Genesis*, 28, 18-19.

(12) Josephus, *Antiquities of the Jews*, ed Loeb, London & Cambridge MA, 1924ff, XI, V:2, and XV, II:2. See also: *Life*, tr William Whiston, John C Whiston, Philadelphia PA, USA.

(13) Wilson, Henry, *Travels in Himalayan Provinces*, John Murray, London, 1841, p129.

(14) Al Beruni, *Hind (India)*, in Arabic, tr Edward Sachau, vol 1 (of two), Trubner, London, 1888. Reprint: S Chand & Co, Delhi, 1964, vol 1, p206. Al Beruni (born 973 AD), the great Muslim scholar, has furnished a very accurate and valuable account of Kashmir. He said: "They are particularly anxious about the natural strength of their country, and therefore take much care to keep a strong hold upon entrances and roads leading into it. In consequence it is very difficult to have any commerce with them. In former times they used to allow one or two foreigners to enter their country, particularly Jews, but at present they do not allow any Hindu whom they do not personally know to enter, much less other people".

(15) Catrou, *History of the Moghul Empire*, tr Alex Moore, John Murray, London, 1836, p195.

(16) Claudius, Buchanan, *Christian Researches in Asia*, Ogle, Edinburgh, 1912, p229. While mentioning his discovery of an ancient manuscript in Hebrew, he says that it was written on a roll of leather about 48 feet in length.

(17) Interview with Mir Alam Badshah Naqashbandi, chief of the Pakhtoon tribe, January 5, 1982. I also met him for the second time in 1989, just before his death. Benjamin Yehoshua, who accompanied me, has recorded his impressions in his book *Mystery of the Lost Tribes*, Delhi, 1989, pp30-32. In an earlier interview, the chief had said: "We are that group of Jews who disobeyed Moses by refusing to eat the heavenly food, *Manan-Salva*. Thereafter, we left Moses and the nomads, and proceeded toward the East. Even the Turks are our brothers, for they also are Israelites who disobeyed Moses, like us. Many centuries ago we came to Kashmir, via Gilgit and Chitral".

A Greek king of Kashmir,
2nd century BC *(Museum of Kashmir)*

2

Ladakh:
Land of the Buddha

The birth of the Buddha was around 563 BC. He was a prince by birth, who renounced the comforts of palace life, to dedicate himself to finding the causes of misery, illness, suffering, old age, decay and death. He led a life of renunciation until he became enlightened. Then he gave his teachings of non-violence, peace and compassion. Buddhism gained ground in India during, and after, his lifetime.

About 300 years after his passing, Ashoka the Great gave patronage to missionary activities, to spread the teachings of the Buddha. He reputedly sent some 80,000 missionaries, monks and nuns to central Asia, China, Sri Lanka, Persia, Babylon, Syria, Palestine and Egypt. Thus, even if the real number of missionaries was smaller than this, Buddhism could be construed to have paved the way for the introduction of Christianity in the world. As my quest for the historical Jesus Christ is connected with Buddhism, and as I was led to this quest initially in Ladakh, through the Buddhist lamas there, I need to introduce this country to my readers.

In 1950, the focus of interest in the Himalayas fell on Tibet when, after the Chinese Maoist revolution, this mainly Buddhist country tried to maintain its independence – and China decided to conquer it. The young 14th Dalai Lama, the temporal and spiritual head of Buddhist Tibet, fled to India. Subsequent events intensified a serious border dispute between China and India. The Chinese occupied a thinly populated part of Ladakh known as the Aksai

The Indus Valley near Leh, capital of Ladakh (*Yoshiaki Sora*)

15

Chin which is strategically important to Tibet, and in 1959, Chinese border guards ambushed an Indian army unit within Ladakh. In 1960 the governments of India and China decided that the officials of the two governments should meet and examine all historical documents relevant to the boundary question.

At this time, I held the post of Director of State Archives, which maintained repositories at Jammu, Srinagar and Leh. I was directed to examine, check and study all historical documents, records, accounts, maps and other material. I had visited Ladakh earlier, but my new assignment led me to make many journeys there in search of source material. During one of my official trips to Ladakh in January 1961, I was snowbound in Leh, the capital, and during this stay I came by chance upon a document relating to Jesus Christ. This was the event which aroused my curiosity, and led me to embark on a quest for the historical Jesus.

Lying 400 miles north of Delhi, north-east of Kashmir, Ladakh is one of the more elevated regions of the world, cradled by the Great Himalaya range to the south, and the Karakoram range to the north. It is a vast arid table-land of sand and recently elevated mountains, with no vegetation. This mountain desert is split by the upper reaches of the river Indus, which flows into Pakistan. It has one of the lowest population densities in the world. In spite of its difficult terrain, Ladakh has its own attraction and charm. Its sandy deserts and its mountains of different hues give the feeling of a lunar surface.

For centuries the region has been an important trade centre on the old Silk Route between central Asia and the Indian sub-continent. But its chief attraction is its Buddhist culture. A visit to the region is an unforgettable experience, and many of the famous explorers of the world, such as Fa-Hien, Ou-King, Marco Polo, Moorcroft, Terbek, Vigne, Cunningham, Notovitch, Forsyth, Sven Hedin and Hino visited this magic land of the Lamas.

The *Ancient Chronicles of Ladakh*, called *La-dvags-rgyal-rabs*, written in Tibetan, were discovered by the German Indologist Hermann Schlagintweit, who had them translated into German. This translation was published in 1866[1]. Ladakh is now known as 'Little Tibet', but earlier it was called *Mar-yul*, or the 'Low Land'

Darad musicians from Kargil, Ladakh, play drums and pipes
(*Kashmir Tourist Office*)

(low relative to Tibet). Fa-Hien, a Chinese monk, who reached
Ladakh in about 400 AD, refers to it under the name of *Kia-chha*.

Ladakh's history goes back to at least 400 BC, when Sargyal
established the Kingdom of Ladakh and Tibet. Not much information is available about subsequent dynasties and rulers. The royal
dynasty of the Ladakhi kings was founded by *Skyid-lde-dyima-gon*
in 842 AD. He extended his sway over Baltistan, right up to Gilgit.
He established his capital at Shay, near Leh. Today, there is a
beautiful palace and a Buddhist monastery at Shey, with a 40ft
(13m) high statue of the Buddha, gold-plated and studded with
gems.

The rule of the Ladakhi kings continued up to 1840, when the
region was invaded and conquered by the Dogra Raja of Jammu.
Later, when the British Government of India *sold* the valley of
Kashmir to Raja Gulab Singh of Jammu, for 75,000 rupees, the
Raja combined all the regions and established the state of Jammu,
Kashmir and Ladakh in 1846.

The people of Ladakh are of mixed race, comprising the Mons, Darads and Mongols. They have practised polyandry since ancient times, as do Tibetans. The people of Ladakh are truthful, good-natured, cheerful, friendly and honest. They are fond of food and drink, and make their guests comfortable and happy by all possible ways and means. The family system in Ladakh is matriarchal, where the wife and mother enjoys authority.

Buddhism in Ladakh is known as Lamaism, of the Yellow (*Gelugpa*) and Red (*Nyingmapa*) sects. Every monastery has *lamas* and *chomos*, just as Catholics have monks and nuns. The whole of Ladakh is dotted with Buddhist monasteries, known as *gompas*. Almost every village has a *gompa*. The most important include Hemis, Shay, Likir, Lamayuru and Alchi. One of the most notable features associated with the *gompas* is the mystery plays, performed with the advent of each spring, a dance of purification performed by the Red Hat *Nyingma* lamas of Hemis.

Nowadays, it is possible to visit Ladakh by road or by air. There is a good motorable road from Srinagar to Leh, and thence to Manali and Simla. Owing to snowfall this road remains open from June to November only, with the Zoji La pass and Drass (13,479ft) – probably the coldest places in Eurasia outside Siberia. This road was completed in 1965, motivated by the military conflict between India and China. Prior to this, Ladakh was accessible only by bridleway, when it took at least two weeks to reach Leh from Srinagar – in the summer months only.

Leh

My story begins in January 1963, when I had to go to Leh to search out documents from the erstwhile royal family of Ladakh, represented by the Queen, Rani Parvati. She lived at Stok, in the old palace, alone, since her two children were studying at Dehra Dun. It was only possible then to reach Leh by military plane, and my colleague and I came in from Jammu, with a hope to return in a day or two.

We went in a jeep to pay a visit to the Queen at the Stok palace. We were received at the entrance by her officials. I bore gifts for the Queen, since this was my first visit, and we had the

Stok Palace, the residence of the Queen of Ladakh *(Joanna van Gruisen)*

customary white silk scarves, to be exchanged with our hostess. We entered a hall which contained regal artifacts – armour, paintings, crockery, costumes and wooden furniture. Then we were led to a well-decorated room, with modern furniture in it. When I raised my eyes, I saw a strikingly beautiful lady, dressed in regal attire, sitting elegantly on a throne. She wore brocades and diamonds, and her headgear, studded with blue turquoise, was very attractive.

We all bowed, and presented our scarves and gifts before her. The Queen thanked us. Then all of us were asked to sit, and were served with local delicacies. When I told her about my mission, she replied that all the family documents were to be at my disposal. She directed her officials to help me, and asked me to visit her next day, when I could have dinner with her.

The Queen of Ladakh is loved by her subjects, who call her *Gyalmoo*, 'the Queen'. Her real name is *Deskit Wangmo*, and her adopted Indian name at the time of her wedding with the king of

Ladakh was *Rani Parvati Devi*. She was married in 1950, and has four children. She is fair and slim, and in her royal dress she reminded me of Queen Mary of Scotland. Her smile was like sunshine. She had become a dowager queen at middle age, and now all her interest lay in educating her children. At a later stage, when I talked to her about her personal agony, she spoke like a philosopher explaining to me the truth about grief and sorrow as expounded by the Buddha.

With the help of local officials and interpreters, I conducted a survey of all historical records, and the work was completed in two days. Now, I wanted to hurry back with these documents to Delhi. After a week, my colleague and I became agitated, because no military aircraft landed in Leh. We made enquiries, and were told that bad weather prevented the flight.

The week had been spent salvaging documents, as well as making visits to Shay palace and Hemis monastery. The Queen of Ladakh had issued special instructions to the caretakers to show me the treasures at both places. I took the opportunity to visit the local Jamia Mosque for prayers on Friday (being Muslim), and kept myself engaged in meeting people. But when the week came to an end, my colleague who was feeling weak, became anxious to depart. No aircraft came. The weather was gloomy. We had completed our mission, and were both rather depressed.

The Moravian Mission Church

Weeks passed and there was no sight of the aircraft, due to bad weather. In order to kill time, I needed some books in English, which they told me were in the Moravian Mission Church. Here I met Reverend Chattan Phuntchuk, who was in charge of the Mission. He took me to the library and placed it at my disposal. I would spend my days perusing books and manuscripts in this library and in delightful talks with my new friend, Rev Phuntchuk.

From him I learned that in the beginning of the 19th century, some German travellers made mention of the ancient relics of Nestorian Christians in Mongolia, Central Asia, Tibet and Ladakh. The Nestorians were a Christian heretic group out-

lawedby the Council of Ephesus, who migrated to Persia and later
as far as Mongolia and China. This news aroused great interest
among the missionaries in Germany. Brothers Heyde and Pagell
decided to visit Mongolia and Tibet. They landed in Calcutta in
1853 and sought permission of the Government of India. For three
long years they waited for this permission – which was never
granted. They utilised these years learning Tibetan from the Buddhists of Ladakh, Lahul and Spiti. This made them abandon their
earlier plan and instead they began evangelistic tours into Zanskar
and Ladakh.

In 1885, the German missionaries succeeded in establishing
the first Moravian Mission at Leh in Ladakh. Next year they built a
church for converts. These missionaries did much useful work in
the field of agriculture, education and medical facilities. Some of
them, like A H Jaeschke, William Heyde, G Sandberg, A H
Francke and Karl Marx (not the political philosopher) compiled
authoritative works on Ladakh. After the First World War, the
Germans were deported from Ladakh and their missionary activities were taken over by British and Swiss nationals. After the
Second World War, the natives took over the church and the
mission. Accordingly, Rev Chattan Phuntchuk assumed charge of
the mission and its activities.

One day, I came across a bundle of diaries written in German
by the Moravian missionaries. Rev Phuntchuk explained to me
that all day-to-day happenings had been recorded by them in these
diaries. It was by chance that I saw the heading on page 118,
written in red ink: 'St Issa'. On enquiry with Rev Phuntchuk, it
transpired that the entry pertained to the visit of Nicolas Notovitch
to Ladakh and to finding some scrolls about St Issa. I took a
photograph of both pages and made notes. I surmised that *Issa*
could be no other person than *Jesus*. Accordingly, on my next visit
to the Moravian Mission, I started to discuss my idea with Rev
Phuntchuk. He evaded all my enquiries, and hence the matter
ended.

Or so I thought.

(1) *Journal and Proceedings of the Asiatic Society of Bengal*, Calcutta, Series 2, VI, 1900, pp393-423. See also: S S Gergan, *Ladags-r-Gyalrabs-Chimed-Ster*, in Tibetan, Srinagar, 1976.

Two pages from the diary of Dr Marx of the Moravian Christian Mission, Leh, which tells about Notovitch's discovery of the Jesus scrolls in Hemis Monastery

1. This 18ft high Buddha is in the heart of the Hemis gompa. (Sylvia Planzer)

2. The Wheel of Life, depicting realms of existence, in a Hemis doorway. (Sylvia Planzer)

3. Looking towards Chinese occupied Ladakh and Tibet from the roof of the Hemis gompa. (Sylvia Planzer)

4. The boatmen on Dal Lake, near Srinagar, still use the centuries-old heart-shaped Hebrew paddle. (Kashmir Tourist Dept.)

5. The Hemis gompa where Tibetan scrolls about Jesus were found. (Holger Kersten)

6. The main courtyard of Hemis. (Sylvia Planzer)

7. The Mystery Play at Hemis – one of the most impressive spiritual art forms in the world, it has not changed for centuries. (Kashmir Tourist Dept.)

8. Shey gompa and its associated dwellings collectively form a large settlement. (Alick Bartholomew)

9. Monks sounding trumpets across the Indus valley from the roof of Shey gompa. (Alick Bartholomew)

10. The tomb of St. Issa at Rozabal in Srinagar, after repairs. (Lino Cremon)

11. (*Left:*) The rectangular wooden sepulchre of Yuzu Asaph at Rozabal. (Lino Cremon)

12. (*Above:*) The sarcophagus, with its silk coverings, and holy texts. (Frank Sacha)

13. (*Above:*) Lamayuru, established in the eleventh century, is suspended between heaven and earth, but finds all its needs in its surroundings.

14. (*Right:*) With a rainfall of about 8mm a year, irrigation from mountain streams is essential. View from Mattro gompa. (Alick Bartholomew)

15. The photograph of the living Jesus, manifested by Sai Baba. (Carol Bruce)

3

The Legend of Jesus in Ladakh

On my return to Kashmir, I translated the two photographed pages of the diary of Dr Marx of the Moravian Mission. These two pages contained controversial information about Jesus Christ. The entry pertained to the year 1890, which mentioned the name Nicolas Notovitch (pronounced 'Notovitch'), a Russian traveller who broke his leg at Hemis in Ladakh, and who was nursed by the Moravian Mission doctors.

Mention is made of the claim made by Notovitch that he had seen Tibetan scrolls about Jesus in the Hemis monastery. These scrolls were explained to Notovitch with the help of a learned Lama during the months he stayed there at the Mission. The scrolls concerned the travels of Jesus in India. This looked interesting, so I thought of pursuing the subject. In this connection, it was necessary to find further information about Nicolas Notovitch.

I wrote to a few friends in India and abroad, and informed them about the diary of the Moravian Mission and its contents. To my good luck, my good German friend Dr Franz Sachse wrote to me that he had seen Notovitch's book in German and he was trying to obtain an English translation from the British Museum Library, London. After some weeks, I received a photocopy of a book called *The Unknown Life of Christ*, by Nicolas Notovitch, published in London in the year 1893. It was translated from the French by Violet Crisps.

Maitreya Buddha at Mulbek, Ladakh *(Yoshiaki Sora)*

Notovitch

Who was this Nicolas Notovitch? He was born in the Crimea in 1858. His parents were Jews but he and his brother Osip Notovitch, during their youth, had converted to the Greek Orthodox faith. He started his career as a journalist and later became an author of about a dozen books. His main interest lay in socio-political studies of the Russian people. He also make a deep study of religion and wrote a book called *Pravda Obevrejah*, which was somewhat anti-Judaic. For this book, he was condemned by Jews and praised by Christians.

Nicolas wrote in French and Russian, and his books were read in political circles. (Hitler makes mention of Notovitch's writings against Judaism in his own biography, *Mein Kampf*.) His books are available in various libraries of Europe. But it was his book on Jesus Christ which established him. The book appeared first in French under the title of *La Vie Inconnue de Saint Issa*, and then in English as *The Unknown Life of Christ*.

During the Turkish War of the late 1870s Notovitch made a series of journeys in the East. After having visited the Balkans, he travelled across central Asia and Persia, reaching India in 1887 AD. Having visited the Golden Temple at Amritsar, Punjab, Notovitch reached Rawalpindi, from where he directed his steps toward what he called 'the valley of eternal happiness', Ladakh. Notovitch went to Kargil, where he started on the Kargil-to-Leh pony track. He had coolies and all the necessary equipment, including horses and tents. At Mulbek, on the Wakha River, he visited two monasteries, and saw the famous rock sculpture of Maitreya Buddha, 24 ft high, carved around 700 AD. Then, in the company of an interpreter, he went to the small Buddhist monastery above the hill.

We crossed a suite of low-ceilinged rooms, whose walls were lined with shelves, displaying various large images of the Buddha, of different dimensions. The lamas much prefer the visits of Europeans to those of Muslims. I asked for an explanation for this from my host, who replied that: "Muslims have no contact with our religion. Quite recently, in their victorious campaign, they converted a number of our people to

Islam by force. As regards Europeans, that is quite another matter: not only do they profess the essential principles of monotheism, but they have almost as much title to be considered worshippers of Buddha as the Lamas of Tibet themselves. The only error of the Christians has been that, after having adopted the great doctrines of Buddha, they have completely severed themselves from him in creating for themselves a different Dalai Lama, ours alone having the gift of seeing, face to face, the majesty of Buddha, and the power of serving as intermediary between earth and heaven.[1]"

Notovitch learned that there existed a common base between Christianity and Buddhism. He asked further questions of the Lama, who said:

We also respect the one whom you recognise as Son of the one God. The spirit of Buddha was indeed incarnate in the sacred person of Issa, who without aid of fire or sword, spread knowledge of our great and true religion throughout the world. Issa is a great prophet, one of the first after twenty-two Buddhas. His name and acts are recorded in our writings.

When Notovitch asked him about these writings, the lama informed him that the principal scrolls were to be found at Lhasa in Tibet, and copies were to be found in the main monasteries. His own *gompa* being a small one, he had no copy of the scrolls. So, Notovitch made up his mind to search out these scrolls from a main monastery.

From Mulbek he proceeded to Leh, and after a few days, started for the great monastery at Hemis, one of the chief monasteries of Ladakh. He was shown sacred relics, paintings and statues. He also witnessed the Purification Dance, performed by masked lamas. (*see plate 7*) He gives a vivid description of the players, their music and the signs given by these dancers. After this, he was led by the head lama to the principal terrace, and entertained, where the head lama explained the dances and spoke on the teachings of Sakyamuni Buddha. Seizing a favourable opportunity, Nicolas Notovitch asked for information on Issa, about

Nicholas Notovitch

whom he had learned from the lama at Mulbek. The head lama
said:

> The name of Issa is held in great esteem by Buddhists but little is known
> about him save by the chief Lamas, who have read scrolls relating to his
> life. There have been an infinite number of Buddhas like Issa, and there
> are 84,000 scrolls extant, replete with details of the lives of each; but
> only a few have read more than a hundredth part of them.
>
> Acting according to established custom, each student or Lamavisit-
> ing Lhasa must make a gift of one or more copies [from there] to the
> convent to which he belongs: our gompa, among others, already pos-
> sesses a large number. Among them are to be found descriptions of the
> life and acts of the Buddha Issa, who preached the holy doctrine in India
> and among the children of Israel, and who was put to death by the
> pagans, whose descendants have since embraced the tenets he then
> propagated, which we believe to be yours[2].

While on an excursion, Notovitch fell from his horse, and his right leg was fractured below the knee. He was carried to Hemis, put in the best chamber, and entertained and nursed by the head lama and other lamas. At last, acceding to his entreaties, the head lama brought two large bound volumes, and read to him the biography of Issa. The scrolls were originally written in Pali, which were later translated into Tibetan and copies were preserved in various Buddhist monasteries. Notovitch carefully noted what was interpreted to him during the days he stayed in the monastery. He makes a further observation:

> *The various [scrolls] which were communicated to me by the Buddhist lama of the monastery of Hemis, which I put in their order of sequence so as to give them consecutive sense and render them conformable to the rules of literary composition, may have actually been spoken by St Thomas, historical sketches having been traced by his own hand or under his direction.*

Notovitch returned to Russia, and showed his notes to the mayor of Kiev, telling him that he wanted to publish his discovery. The mayor dissuaded him from publishing these notes. A year later, Notovitch went to Rome, and showed his manuscript to a cardinal at the Vatican. He also dissuaded him by saying that publication would create a crowd of enemies against him. At the same time, the cardinal offered him money as a recompense for his expenses on the journey, and asked him to hand over the notes to him. Notovitch refused to be bribed, and went to Paris, to seek a publisher for his work. He spoke to Cardinal Rotelli, his acquaintance in Paris, who also opposed publication of his work.

However, these notes were finally published in French as *La Vie Inconnue de Saint Issa*, in 1890, then in New York as *The Life of Saint Issa*, also in 1890, and finally in 1895 in London as *The Unknown Life of Christ*. The book later appeared in German, Spanish and Italian. Notovitch's book created a lot of controversy among Christian scholars. Information about the presence of Jesus in India prior to his crucifixion shook the foundations of Christianity. The reaction was almost one of panic: some scholars doubted the veracity of Notovitch's claims, others doubted the very existence of Notovitch, and others the existence of the Buddhist monastery at Hemis. There were widespread accusations that the alleged sojourn of Jesus was a forgery and a fraud.

Notovitch responded publicly by announcing his existence, along with the names of people he met on his travels in Kashmir and Ladakh. He also mentioned that the Vatican Library possessed 63 complete or incomplete manuscripts, from India, China, Egypt and Arabia, in various languages, referring to Jesus. He also offered to return to Tibet in the company of recognised orientalists to verify the authenticity of the verses contained in his compilation. In the French journal, *La Paix*, he affirmed his belief in the Orthodox Church, and advised his detractors to restrict themselves to the simple issue of the existence of the Buddhist scrolls at Hemis.

The Scrolls Verified

In 1812, Meer Izzut-oolah went to Ladakh, and then visited central Asia. After his return, he printed his notes in his native Persian, later translated into English by Henderson[3]. Meer Izzut-oolah was in the service of the East India Company, which administered the Indian dominion on behalf of the British parliament prior to 1857. He was deputed to central Asia to collect information about the strategic, social, political and military strengths of the kingdom of Bokhara in central Asia.

> *They keep sculptured representations of departed saints, prophets and lamas in their temples, for contemplation. Some of these figures are said to represent a certain prophet who is living in the heavens, which would appear to point to Jesus Christ. I was informed by an aged man that he had ascertained beyond all doubts that some portions of the Bible had been revealed to the Tibetans. They assert that their original scripture was in a language that has now become unintelligible.[4]*

These interesting observations, made in 1812, point to the existence of a figured representation of Jesus in the Buddhist monas-

teries. But the most important observation pertains to some portions of the Bible having been put into the Buddhist scriptures.
Nicolas Notovitch makes mention of the scrolls in the year 1893,
but Meer Izzut-oolah has provided a hint from as far back as 1812.
This hint gives further support to the claim of Notovitch that he
did see the scrolls at Hemis.

I felt convinced of the sincerity of Notovitch, and tried to find
if any others had seen these scrolls. I did find that in 1922, a Hindu
monk, Swami Abhedananda, disciple of the late 19th century
Vedantist, Swami Ramakrishna, had been to Hemis, and had
found out about St Issa.

Swami Abhedananda, born in 1860, adopted a monastic life
from childhood, travelling throughout India between 1888 and
1895. After having attained sainthood, he left for North America,
and lived there for 25 years, up to 1921. He lectured on spiritual
topics in North and South America, Europe and elsewhere, returning to India in 1922. He was fascinated by Jesus Christ, and his
curiosity was aroused after reading Notovitch's book. He went to
Leh on a fact-finding mission[5], finding the scrolls at Hemis. He
was told that the account of the life of St Issa was true, and was
shown a copy of an original manuscript lodged in Lhasa, Tibet.
Below is a quote from a book on his travels, by a disciple, written
in Bengali:

> *He reached the Hemis monastery on 4th October 1922, and discovered
> a manuscript of the unknown life of Jesus, the Christ, which was
> previously recorded by the Russian traveller, Nicolas Notovitch, and
> with the help of a senior lama, he obtained a translated copy of the
> important portions of the life of Jesus, and had it incorporated in
> Bengali, in his book 'Kashmir O Tibbate'[6].*

This convinced me that a time will come when the scrolls will be
found in Hemis, or in some other Tibetan Buddhist monastery. In
his memorandum to his publisher, Notovitch said that he learned
from the head lama of Hemis that there existed very ancient
records about the life of Jesus Christ, in the archives at Lhasa in
Tibet. The same is related by Swami Prajnananda, in an interview

The Author with Ladakhi guide in search of Buddhist scrolls about Jesus

with Richard Dick, husband of the film actress Janet Bock. The Swami says that the original scroll is in Pali, and this manuscript was housed in the Marbour monastery in Tibet, but that now there is no trace of it[7].

Suppression

I returned to Ladakh several times, to find the scrolls, but in vain. Rev Chattan Phuntchok had left for Darjeeling, and was no longer in charge of the Moravian Mission. I inquired about the diaries of the Mission doctors, from which I had taken photographs of the two pages. The diaries were not there. I felt sad I could not see the scrolls about Jesus in Hemis monastery. Maybe the Lamas have concealed them.

Maybe Ahmed Shah had obtained the scrolls? I made this conjecture after reading what Nicolai Roerich writes about his meeting with the head lama of Hemis, who informed him that "many Mohammedans would like to possess the manuscripts".

This statement is significant because it is not clear why Muslims would want to obtain the scrolls. Was he hinting at Ahmed Shah? Amongst Muslims, it is only the *Ahmadiyyas* (about whom more later) who would be interested in obtaining the scrolls, for their missionary work. Had they succeeded, they would have published it. I think the lamas concealed the scrolls out of fear for their safety.

The revelations made by Nicolas Notovitch became a red rag to the Church, and they made plans to refute his discovery and at the same time steal these scrolls. An American mission made ample preparations to visit Ladakh to verify the findings made by the Russian author. Such attempts were made by the Christian Church in India also. Some even denied the existence of any Buddhist monastery at Hemis, while others denied existence of any Russian by the name of Nicolas Notovitch.

However, frequent visits of foreigners to the Hemis monastery created doubts in the minds of the lamas, who may have taken extra care to conceal these verses in their scriptures. Snellgrove[8], who visited Ladakh in 1974, admitted that the lamas seemed convinced that all foreigners steal if they can, and there have in fact been quite serious losses.

A confirmation of the discovery by Nicolas Notovitch came in 1928, when Professor Nicolai Roerich led an expedition through central Asia to Ladakh and Kashmir. He refers to manuscripts and legends about Christ in various regions of Asia. In his book *The Heart of Asia* he records that he visited Hemis and was shown a number of scrolls. He testified that such documents and manuscripts about Christ normally lie in the darkest part in the underground store rooms of the Hemis monastery.

Significantly, he was also told by the Head Lama that many Muslims would like to possess the scrolls[9]. This relates back to the 1890s, when the Church Mission in India engaged the services of Ahmed Shah and Professor Douglas to destroy the Tibetan 'gospels'. Ahmed Shah spent four years in Ladakh, admitting in his book *Four Years in Tibet*[10] that his sole aim in visiting Ladakh was to "refute the findings of Nicolas Notovitch"[11]. Professor Douglas, of the Government College, Agra, visited Ladakh for 'investigations', and wrote that the work of Notovitch was literary

The Author with guides in Leh

forgery[12]. Since that time, many would support John Forsström's statement[13] that it has been the continuing practice of the Church to "trace, buy, confiscate and steal ancient documents referring *inter alia* to Jesus' life in India, and his death in Kashmir".

In 1921 an adventurous lady traveller named Henrietta Merrick visited Hemis and was informed about the legend of Jesus Christ contained in the precious documents. She wrote:

> *In Leh is the legend of Jesus who is called Issa, and the Monastery at Hemis holds precious documents fifteen hundred years old which tell of the days that he passed in Leh where he was joyously received and where he preached.[14].*

I think that, owing to their fears of foreign interest, the lamas may have concealed the scrolls, as Roerich suggested, in their darkest underground cells. My failure to locate these scrolls was disappointing, but I did make one discovery. I located a Tibetan manuscript which was an 1802 translation from an ancient Chinese manuscript, *The History of Religion and Doctrines – the Glass Mirror*[15]. (*see Chapter 20*)

A book compiled by Elizabeth Clare Prophet[16] brings together the testimony of four eye-witnesses to the Tibetan scrolls, which, taken together, reveal details of the pilgrimage of Jesus from Jerusalem to India, between the ages of 12 and 29, in which he was both a student of Buddhist teachings and a teacher in his own right. The book includes excerpts from the writings of Notovitch, Swami Abhedananda, Roerich and a traveller called Elizabeth Caspiri.

---

(1) Notovitch, Nicolas, *The Unknown Life of Christ*, Rand McNally, Chicago, 1894 & Hutchinson, London, 1895, p51.

(2) Notovitch, Nicolas, *The Unknown Life of Christ*, p120.

(3) Meer Izzut-oolah, *Travels in Central Asia*, tr Henderson, Foreign Dept Press, Calcutta, 1872.

(4) *Ibid*, pp13–14.

(5) Bock, Janet, *The Jesus Mystery*, Aura Books, Los Angeles, 1980, p20.

(6) Ghose, Ashutosh, *Swami Abhedananda, The Patron Saint*, Calcutta, 1967. Also Ghose, Ashutosh, *Kashmir O Tibbate*, Ramakrishna Vedanta Math, Calcutta, 1927, p230.

(7) Bock, Janet, *ibid*, p22.

(8) Snellgrove, David, *The Cultural Heritage of Ladakh*, 1977, p127. Also: Forsström, Johan, *The King of the Jews*, Nugedoga, Sri Lanka, and East West Books, Hango, Finland, 1987, p197.

(9) Roerich, Nicolai, *Altai Himalaya*, New York, 1929, pp89–90; Roerich, Nicolai & Grant, Frances, *Himalaya, A Monograph*, New York, 1926.

(10) Shah, Ahmed, *Four Years in Tibet*, Lazarus & Co, Benares, 1906.

(11) *The Museum*, Vol 24, 1972, Newark Museum Association, 49 Washington St, Newark NJ, USA, p51.

(12) Douglas, Professor Archibald, article in *The Nineteenth Century*, April 1896.

(13) Forsström, Johan, *The King of the Jews*, East-West Books, Hango, Finland, 1987, p187. This book has a useful bibliography of books dealing with Buddhism and Christianity.

(14) Merrick, Henriette, *In the World's Attic*, Putnams, New York, 1931, p215. See also Harvey, Mrs, *The Adventures of a Lady in Tartary, China and Kashmir*, London, 1854, 3 vols.

(15) Le-zan Chhes-kyi Nima, *Grub-tha Thams-chand kyi Khuna dan Dod-Thsul*

Ston-pe Legs Shad Shel-gyi Melong, (Tibetan, translated from Chinese), or *The History of Religions and Doctrines – The Glass Mirror*, in the collection of S S Gergan, Srinagar, Kashmir.

(16) Prophet, Elizabeth Clare, *The Lost Years of Jesus*, Malibu, USA, 1984, p317. See also Bock, Janet, *The Jesus Mystery*, Aura Books, Los Angeles, 1980. Edmunds, A J, *Gospel Parallels*, from Pali texts, Chicago, 1900; Lillie, Arthur, *India in Primitive Christianity*, London, 1909. An ancient Aramaic manuscript was obtained by Rev G J R Ouseley from a Tibetan monastery in 1881. It has been published by Edmond Bordeaux Szekely in 1981 under the title of *The Essene Gospel of Peace*. It shows very close affinity between the teachings of Buddha and Jesus Christ.

Ley, capital of Ladakh *(Yoshiaki Sora)*

4

What the Lamas knew about Issa

At Hemis, Nicolas Notovitch obtained 244 verses about the life and acts of *Issa* – for such is the name which Jesus was known by in the East. In the following pages, I give a condensed version[1].

1. The earth trembled and the heavens wept, because of a great crime, which has been committed in the land of Israel.

2. For they tortured and murdered the great and just Issa, who had incarnated in a simple mortal frame to do good for people and destroy the evil spirit in them.

3. He came to bring humankind back to a life of peace, love and happiness.

4. The people of Israel, who had dwelt on a fertile soil and who had possessed large flocks, excited the anger of God by their sins.

5. God inflicted upon them a terrible chastisement, in taking from them their land, cattle and possessions. Israel was reduced to slavery under the Pharaohs who ruled over Egypt.

6. In their great calamity, the people of Israel remembered their heavenly protector. They wept and implored his grace and mercy.

7. The new Pharaoh had two sons, of whom the younger was Mossa [Moses], who was good and compassionate.

8. The learned Israelites who had taught Mossa diverse sciences, requested him to intercede with the Pharaoh in their favour.

37

9. The Pharaoh gave Mossa an order to take all the Jewish slaves to another city away from the capital.

10. Mossa then led them instead into the land they had lost by their many sins. He gave them laws and enjoined them to pray always to the invisible Creator.

11. The kingdom of the Jews became the most powerful of all the earth and the glory of the riches of Israel spread throughout the world [in the time of Solomon].

12. Unfortunately, the fidelity of the Israelites to their God did not last. They forgot the laws Mossa had written for them.

13. God determined to exercise his chastisements upon them once more. Pagans from the country of Romeles [Rome] invaded the country of the Jews and devastated it. They were reduced to slavery.

14. They groaned and lamented, and in this extreme distress remembered God. They implored and besought his forgiveness.

15. At this moment, the all-merciful Judge decided to become incarnate in human form.

16. Soon after, a marvellous child was born unto the land of Israel. God himself spoke by the mouth of this infant who was given the name of Issa.

17. This divine child spoke of the one and indivisible God, and people from all parts came to hear him.

18. When Issa had attained the age of thirteen years, many rich and noble families became desirous of having him as their son-in-law.

19. Then it was at this juncture that Issa left his parents and departed from Jerusalem towards Sindh along with the merchants.

20. In the course of his fourteenth year the young Issa came to this [eastern] side of the Sindh. His name spread far and wide.

21. The devotees [Jains] of the god Djaine prayed him to dwell among them but he left the country of the five streams and went to Orsis.

22. *The white [Hindu] priests of Brahma made him a joyous welcome. They taught him Vedas, healing by prayer, and how to drive out evil spirits.*

23. *He passed six years at Jagganath, Rajagriha, Benares and other holy cities.*

24. *The white priests, becoming acquainted with the discourses of Issa addressed to the Sudras [the untouchable caste], resolved upon his death. But he, warned of this danger, left Jagganath by night and reached the country of Goutamides.*

25. *Six years later, Issa, whom the Buddha had elected to spread his holy word, became a perfect expositor of the sacred canon.*

26. *Then he went towards the west, preaching to diverse people the sure means of merging oneself in the Eternal Spirit. He said:*

"He who has regained his original purity will die having obtained remission for his sins. Even as a father would act towards his children, so will God judge men after their deaths, according to the laws of his mercy. All things have been sacrificed to man, who is directly and intimately associated with me – his Father."

27. *The neighbouring countries resounded with the prophecies of Issa, and when he entered into Persia, the priests forbade the people to listen to him.*

28. *Issa went from one town to another, strengthening the courage of the Israelites with the word of God. They were succumbing to the weight of their despair. Thousands of people followed him, to hear him preach.*

29. *But the chiefs of the towns became afraid of him and they made it known to the principal governor at Jerusalem that a man named Issa had arrived in the country and that he was stirring up the people against the authorities.*

30. *Issa taught the people of Israel for three years, and all that he had predicted came to pass. During this time, the disguised servants of Pilate watched him closely.*

*31. Pilate, becoming alarmed at the great popularity of Issa, com-
manded his soldiers to arrest him. He was thus arrested and put in a
subterranean cell. They tortured him in many ways in the hope of
forcing him to make a confession.*

*32. By the order of the governor, the soldiers led Issa and the two
thieves to the place of execution, where they nailed them to crosses.*

*33. All day the bodies of Issa and the two thieves remained suspended.
At sunset the suffering of Issa came to an end. He lost consciousness and
the soul of this just man left his body, to become absorbed in the Divine.*

*34. His parents buried him near the spot of his execution. The crowd
came to pray over his tomb and the air was filled with groans and
lamentations.*

*35. Three days later, the governor sent his soldiers to carry away the
body of Issa to bury it elsewhere, fearing otherwise a popular insurrec-
tion. But the crowd found the tomb open and empty.*

After reading the above, I was spell-bound! Here were hidden
details of eighteen missing years in the life of Jesus, about which
the Gospels are silent. The only account of the intervening years
were given in a few sentences in the *Holy Bible:*[2]

*And when they had performed everything according to the law of the
Lord, they returned into Galilee, to their own city Nazareth. And the
child grew, and waxed strong in spirit, filled with wisdom; and the
favour of God was upon him.*

    *Now his parents went to Jerusalem every year, at the feast of the
Passover. And when he was twelve years old, they went up [to
Jerusalem] according to custom. And when the feast was ended, as they
were returning, Jesus tarried behind in Jerusalem.*

    *His parents did not know it, but supposing him to be in the
company, they went a day's journey, and they sought him among their
kinsfolk and acquaintances. And when they did not find him, they
returned to Jerusalem, seeking him.*

    *After three days they found him in the temple, sitting among the
teachers, listening to them, and asking them questions. And all who
heard him were amazed at his understanding and his answers. And*

Monk reading at a door overlooking the valley, Shey gompa *(Mari Franklin)*

*when they saw him they were astonished; and his mother said to him,
"Son, why have you treated us so? Behold, your father and I have been
looking for you anxiously." And he said to them, "How is it that you
sought me? Did you not know that I must be in my Father's house?"
And they did not understand the saying which he spoke to them. And he
went down with them and came to Nazareth, and was obedient to them;
and his mother kept all these things in her heart.*

That is all that is contained in the Gospels concerning eighteen
years in the life of Jesus – the next event recounted in his life is his
baptism by John, at the age of 29 years. This naturally requires
explanation. As do many further matters concerning the life of
Jesus. In order to do this, we need to go back to the beginning of
Jesus' life, and re-examine other records than the authorised Bible.

---

(1) Nicholas Notovitch published his translation of the Tibetan Gospel, in
French, English and other languages. In 1890, the work appeared under the
title of *The Life of St Issa*, in New York. In 1894, another edition appeared in
France, called *La Vie inconnue de Jesus Christ*. During the same period, another
French edition came out called *La vie de St Issa*, which was translated by
Heyina Loranger and Violet Crispe, appearing in London and Chicago as *The
Unknown Life of Christ*. The German edition carries the title *Die Lucke im Leben
Jesus*, Stuttgart, 1894.
(2) Holy Bible, *Luke*, 2, 39-48.

5

The Birth of Jesus

Joseph and Mary

The tradition of compiling genealogies was very common among the Jews. Such compilations could be genuine or fictitious. *Matthew* and *Luke* have given genealogies of Jesus but both contain discrepancies. While the genealogy prepared in *Matthew* contains 41 names[1], *Luke* mentions 77 names[2] in ascending order, from Adam to Jesus. Both genealogies speak of Joseph as husband of Mary and father of Jesus.

After going through these, I felt that the Gospel genealogies have not been compiled on the basis of the biological descent, but to fulfil the requirements of mythological prophecies. Secondly, while the genealogy of Joseph has been compiled in one way or the other, no such attempt has been made in case of Mary. Thirdly, both genealogies of Jesus are self-contradictory and irreconcilable.

Apart from the authorised Gospels, there are the unrecognised works, known as the *Apocryphal Gospels*, which can furnish more information. There are about fifty of them discovered so far, all declared heretical by the Church centuries ago. Most of these works were destroyed under various decrees of the Church, but some copies have survived and seen the light of day.

Concerning Mary the Mother, the *Gospel of James* says that Mary was the daughter of Joachim and his wife Hanna[3]. Her cousin Elizabeth was married to Zechariah, a high priest, who arranged for Joseph and Mary to be married. Elizabeth belonged to the family of Aaron[4]. Joachim was a wealthy farmer of Nazareth

43

who had prayed to the Lord to bless him with a child. An angel appeared before Hanna and assured her that the Lord would bless her with a child. She made a promise that she would take it for service in the Temple, as a gift to God.

Eventually, Mary was born to Hanna. She was taken to the temple at the age of three and placed under the charge of the priest[5]. She stayed until she was twelve. Jesus was born to Mary when she was fourteen years of age[6]. Mary also gave birth to other children, considered to be brothers and sisters to Jesus, even though his own paternity was from a different source[7]. The people of Nazareth considered James, Joses, Judah and Simon as brothers of Jesus:

> On the sabbath he began to teach in the synagogue; and many who heard him were astonished, saying, "Where did this man get all this? What is the wisdom given to him? What mighty works are wrought by his hands! Is not this the carpenter, the son of Mary and the brother of James and Joses and Judas and Simon, and are not his sisters here with us?"

The names of his sisters are not given. From the time of the holy family's return from Egypt, Joseph is never again mentioned significantly. Also, Joseph never mentions Jesus as being his son, though Mary does describe Joseph as the father of Jesus[8]. However, on the death of Joseph, Jesus is said to have uttered the following lamentation:

> Not a single limb of it shall be broken, nor shall any hair of thy head be changed, nothing of thy body will perish: O! my father Joseph.[9]

The Virgin Birth

Mystery surrounds the conception and birth of Jesus. It is an article of faith with Christians to believe that Jesus was conceived when Mary was a virgin. The concept of virgin birth was very popular during the second century AD, becoming a key item of Church doctrine. Complications have arisen due to the fact that in order to meet objections, the compilers of the revised Gospels resorted to interpolations.

According to *Matthew*, Mary was found with the child of the Holy Ghost before her marriage with Joseph. While Joseph pondered on these things, an angel appeared to him in a dream, saying that he should not worry but take his wife Mary to his house[10]. According to *Luke*, the angel Gabriel came to Mary to inform her that the Holy Ghost would overlight her and she would bring forth a son[11].

The *Protevangelium Jacobi*, or *Gospel of James*[12], gives some information about Mary and her marriage with Joseph. According to this Gospel, Mary grew up in the Temple, where she was visited and fed by the angels. When she was twelve years old, she witnessed an angelic apparition. The high priest of the Temple prayed concerning her. An angel appeared to him saying: *"Go forth and assemble those that are bachelors. Let them bring a rod and to whomsoever the Lord shows a sign, his wife shall she be"*. When they had gathered together, they went to the high priest. The rods were thrown in the fountain outside the Temples. When Joseph's rod emerged, a dove came down and sat beside it. Thus Joseph was selected by a divine sign. Hence Joseph took Mary to his house[13].

The theory of virgin birth propounded by *Matthew* and *Luke* finds no corroboration from *Mark* or *John* or the *Epistles*. Maybe, by virgin birth, both Gospels may have meant a miraculous birth in more simple terms. In religious mythology, all manner of miracles are possible. It is worth noting that, in more ancient times, while the Egyptians regarded the Pharaoh as a god, the Sumerians and Assyrians regarded a king as the *son* of God. Some Sumerian myths tell us of gods who came down to impregnate women, and then to return to the stars.

Perhaps we would have solved the question of the tradition of divine birth if the censors of Rome had not destroyed the manuscripts of the ancient mystery cults, and the later Christian compilers had not thrown out other manuscripts in producing the New Testament. *The Book of Enoch*, for example, gave the names of angels who had coupled with virgins of earth[14].

The Essene version

On the question of the virgin birth, I have had long and fruitful discussions with Christian friends. How could Jesus be born in a different way, and why should normal laws of nature be dispensed with for his sake? Maybe the earlier compilers of the Gospels wove these mysteries around the person of Jesus Christ so as to glorify him. It was during these discussions that a friend advised me to study the works of the Essenes, known as the *Dead Sea Scrolls*.

Who were these Essenes? At the time Jesus was born in Judaea, there existed many sects among the Jews. The principal and important among these were Sadducees, Pharisees and Essenes. The last sect, though very important, is not mentioned in the New Testament. But the historian Josephus wrote that "the Essenes are the most honest people in the world and are as good as their word, very industrious and enterprising and showing great skill and concern for agriculture. They exercise justice and equality in their dealings with all people, despise sensuality, willingly adopt the children of other people, avoid riches and worldly gains and are members of the same brotherhood"[15].

During my study it transpired that for better understanding of the New Testament, it was essential to study all the writings of the Essenes including the Dead Sea Scrolls. It also became clear that the Essenes did play an important role in the upbringing of Jesus. The Essenes have a different version about the birth of Jesus. I quote to explain their point of view:

I will tell you of the parentage of this man, who loved all men and for whom we feel the highest esteem. He was from his infancy brought up for our brotherhood. Indeed, he was predicted by an Essene, whom the woman thought to be an angel. This woman was given to many imaginings, delving into the supernatural and into the mysteries of life. Our brother the Essene has acknowledged his part in these things and has persuaded the brotherhood to search for and protect the child secretly.

Joseph, who was a man of great experience in life and of deep devotion to the immortal truth, was influenced, through a messenger of our Order, not to leave the woman nor to disturb her faith in the sacredness of her experience. He was told to be a father to the child until our brotherhood should admit him as a novice. Thus, during their flight to Egypt, Joseph, his wife and the child were secretly protected and guided by our brotherhood[16].

The issue regarding the virgin birth of Jesus thus came clear. This account claims that no angel of God had come to meet Mary, but it was a member of the Essene brotherhood who had either been active or facilitative in fathering Jesus. This establishes a strong connection between Jesus and the Essenes.

The above-quoted passage further informs that Joseph was told to be a father of this child until Jesus was admitted to the Order as a novice. Secondly, Joseph is told not to disturb the faith of Mary in the sacredness of her experience – he had been troubled by her pregnancy before their marriage. Here is a clear hint about the mystical rituals observed by such people as the Indian Tantrics. The *Tantra* advocates worship of the *Shakti* – the feminine energy – in conjunction with *Shiva* or *Shakta* – the male element, the highest state of mystical union between god and consort. The *Tantra* makes use of the symbolism of sexual union, which is designated as *maithuna* or heavenly coitus. It is possible that the Essene had performed this very type of ritualistic copulation with Mary, and this experience had been viewed as sacred and holy. As Joseph was himself a member of the Essene Order, he had agreed to be the father of the child.

The date of Jesus' birth

The date of Jesus' birth is very much open to question. *Luke* and *Matthew* have given some indication in this direction:

> *And there were in the same country shepherds abiding in the fields, keeping watch over their flocks by night*[17].
>
> *Now when Jesus was born in Bethlehem of Judaea in the days of Herod the king, behold, there came wise men from the east to Jerusalem, saying "Where is he who has been born king of the Jews? For we have seen his star in the East, and have come to worship him"*[18].

The Church has fixed Christmas, 25 December, as the date of the birth of Christ. But this month remains very cold in Palestine and no sheep would be in the fields and no shepherds would watch over their flocks by night – during December, Palestine is frosty, and flocks are put out to grass between March and November. It appears that someone made a mistake[19].

A further probe in this matter revealed that the Romans celebrated the 25th December, every year, as the birthday of Mithra, who was worshipped by them as the saviour of mankind – the festival was called *Dies Natalis Invicti*, or the birthday of the unconquered[20]. When Romans adopted Christianity, they converted the Mithra festival into a Christian festival.

This date was arbitrarily fixed by a Scythian monk, Dionysius Exignus in the year 533[21], in the pattern of Paul, who successfully grafted the Christian teachings with the beliefs of the Romans. Also, Exignus arranged dating to move directly from 1 BC to 1 AD, which would suggest a mystical reasoning behind the dating system[22].

Prior to Exignus, the date of birth of Jesus had been fixed as 6th January, which is still being celebrated in the Orthodox Church, the Balkans and Mexico. It transpired that as *Aeon* was born on the 6th January, and his birth used to be celebrated in Egypt and Asia Minor, the Church arbitrarily borrowed this date and applied it to Jesus Christ[23]. The question arises as to why this date was subsequently changed. However, *Luke* has clearly hinted that Jesus was born in the summer and not in the winter – as the animals are put to grass between the months of March and November, his date of birth needs to be looked for between these months.

As regards the year in which Jesus was born, both *Luke* and *Matthew* have mentioned the reign of Herod. We know that Herod was designated king of Judaea by the Romans in 40 BC. *Luke* has also mentioned that Mary brought forth her son when Cyrenius was the governor of Syria[24]. Cyrenius is better known as Quirinius in history, who went as Legate to Syria in 6 AD. But it is also recorded on an inscription discovered at Antioch that he went to Syria on a military mission and established his seat of government there between 10 and 7 BC[25]. Hence, we are probably accurate to date Jesus' birth around 7 BC.

Another hint comes from *Matthew* when he says that at the time Jesus was born, a star was seen – in fact, three stars have been mentioned, namely the Star of the Magi, the Star of Horus and the Star of Bethlehem. These stars could have been comets, which did appear between 6 and 7 BC[26], or they could refer to the three successive conjunctions of Jupiter and Saturn in the constellation Pisces (discovered by Kepler), or the triple conjunction of Jupiter, Saturn and Uranus at that time. Stars and comets have not only impressed human beings but have a special significance for astronomers and astrologers of the world. Their appearances have been recorded by the Indians, Tibetans, Egyptians, Greeks, Persians and Chinese.

The Visit of the Wise Men

Matthew connects the birth of Jesus with the visit of the wise men from the East who came to Jerusalem and made enquiries about the infant. It is very significant that for the first time, an intimate connection is established between Jesus and the East. Let me quote from the Gospel[27]:

> *Now when Jesus was born in the days of Herod, behold, there came wise men from the East to Jerusalem, saying, "Where is he that is born king of the Jews? For we have seen his star in the East, and are come to worship him".*
>
> *And when they were come into the house, they saw the child with Mary his mother and they fell down and worshipped him. Then, opening their treasures, they offered him gifts, gold and frankincense and myrrh. And being warned in a dream not to return to Herod, they departed to their own country by another way[28].*

Who were these wise men from the East? It is clear to me that these wise men could be no other than Buddhists. I have my own reasons for coming to this conclusion, after making a thorough study of Buddhism in Ladakh and Tibet.

Long before the birth of Jesus, Buddhist missionaries had gone to Iran, Syria and Rome – for example, a Buddhist mission from the East was welcomed at the court of Ptolemy Philadelphus,

some time in the 3rd century BC[29]. It is a misunderstanding to think that Buddhists believe in one Buddha: in the Buddhist pantheon there are various Buddhas and Bodhisattvas. The term *Bodhisattva* stands for future Buddhas, Buddhas in the making. As such, Buddhists make a regular search for them, believing in the reincarnation of Buddhas or Enlightened Ones.

In Tibet and Ladakh, special rituals are conducted for finding Bodhisattvas, or *tulkus*. When a head lama passes away, monks are required to find his successor. They find the baby into whose body the soul of the departed lama has taken refuge. A careful study of cosmic signs is conducted by lamas[30], using astrology. Personal belongings of the lama, including his cup and other presents, like gold, gems, holy water and incense are placed before the baby, mixed with other articles. If the baby touches the cup of the deceased lama, and passes other tests, he is considered as an incarnate lama, and much rejoicing breaks out.

The above would clearly hint that arguably the wise men from the East were no other than Buddhist priests. They were in search of their *tulku*. Having found from their astrological and occult studies that an Enlightened One had been born in Judaea, they reached Jerusalem. They had seen his advent through cosmic signs and after having found him, they prostrated before Jesus and presented their gifts, which included gold, frankincense and myrrh. After having recognised Jesus as a future Buddha, they returned to their country, quietly, by another way. As would be the custom with Buddhist lamas, they would come again later to take the child for education and worship.

50

(1) *Matthew*, 1, 1-17.

(2) *Luke*, 3, 23-38.

(3) Robinson, Forbes, *The Coptic Apocryphal Gospels*, Methuen & Co, London, 1902.

(4) *Luke*, 1, 5.

(5) The *Gospel of James* or *Protevangelium Jacobi*, v11, I. This was discovered in the 16th century, and is included in Forbes Robinson's *Coptic Apocryphal Gospels*. For further particulars, refer to Hastings, J, *Dictionary of the Apostolic Church*, T & T Clark, Edinburgh, 1918. Also Nazir Ahmad Khwaja, *Jesus in Heaven on Earth*, p131.

(6) Hiren, Yrjo, *The Sacred Shrine*, Macmillan, London, 1912.

(7) *Mark*, 6, 3.

(8) *Luke*, 1, 48. "And when they saw him, they were amazed; and his mother said unto him, *Son, why hast thou thus dealt with us? Behold, thy father and I have sought thee, sorrowing*".

(9) Hastings, J, *Dictionary of the Bible*, T & T Clark, Edinburgh, 1904, p434.

(10) *Matthew*, I, 20. "The angel of the Lord appeared unto him in a dream, saying, *Joseph, fear not to take unto thee Mary thy wife*". The Essenes gave a different version: "And Joseph, through a messenger of our Order was influenced not to leave the woman, nor disturb her faith in the sacredness of her experience, and to be father to the child". From *The Crucifixion by an Eye-Witness*, p40.

(11) *Luke*, I, 30-35.

(12) Yrjo Hiren, *The Sacred Shrine*, Macmillan, London, 1912, pp200-206; *The Ante-Nicene Christian Library*, 25 vols, T & T Clark, Edinburgh, 1869; Robinson, Forbes, *The Coptic Apocryphal Gospel*, Methuen, London, 1902; James, Montague, *The Apocryphal New Testament*, Oxford, 1924; Salmond, *The Writings of Hippolytus*, T & T Clark, Edinburgh, 1902.

(13) The *Gospel of James*, as quoted in Nazir Ahmad, Khwaja, *Jesus in Heaven on Earth*, Azeez Manzil, Lahore, 1973, pp130-136. First published by the Woking Muslim Mission and Literary Trust, Woking, UK.

(14) *The Book of Enoch*, 2 vols, tr R H Charles, Clarendon Press, Oxford, 1893; James, M R, *The Apocryphal New Testament*, Oxford, 1926; Charles, R H, *The Old Testament Apocrypha and Pseudepigrapha*, 2 vols, Oxford, 1913.

(15) *Encyclopaedia Britannica*, art. Essenes; *Historia Antiqua Judaico* or *Antiquities of the Jews* by Josephus, Flavius, edited by Loeb, London & Cambridge MA, 1924ff; Dupont-Sommer, A, *The Jewish Sect of Qumran and the Essenes*, Macmillan, New York, 1956; Allegro, John, *The Dead Sea Scrolls: a Reappraisal*, Penguin, Middlesex, 1964; Allegro, John, *Dead Sea Scrolls: The Mystery Revealed*, New York, 1981; Cannon, Dolores, *Jesus and the Essenes*, Gateway Books, Bath, 1992.

(16) *The Crucifixion by An Eye-Witness*, Indo-American Book Co, Chicago, 1907, pp40-44. This book is a translation from a Latin manuscript in the possession of the Masonic Fraternity in Germany. It was first published in

1873, but was withdrawn from circulation, and all plates were destroyed. One copy survived, and the book was re-published in 1907. It contains the translation of a letter written by a member of the Essenes to another member in Alexandria, just seven years after the crucifixion. It narrates an eye-witness account of the story of the crucifixion, his removal from the cross, and resuscitation.

(17) *Luke*, 2, 8.

(18) *Matthew*, 2, 1-3.

(19) Keller, Werner, *The Bible as History*, Hodder & Stoughton, London, 1956, pp338-339.

(20) Davies, Powell, *The Meaning of the Dead Sea Scrolls*, New York, 1956, p90.

(21) Nazir Ahmad, Khwaja, *Jesus in Heaven on Earth*, pp83-84.

(22) Davies, Powell, *The Meaning of the Dead Sea Scrolls*, New York, p90.

(23) Forsström, Johan, *The King of the Jews*, 1987, p44.

(24) *Luke*, 2, 1-7. "And it came to pass in those days, that there went out a decree from Caesar Augustus, that all the world should be taxed. And this taxing was first made when Cyrenius was governor of Syria".

(25) Keller, Werner, *The Bible as History*, p330.

(26) *ibid*, p334. We do know that the wise men from the East were guided to baby Jesus by a star, which has been given many names, such as, the 'Star of the Three Kings', the 'Star of Horus' and the 'Star in the East'.

(27) *Matthew*, 2, 1-10.

(28) *Matthew*, 2, 11-12. The gifts of gold, frankincense and myrrh had special significance. Gold signifies royalty, frankincense divinity and myrrh hints toward spirituality.

(29) Muses, G A, ed, *The Septuagint Bible*, Falcon's Wing Press, Colorado, 1954, p xxi, Introduction. Ottley, R R, *Introduction to the Old Testament in Greek*, revised edition, Cambridge, 1914: "A Buddhist mission from the Ganges found a welcome at his [Ptolemy Philadelphus'] court; and the reign which produced Manetho's Greek history of Egyptian institutions may well have yielded also a translation into Greek of Hebrew sacred books".

(30) Hassnain, Oki & Sumi, *Ladakh the Moonland*, Light and Life publishers, New Delhi, 1975, p74. "Succession of incarnate lamas is a complicated affair. It is based on various tests based on a religious sanction. According to them, when a person dies, his spirit is born again in another body. Such an incarnation is perpetuated involuntarily through the forces of *karma*. The position of an incarnate lama or *Rinpoche*, being high and esteemed, means he is sure to come again, in the next life, to lead and show the path to Buddhahood".

6

Jesus' childhood

The Buddhist Version

I must now revert back to the version recorded by Nicolas Notovitch at Hemis about the birth of Jesus. Here I quote:

> At this time came the moment when the all-merciful Judge elected to become incarnate in a human being. And the Eternal Spirit, dwelling in a state of complete rest and supreme beatitude, awoke and detached itself, for an indefinite period, from the Eternal Being, so as to show forth, in the guise of humanity, the means of self-identification with divinity, and of attaining eternal felicity. And to demonstrate by example how humanity may attain moral purity, and by separating his soul from its mortal coil, the degrees of perfection necessary to enter into the kingdom of heaven, which is unchangeable, and where happi-ness reigns eternal.
>
> Soon after, a marvellous child was born in the land of Israel, God himself speaking by the mouth of this infant of the frailty of body and the grandeur of the soul.
>
> The divine child, to whom was given the name of Issa, began from the earliest years to speak of the one and indivisible God, exhorting the souls of those gone astray to repentance and the purification of the sins of which they are culpable. People came from all parts to hear him, and they marvelled at the discourses proceeding from his child's mouth. All the Israelites were of one accord in saying that the Eternal Spirit dwelt with this child[1].

Jesus in Egypt, 6–4 BC

The *Gospel according to Matthew* informs that Joseph took his wife and Jesus to Egypt and was there until the death of Herod (4 BC). No other information is available about them. However, the Apocryphal works point to numerous places where Jesus stayed, along with his parents, in the monasteries of Wadi-el-Natrun, Mataria and Al-Moharraq[2]. Mataria was also known as the 'Herbal Garden' and was renowned for its unique fruits and flowers[3]. These monasteries belonged to the Essenes, who according to Philo of Alexandria totalled four thousand souls[4]. The village of Mataria lies on the right bank of the Nile, and it was here that the Holy Family found refuge. At present, the Church of the Holy Family exists in the Herbal Garden, which also has a fig tree with a hollow trunk in which, according to a Coptic legend, Joseph and his family once hid themselves.

During their stay in Egypt, the Essene brotherhood provided all facilities to Joseph, Mary and Jesus. They were conducted as guests to their dwelling near the slope of a mountain where the Romans had built a temple dedicated to Jupiter. They were also introduced to the Essene congregation where they learned prayer ceremony as well as the eating of consecrated bread and drinking of holy wine. Let me quote from an Essene work:

> At the introduction ceremony, Joseph was placed among the half circle of men on the right hand and Mary, his wife, among women on the left hand. There they, with our brethren, ate the bread and drank the wine and all together sang the holy hymns.
>
> Further, Joseph here vowed before the elder of our brotherhood that he would renounce forever any claim on the child, who henceforth would belong to the order. He was then made acquainted with the salutation and sign of the holy brotherhood[5].

Josephus has described the Essenes as a secret brotherhood, opposed to the Pharisees and Sadducees. They held their meetings away from towns in their own monasteries. They wore white garments and were interested in the healing properties of herbs and stones. A wing of the Essenes was known as the *Therapeutees*, who lived in mixed communities but observed celibacy. The members of this order lived separately but danced every seventh week after supper, singing hymns and dancing until dawn[6]. Another wing of the Essenes was known as the *Sampsaeans*, who mostly lived by the eastern shores of the Dead Sea.

Josephus called the Essenes 'the most perfect of all the sects in Palestine'. According to him, members of the order embraced non-violence and enjoyed a high moral reputation amongst the Jews. They were vegetarians, and did not believe in animal sacrifice. All this leads us to believe that the Essenes *could* be the Buddhists of a western stock, maintaining secrecy over their identity or influences.

Buddhist missionaries made their appearance in Egypt soon after the time of Alexander the Great[7], who died in 323 BC. Two hundred years after the passing away of Sakyamuni Buddha, just before Alexander's time, Buddhists divided themselves into two main sects, the *Theravadins* and the *Sarvastivadins*[8]. There could be a connection between the *Therapeutees* and *Sampsaeans* mentioned by Eusebius and John Allegro, and the *Theravadins* and the *Sarvastivadins* of the Buddhists.

During their stay in Egypt, the holy family remained under the protection of the Essenes, who will have given Jesus much care and attention. They absorbed themselves in study, contemplation and meditation, and during his formative years, Jesus will have followed their example. When the peril of Roman suppression in Galilee was over, Joseph went to Nazareth, and from there, returned to Jerusalem[9].

Youth

After his return from Egypt, Jesus spent his childhood in Nazareth. His father Joseph worked as a carpenter and lived in a little house with clay walls. By now, Jesus was literate, wise and skilled in his father's profession, being able to make wooden tools for use in agriculture[10]. Nazareth is surrounded by hills and is peaceful. Its fields were full of wheat and its gardens had date-palms, figs and pomegranates. In those days, a military road passed through it and an ancient caravan route between Damascus and Egypt crossed the plain of Jezreel, south of Nazareth.

While Jesus loved to read the *Psalms of David*, his mother Mary absorbed herself in prayer and devotion. When he was twelve years old, his parents took him to Jerusalem for the Passover feast mentioned in the previous chapter, and was lost, then to be found in the Temple. Although Jesus was respectful of his parents after that, it was clear that Jesus was now not interested in a carpenter's work but had decided to devote himself to God.

The following incident also reveals that at the age of twelve, Jesus was fully conversant with the scriptures. When he spoke with the scribes in the temple, his knowledge of the doctrines gave offence to the Pharisees.

> *When Jesus spoke with the scribes concerning holy things, his doctrines gave deep offence to the Pharisees in Jerusalem. They knew him to be from Galilee, and they despised him as they despised all people from Galilee. When the divine child had spoken publicly in the Temple, the Essenes were apprehensive of the dangers that threatened him. They knew that the Pharisees were in private council, determined to banish him from the synagogue of Sopherim. Thus it came to pass that Jesus was lost from his parents in the large city which then contained many people from the whole country, because of the Passover. At last, on the fourth day, Jesus was found by his parents, according to the information given by the Essenes.* [11]

This is an alternative story to that given in *Luke*[12]. When they arrived home in Nazareth, Joseph and Mary will have had to adjust to what Jesus had told them at the Temple, that he was not interested in the profession of carpentry, but instead would like to serve God, as a priest or similar[13]. This was inevitable, because of Jesus' involvements with the Essenes from early life, and demonstrated in Jesus' aversion to the Pharisees. Like the Pharisees, the Essenes meticulously observed the laws of Moses, the sabbath and ritual purity, professing belief also in immortality and divine punishment of sins. But unlike the Pharisees, the Essenes denied the resurrection of the body, and refused to immerse themselves in public life. With few exceptions, they shunned Temple worship, content to live ascetic lives of manual labour in relative seclusion. The sabbath was reserved for day-long prayer and meditation on the *Torah*. Those who qualified for membership swore piety to God, justice toward people, hatred of falsehood, love of truth and faithful observance of other tenets of the Essenes[14].

Josephus records that Jesus was noted for his learning, and was often consulted by the priests and doctors of Jerusalem. He seemed to spend much of his time in Jerusalem, which was about twenty miles from Qumran, where he would visit the Essenes, discussing philosophical issues with them. The Essenes disliked the Roman subjugators of Palestine, and in order to provide moral support for the movement against the Romans, they trained preachers, including the growing John and Jesus.

Initiation

Jesus met John the Baptist in Nazareth and they became friends, their attachment ripening into close brotherliness with each other. They would often wander into the wildest parts of the mountain regions and visit the Essene retreat on the mountain where Masada stands. Here the elder of the brotherhood, Nabbin, would teach them wisdom and virtue. When Joseph heard about it, he remembered his vow and duty towards the Essene brotherhood. He then, for the first time, made known to Jesus that he was not his real father[15]. Now, it was decided that Jesus should be initiated into the order. Here is the account of the initiation ceremony:

> At the appointed time they saw, in the evening, the fire signal ascend from the mountain. When they were arrived at the temple they were met by the brotherhood. According to our rules, Jesus and John were initiated into our order, after the following manner: both were instructed and shown the way to enter into the assembly, where the brethren were seated in four separate groups according to the four degrees. Over the scene, the crescent moon shed its light.
>
> The two were placed before the brethren. There they made their vow, the brethren, in their white robes, placing their right hands upon their breasts, with the left hanging down at the side. And this was done as a token that none but the pure in heart shall see that which is sacred

*and holy. And the two vowed indifference to the treasures of the earth,
to worldly power or name, and by the brotherly kiss they vowed
obedience and secrecy.*

*And, in obedience to our custom, when these two had made their
vow they were conducted into a lonely cavern where, for three days and
nights, they were subjected to self-examination and trial. In the evening
of the third day they were again brought before the assembly to answer
questions put to them, and then to pray. Having received the brotherly
kiss, they were clothed in white robes, emblem of sacred purity, and the
trowel, emblematic of the labours of our brotherhood, was put in their
hands.*

*Having sung the sacred hymns and partaken of the feast of love by
themselves, they were dismissed. When the year of trial and self-
examination was passed, they were again, under the new moon, admitted into the order, this time as real members, and initiated into the
higher science. Thus it came to pass that John returned to live in
solitude and wilderness while Jesus returned to Nazareth[16].*

As far as the four Gospels are concerned, the story of Jesus stops
abruptly at the age of twelve. Nothing is known about the subsequent eighteen years, until he assumed his ministry and was put
on the cross. There is not a single reference to Jesus in the Gospels
during this entire period. This raised many suspicions in my mind.
I felt disgusted with the Church for having removed or destroyed
this information. Hence for the 'lost years', from the age of 12 to
30, I tried to find information from other sources, predominantly
in the East.

My researches persuaded me that now was the right time to
find out all the available oriental sources of information. I visited
many libraries, and to my astonishment found that many books in
Sanskrit, Persian, Urdu and Kashmiri contained useful and interesting information about Jesus Christ. It was a strange coincidence
that besides entrusting archives and archaeology to me as director,
the state government also entrusted libraries and research to me.
God had been kind, and all institutions, store-houses of culture,
were at my disposal. I was to look after thousands of manuscripts
and handwritten scrolls in Sanskrit, Tibetan, Arabic, Persian,

Urdu and other languages.

For the next ten years, I made many trips to find different manuscripts, which contained startling evidence about the journeys of Jesus to India. I had found a mine of information, and in my enthusiasm, I gave several interviews to journals. This created a band of friends throughout the world, who offered to help me in research work. But at the same time, many hurdles came in my way and I suffered due to my revelations about Jesus and his life in Kashmir – and this is not the occasion to tell that story! I continued my researches further, as you will see in subsequent chapters.

---

(1) Notovitch, Nicolas, *The Life of Saint Issa*, R F Fenno & Co, New York, 1890, IV, 1-8. See also: Notovitch, Nicolas, *The Unknown Life of Christ*, Hutchinson, London, 1893. A book has been published under the title *The Unknown Life of Jesus Christ*, by Nababharat Publishers, Calcutta, 1981, containing chapters IV, V and VI, recorded by Swami Abhedananda in 1922.
(2) Ameen, Hakim, *St Mark and the Coptic Church*, p8. A full description is given in Levi, *The Aquarian Gospel of Jesus the Christ*, California, 1978, pp50-55.
(3) Keller, Werner, *The Bible as History*, p341.
(4) Nazir Ahmad, Khwaja, *Jesus in Heaven on Earth*, p218.
(5) *The Crucifixion by an Eye-Witness*, pp41-42.
(6) Eusebius of Caesarea, *Historica Ecclesiastica*, ed E Schwarz, New York, 1914, Vol 2, XVII, pp22-23; Josephus, Flavius, *The Wars of the Jews*, T Nelson & Sons, London, 1873; Dupont-Sommer, *The Jewish Sect of Qumran and the Essenes*, tr R D Barnett, Macmillan, 1955.
(7) Forsström, Johan, *The King of the Jews*, p289.
(8) Aziz-us-Samad, Ulfat, *Great Religions of the World*, Lahore, 1976, p44. According to Josephus, the Essenes were called *Therapeuts*, which means a physician. But Philo of Alexandria (ca 20 AD) wrote that the Therapeuts were those who retired into solitude and passed their time studying religion and nature. See *The Crucifixion by an Eye-Witness*, Chicago, 1907.
(9) *The Crucifixion by an Eye-Witness*, pp41-43.
(10) Nazir Ahmad, Khwaja, *Jesus in Heaven on Earth*, p114.
(11) *The Crucifixion by an Eye-Witness*, pp44-47.
(12) *Luke*, 2, 42-46. "And when he was twelve years old, they went up to Jerusalem. As they returned, the child Jesus tarried behind. And it came to pass that after three days they found him at the Temple".
(13) *Luke*, 2, 48-49. This incident establishes the relationship of love between Jesus and God. At another place he says: "My Father is greater than I", (John, 14, 28).

(14) *Encyclopaedia Britannica*, Micropaedia, Vol III, p965; Szekely, Edmond Bordeaux, *The Essene Code of Life*, San Diego, 1977.

(15) *The Crucifixion by an Eye-Witness*, p49. "In the beginning was the Word, and the Word was with God. And the Word became flesh and dwelt among us", (John, 1, 1-2). On earth, Jesus called himself the Son of God and the Son of Man. See also: Fuller, R H, *The Foundations of New Testament Christology*, Collins, London, 1965, for an understanding of these titles of Jesus.

(16) *The Crucifixion by an Eye-Witness*, pp49-53. "And Jesus greatly loved the Vedic hymns and the Avesta; but more than all he loved to read the Psalms of David and the pungent words of Solomon. The Jewish books of prophecy were his delight; and when he reached his seventh year he needed not the books to read, for he had fixed in memory every word", from *The Aquarian Gospel of Jesus the Christ*, p50.

7

The Early Travels of Jesus

Jesus' first journey to India

One of the most interesting episodes in the life of Jesus is the account of his first journey to India. The basis of this account was given by Roerich from the Tibetan scrolls he found in 1925[1]. Jesus was thirteen years old when he departed for India[2]. The *Sutra* known as *Natha Namavali* also asserts that Jesus, called *Isha Natha*, came to India at the age of fourteen[3].

The *Gospel of the Hebrews*[4] informs us that Jesus journeyed towards India via Assyria and Chaldea (Mesopotamia) in a train of merchants. In those days the trade route from Jerusalem to Sindh passed from Damascus to Kharax (on the confluence of the Tigris and Euphrates rivers) then through Nisibis and Babylon. From Kharax, one could proceed to Sindh by ship, or by road through Persia. This latter route passed through Elam to Hormuz, and then to Sindh. The caravan of merchants which Jesus joined may well have followed this very route, though we have no definite proof.

Was it really possible to travel from Palestine to India 2,000 years ago? Around 326 BC, Alexander the Great and his army reached the banks of the river Jehlum in Northern India. The Silk Roads, connecting China with the Middle East, through central Asia, was used even earlier. The Silk Road starts at Sian in China, passing through Kansu province to the Gobi desert, where it divides into two branches between Tun-huang and Kashgar, one via Turfan, and the other via Khotan and Yarkand.

From Kashgar, the road crosses the High Pamir to Sa-

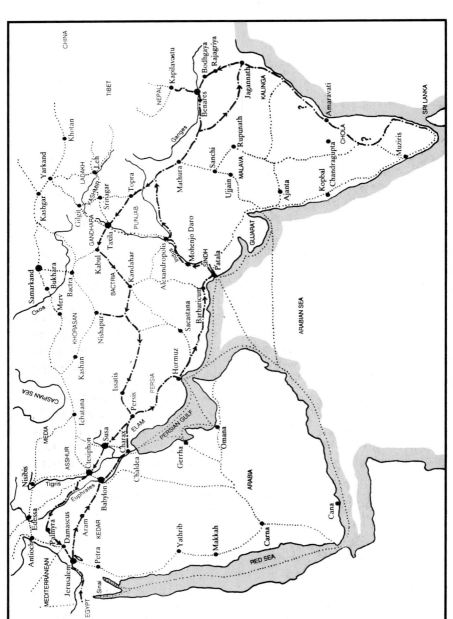

Jesus' first journey to India, 13–27 AD

markand, Bokhara and Merv. A side road from Yarkand leads to
Leh in Ladakh and Srinagar in Kashmir, proceeding to India. From
Merv, the main road passes through Persia and Mesopotamia to
meet the Mediterranean Sea at Antioch and Tyre. From Damascus,
roads led to Rome, Egypt, Arabia and Ethiopia. These routes have
been used for commerce and migration by Greeks, Israelites, Kassites, Aryans, Sumerians, Assyrians and others.

The Indus civilisation, flourishing at Mohenjo-Daro, Harappa
and Taxila around 2,000 BC, was an extension of Mesopotamian
culture, which itself was connected with Egyptian culture. Archaeologists have unearthed relics and artifacts of similar features and
motif in Iraq, Iran, central Asia and north India. So it is evident
that cultures from Egypt to India were manifestations of a single
root culture with regional variations. For this to be possible there
must have been considerable movement from one region to another in ancient times. It is thus quite possible for Jesus to have
travelled from Palestine to India during his lifetime.

Jesus' first destination was Sindh, where the Indus river and its
tributaries, the Ravi, Beas, Chinab and Jehlum rivers, join the
Arabian Sea. The ancient city of Patala stood on the Indus delta.
Jesus' stay in Sindh was probably short, and he went on through
the Punjab and Rajputana until he finally reached Orissa.

During his journey, Jesus would have come into contact with
followers of Jainism. This is mentioned in Notovitch's notes in
chapter 4, para. 21. This religion was founded by Varadhamana
Mahavira (599-527 BC), who advocated purification of the soul
through leading a pure life, through non-violence, noble actions
and thoughts, kindness to all beings and vegetarian diet. The Jains
perhaps begged him to stay with them, but Jesus journeyed on to
his destination – the temple of Jagannath at Puri in Orissa[5].

Jagannath and Varanasi
The temple of Jagannath is a very big institution. The main temple
in the centre is surrounded by numerous temples, halls and clois-
ters on four sides. Evidence suggests that Jesus stayed here for six
years. During this period, he also visited Rajagriha, Varanasi
(Benares), and other holy cities. Varanasi is the holy city of Hindus

on the banks of the river Ganges, and here he will have been introduced to the Vedas by the priests. They came to this city from all parts of India for prayer and meditation. Pilgrims bathe in the water and sprinkle water in the air facing the sun. The dead are cremated on the bank of this sacred river and ashes thrown in the water. Since ancient times, pilgrims have stood at the banks of the Ganges, chanting prayers and performing bathing rituals.

Jesus gave his first sermon among the people at Varanasi, in which he spoke about the equality of all people before God. He said:

God the Father establishes no difference between his children, who are equally dear to him. Respect God, bow down your knee before Him only, and to Him only may offerings be made.

The eternal Judge, the eternal Spirit, is the one and indivisible soul of the universe, which alone creates, contains and animates the whole. He alone has willed and created. He alone has existed from eternity and will exist without end. He has no equal, neither in the heavens nor on this earth.

The Great Creator shares His power with no-one, still less with inanimate objects, for He alone possesses supreme power. He willed it and the world appeared. By one divine thought he united the waters and separated them from the dry portion of the globe. He is the cause of the mysterious life of humanity, in whom He has breathed a part of his being. And He has subordinated to humanity the land, the waters, the animals and all that He has created, and which He maintains in immutable order by fixing the duration of each.

The wrath of God shall soon be let loose on humanity, for it has forgotten its Creator and filled its temples with abominations, and it adores a host of creatures which God has subordinated to it. They that deprive their brothers of divine happiness shall themselves be deprived of it.

Help the poor, assist the weak, harm no-one, do not covet what you do not have and what you see in the possession of others[6].

The Brahmin priests resented the ideas of Jesus and became his enemies. They asked him to abandon the company of the low-

Chortens, in which are buried sacred texts, are found in great numbers in Ladakh (*Yoshiaka Sora*)

caste Shudras. Jesus felt disgusted and left Jagannath for the birthplace of Sakyamuni Buddha.

Jesus amongst the Buddhists

A study of Buddhist scrolls preserved in the Hemis monastery of
Ladakh exposes interesting information about the founder of Buddhism. I will try to summarise it briefly.

Only seven Buddhas are exalted among 1002 Buddhas.
Sakyamuni Buddha is the supreme Buddha and he has powers over
transmigration of souls. When Buddha looked for a race, a country, a time, and a mother, he entered the womb of the Queen
Maya. He had 32 marks of greatness and possessed 80 physical
perfections. He grew up into a beautiful youth and acquired profi-
ciency in five branches of science. His father, who was the Chief of
the Shakya clan in Kapilavastu, Nepal, selected a princess to be his
wife.

When the prince saw the unbearable misery of birth, the cruel
afflictions of illness and old age and the agony of decay and death,
Buddha renounced the princely world to find salvation. He travelled to many parts of India and was reduced to a skeleton through
the practice of rigid austerities. He reached Gaya and meditated
under the Bodhi tree. After having conquered fear as well as desire,
he found divine vision. Thus he attained omniscience.

Buddha declared the Noble Eightfold Path as his message for
salvation from misery and pain: right views, right intentions, right
speech, right action, right livelihood, right effort, right mindful-
ness, and right meditation.

Dating the life of Buddha is difficult – he lived between about
563 and 483 BC. After the Kalinga war, some 270 years later,
Ashoka Maurya (269-232 BC), emperor of north India, adopted
Buddhism. He made it his life mission to spread the teachings of
Buddha. He sent Buddhist missionaries to many countries. It was
during this period that the Buddhist monks came into contact with
Pythagoreans in Greece and Essenes in Judaea. Ashoka succeeded
in his endeavours in India, Sri Lanka and the Far East[7].

When Jesus arrived in Kapilavastu in Nepal, the Buddhists
received him and he lived with monks in a monastery. He wit-

nessed their religious rites and participated in prayer and meditation. A time came when he had grasped the teachings of Buddha, attained mastery in the Sutras, the Vinayas and the Abhidharma, and began to give sermons like the Master. The monks included him in the list of outstanding masters or *Arhats*. After a few years, they even accepted him as a Bodhisattva. The chief monk, in a special congregation of the monks, declared:

We stand today upon a crest of time. Six times ago a master was born who gave glory and light to man. And now a master sage stands here. This Hebrew prophet is a rising star of wisdom. He brings to us a knowledge of God. All the world will hear his words, will heed his words and glorify his name[8].

Jesus lived among the Buddhists for six years[9]. He wanted to move on, but they requested him to stay. When he insisted, they agreed with a heavy heart, saying that "Buddha had chosen him to spread his holy word".

Return Westwards

Then he left Nepal and went towards the west, preaching to diverse people the supreme perfection of humanity, in words such as these:

He who shall have regained his original purity will die having obtained remission for his sins, and he will have the right to contemplate the majesty of God. The Eternal Law-giver is One. There is no other God but He. He has not shared the world with anyone, neither has He informed anyone of his full intentions.

Cease to seek for heaven in the sky. Open up the windows of your hearts, and like a flood of light, heaven will come and bring a boundless joy. Then toil will be no cruel task[10].

Even as a father shows kindness towards his children, so will God judge people after death, in conformity with His merciful laws. He will never humiliate His child by casting his soul for punishment into the body of a beast[11].

Everything has been sacrificed to man, who is directly and intimately united to Him, his Father. Therefore the man shall be severely judged and chastised by divine law who causes the sacrifice of His children[12].

Man can be naught before the Eternal Judge, just as animals can be naught before man. Therefore, I say unto you, leave your idols and perform not rites which separate you from your Father and bind you to the priest, from whom heaven has turned away[13].

His words spread among the people through whose country he passed. Some priests demanded of him to perform miracles. But Jesus answered that miracles of God had been wrought from the day this universe was created. These miracles are performed every day and every moment; whosoever sees them not is deprived of one of the most beautiful gifts of life. He told them to perceive God with their hearts and not with their eyes. He advised them not to deceive any one, to abstain from debauchery and to try to attain supreme bliss by purification of the soul[14].

Jesus arrives in Persia

On his return journey, Jesus had to pass through Punjab. He joined a caravan of merchants, who were coming by way of Kashmir. When they heard him speaking like a prophet, they became followers. He showed many miracles and healed the sick among them. When they came to know that Jesus wanted to proceed towards Persia, they gave him a Bactrian beast for riding[15].

When he entered Persia the priests became afraid and forbade the people to listen to him. Nevertheless, villagers welcomed him. The priests asked many questions regarding Zoroaster. He said to them:

I preach no new God but our celestial Father, who existed before the beginning and will exist until after the end. You pretend that you must adore the sun and the genii of good and evil. But I say unto you that the sun does not act spontaneously, but by the will of the invisible Creator, who has made it. Who then has caused this star to light the day, warm man at his work and vivify the seeds sown in the fields?

There is no God other than the God of good! He, like the father of a family, does only good to his children. He forgives their transgressions if they repent: honour the day of Judgment, for God will inflict a terrible punishment upon all those who have led His children astray[16].

Jesus left Persia and continued his journey towards the land of Israel. He arrived back in about 22 AD. He found that the Israelites were filled with despair due to sufferings inflicted on them by their rulers. Jesus exhorted them not to despair and to have faith in God. They came in multitudes to listen to his words. He told them that redemption from the yoke of sin was near and they must not neglect the laws of God and those of Moses. He said:

Enter into your temple, into your heart; illuminate it with good thoughts, with patience and unshakeable faith in your Father. Do that which is agreeable to God, for in doing good to your fellow men, you perform a ceremony that embellishes the temple wherein abideth Him who has created you[17].

The material I have uncovered concerning this period of Jesus' life gives a basic structure to his eighteen missing years – vital years which the Gospels *somehow* forgot.

---

(1) Roerich, Nicolai, and Grant, Francis, *Himalaya: a Monograph*, New York, 1926, pp148-153.

(2) Forsström, Johan, *The King of the Jews*, p176, quoting *Jami-ut-Tawarikh*, by Faqir Muhammad ben Qazi Muhammad Raza, that "Jesus was thirteen years old when he left for the far-eastern countries". However, *The Life of St Issa*, by Nicolas Notovitch, mentions: "In his fourteenth year, young Issa came to the Sindh".

(3) Serrano, Miguel, *The Serpent of Paradise*, Rider & Co, London, pp142-143.

(4) While only four gospels are included in the *Holy Bible*, twenty-six gospels stand excluded. Out of these, the *Gospel of Thomas*, the *Gospel according to the Hebrews*, the *Gospel according to the Egyptians*, the *Gospel of Peter*, the *Gospel of the Ebionites*, the *Gospel of Barnabas* and the *Gospel of James* are of particular importance, because these are of the same general type as the Canonical Gospels. For studying all the unrecognised Gospels, consult the following: *The Ante-Nicene Christian Library*, 25 vols, Edinburgh, 1869; Andrews, *Apocryphal Books of the Old and New Testament*, London, 1906; James, Montague, *The Apocryphal New Testament*, Oxford, 1924; Schonfield, Hugh, *The Authentic New Testament*, London, 1956.

(5) Notovitch, Nicolas, *The Life of St Issa*, v, 1-3.

(6) Notovitch, Nicolas, *The Life of St Issa*, V, 11-27.

(7) Bock, Janet, *The Jesus Mystery*, Los Angeles, 1980, p89; Forsström, Johan, *King of the Jews*, pp275-285.

(8) Levi, *The Aquarian Gospel*, California, 1972, 32: 42-43.

(9) Notovitch, Nicolas, *The Life of St Issa*, VI, 4.

(10) Levi, *The Aquarian Gospel*, 33, 1-10.

(11) Notovitch, Nicolas, *The Unknown Life of Jesus Christ*, Hutchinson, London, 1895, VI, 2.

(12) Notovitch, Nicolas, *The Life of St Issa*, VI, 13. This verse has been differently worded in *The Unknown Life of Christ*: "All things have been sacrificed to man, who is directly and intimately associated with Me his Father; therefore he who shall have stolen from Me My child, will be severely judged and chastised by the divine law".

(13) Notovitch, Nicolas, *The Life of St Issa*, VI: 11-15.

(14) Notovitch, Nicolas, *The Life of St Issa*, VII, 4-13.

(15) Levi, *The Aquarian Gospel*, 37: 1-17.

(16) Notovitch, Nicolas, *The Life of St Issa*, VIII: 6-20.

(17) Notovitch, Nicholas, *The Life of St Issa*, IX, 12.

Decorative wheels on the roof of Hemis Monastery *(Sylvia Planzer)*

8

Jesus' initiation

When Jesus arrived back in Palestine, he stayed in many small towns and villages populated by Jewish communities. People of the bigger towns had adopted Greek dress and a Roman way of life. Palestine was crowded and the majority of the Jews earned a meagre livelihood in manual labour. There was a time when they had been the rulers of the country, but now, their position was no better than slaves or subjects of the Romans. In their heart of hearts, they hated the Roman rule. Having suffered the oppression of the Roman conquerors, they looked for the advent of a redeemer, the Messiah.

Jesus back in Egypt

Jesus had been away from the land of his birth for about nineteen years. He also longed to see his Essene friends in Egypt and inform them about his experiences in the East. He was received with great honour by the brotherhood and the aged teachers praised his wisdom. However he told them he wished to gain further heights and to pass harder tests.

After receiving his mystic name from the hierophant, Jesus passed the first test. In honour of this distinction, he received a scroll on which was written just one word: Sincerity.

After this Jesus passed the second test and the hierophant placed a scroll in his hands, on which was inscribed: Justice. Then Jesus passed the third test and received a scroll on which was written: Faith. Then

71

passed the fourth test and the hierophant placed a scroll in his hands, on which was written: Philanthropy.

Jesus spent 40 days in a monastery in deep meditation. He had conquered self and could now talk with nature. He passed the fifth test and the hierophant placed in his hand another scroll, on which was written: Heroism. After this, Jesus passed the sixth test and he received a scroll, on which was inscribed: Love Divine.

And when Jesus passed the seventh test, the hierophant placed a diadem on his brow and said: "You are the Christ!". Then a voice that shook the very monastery was heard and it said: "This is the Christ". Every living creature said: "Amen!". He had become immortal.[1]

At the time Jesus was in Egypt, an extraordinary event occurred there. An age of history was recognised to have passed, and in order to note the course of nations, peoples, tribes and tongues, seven sages met at a fixed place. Jesus was invited to attend the meeting, where he delivered an address, in which he said:

The history of life is well condensed in these immortal postulates: 'There are seven hills on which the holy city shall be built; there are seven sure foundation stones on which the universal church shall stand'. The words I speak are not my own; they are the words of Him whose will I do.

And from men of low estate I will select twelve men, who represent twelve immortal thoughts, and these will be the model of the church. And when a better age shall come, the universal church will stand upon the seven postulates. And in the name of God, our Father God, the kingdom of the soul shall be established on the seven hills. And all the peoples, tribes and tongues of earth shall enter in. The prince of peace will take his seat upon the throne of power; the triune God will then be All in All.

When Jesus finished his discourse, all the seven sages said: "*Amen!*". After this, no word was said and Jesus left the assembly and went his way back to Jerusalem[2].

Jesus in Greece

In the *Gospel of John*, it is stated that some Greeks came to worship Jesus. They asked him some questions and he told them that if any man sought to serve him, let him follow him[3]. For our study this reference is important because it connects Jesus with Greece. Jesus longed to visit the Greek masters, so he crossed the Carmel hills and took a ship for Greece. After reaching Athens, he stood in the Amphitheatre, where the Greek masters had assembled to hear him. He said:

> *Masters! I come not here to speak of philosophy. But I will tell you of a life beyond; within a real life that cannot pass away. Return, O mystic streams of Grecian thought, and mingle your clear waters with the flood of Spirit-life! And then the spirit consciousness will sleep no more, and man will know, and God will bless.*

When he sat down, the Greek masters were astonished at the wisdom of his words[4].

Jesus in Britain

Joseph of Arimathaea, a rich and influential Essene, was an importer in the tin trade between Cornwall and Phoenicia. There are legends that during one of his journeys to Britain, he was accompanied by Jesus[5]. This would have occurred at the end of Jesus' travels to India and Tibet. Joseph was not only a wealthy person but also counsellor to the Jewish Sanhedrin. As an uncle of Mary, he was related to Jesus, possibly a guardian, and took much interest in his welfare. There is also a tradition in Brittany that Mary's mother was from Cornwall[6], in which it is suggested that Jesus' fair complexion came from this origin.

Jesus is said to have stayed at Glastonbury, for quiet study, prayer and meditation, in a small house of mud and wattles, near the Chalice Well[7]. St Augustine wrote, to Pope Gregory the Great, that Jesus had even built a church at Glastonbury[8]. Gildas, the first British historian (516-570) states that Jesus "afforded his light to this island during the height of the reign of Tiberius'"[9]. Tiberius ruled between 14 and 37 AD and 'the height of his reign' was 25-27

AD. As such it is possible to fix the date of the visit of Jesus to Glastonbury at about 26–27 AD.

During that period, the Druid culture flourished in Britain. Forty Druid tribes had universities for the study of natural philosophy, astronomy, arithmetic, geometry, medicine, poetry and ritual[10]. Jesus evidently wanted to learn the secrets of Druidism. The natives of Glastonbury were peace-loving, cultured and domesticated. The Druids believed in a trinity, and three golden rays were the emblem of Druidism. They also had a messianic tradition, the Celtic Messiah being known as *Esus*.

The legends about Jesus at Glastonbury have persisted during the last two thousand years and cannot be dismissed easily. It is not a strange coincidence that around 37AD, at that time after Jesus' crucifixion when Joseph of Arimathaea and his group were reputed to have sailed to Glastonbury to settle[11], a wattle church was built on what was to became the site of the Abbey, which survived until the 1100s. Joseph's arrival gave birth to the *Culdees*, or *quidam advanae*, the 'strangers', or christianised Druids, who established centres safe from later Roman pressure on islands off the west of Britain[12].

---

(1) Levi, *The Aquarian Gospel*, pp87-97.

(2) Levi. *The Aquarian Gospel*, p60, 2-21.

(3) *John*, 12, 20-26. John informs that some Greeks sought Jesus and requested Philip to arrange their interview with him. "And Jesus answered them, saying, *The hour has come, that the Son of Man shall be glorified. He that loveth his life shall lose it; and he that hateth his life in this world shall keep it unto life eternal*".

(4) Levi, *The Aquarian Gospel*, pp83-85.

(5) This was first put forward by Rev R W Morgan in *St Paul in Britain*, Covenant, London, 1860, on the basis of legends, traditions and oral history; further amplification exists in the following books: Corbett, Percy, *Why Britain?*, R J Press, Newbury, UK, 1984; Dunstan, Victor, *Did the Virgin Mary Live and Die in England?*, Megiddo Press, UK, 1985; Jowett, George, *The Drama of the Lost Disciples*, Covenant, London, 1961; Dobson, C C, *Did our Lord visit Britain*, Covenant, London, 1936; Lewis, Rev L S, *St Joseph of Arimathaea at Glastonbury*, James Clarke, UK, 1922 & 1976; Taylor, J W, *The Coming of the Saints*, London 1906, Covenant 1969, Artisan USA, 1986.

(6) Lewis, L S, *St Joseph of Arimathaea at Glastonbury*, ch 4; Dunstan, Victor, *Did the Virgin Mary Live and Die in England?*; Matthews, John, *A Glastonbury Reader*, Aquarian, 1991; Hagger, Nicholas, *The Fire and the Stones*, Element,

UK, 1991. "Another Cornish story is to the effect that Joseph of Arimathaea came in a boat to Cornwall, and brought the boy Jesus with him, and taught him how to extract tin and purge it from its wolfram", Baring-Gould, *The Book of Cornwall*, quoted in *Did Our Lord visit Britain?*, p13.

(7) Dobson, C C, *Did Our Lord visit Britain?*, Covenant, London, 1936. The Chalice Well, being one of the most revered ancient sites in the Isle of Avalon, is connected with Jesus before and after the crucifixion, in several legends and traditions. The name *Chalice* alludes to the cup used in the Last Supper, which Joseph is reputed to have brought with him. Information about the Chalice Well is available from the Chalice Well Trust, Glastonbury, Somerset. The Trust was founded by Wellesley Tudor Pole in 1959.

(8) *Epistolae ad Gregorium Papam*, quoted in Rev R W Morgan's *St Paul in Britain*, Covenant, London, 1860.

(9) Lewis, Rev L S, *St Joseph of Arimathaea at Glastonbury*, James Clark, 1922; Dobson, C C, *Did Our Lord visit Britain?*, Covenant, London, 1860.

(10) Hill Elder, Isabel , *Celt, Druid and Culdee*, Covenant, London, 1947 & 1973, pp48-63.

(11) Lewis, H A, *Christ in Cornwall?*, in Matthews, John, *A Glastonbury Reader*, Aquarian, 1991. Dobson, C C, *Did Our Lord visit Britain?*, Covenant, London, 1936.

(12) Hill Elder, Isabel, *Celt, Druid and Culdee*, pp78-88, quoting Baronius add ann 306, Vatican MSS, *Nova Legenda Anglia*, II: "Certain friends and disciples of our Lord, in the persecution that followed his Ascension, found refuge in Britain in AD 37". I myself have visited Glastonbury and other sites, and feel satisfied that the tradition of Christianity reaching Britain before its advent in the Roman Empire is correct.

9

Jesus' Ministry in Israel

Jesus was twenty-nine years old when he returned to Israel. During his absence, the Romans had caused the Israelites to endure ever more atrocious sufferings, and they were filled with despair. This went back to 63 BC, when the spiritual and political independence of Israel came to an abrupt end. It was in this year that Pompey, the Roman general, marched into Palestine with his army[1]. Pompey stormed Jerusalem and broke into the Temple, being welcomed as a deliverer by the Pharisees. But disillusion set in, and several failed revolts followed.

In 37 BC the Romans placed Herod of Idumaea on the throne. He was a tyrant, but he did beautify the Temple and built many fine buildings. The last part of his reign was made miserable by family disloyalty. These conflicts continued after his death, with the result that the Romans started installing military governors instead (6 AD). The Jewish priests, meanwhile, preached the coming of a Messiah – who could restore their political power. It was in these days that John the Baptist started preaching in the wilderness of Judaea, saying:

> *Repent, for the Kingdom of Heaven is at hand. For this is he that was spoken of by the prophet Isaiah, saying: "The voice of one crying in the wilderness: prepare the way of the Lord, make his paths straight.*[2]

John the Baptist
Little is known about John the Baptist, except that he was the son

76

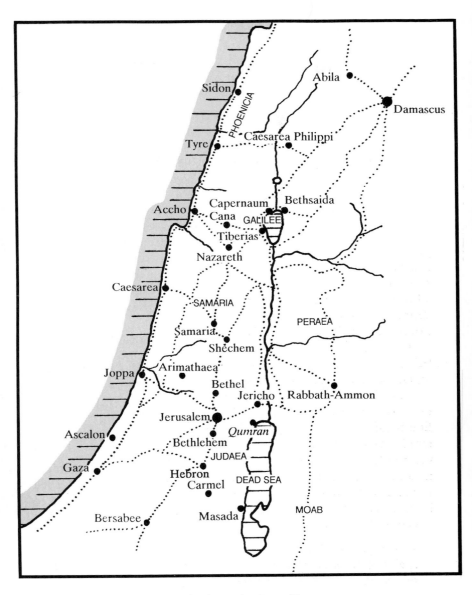

Palestine at the time of Jesus

of a priest called Zechariah, and was born miraculously to Elizabeth. Elizabeth was the cousin of Mary, and both confided in each
other. Zechariah had been informed by an angel:

> *Fear not, Zechariah, for your prayer is heard; and your wife Elizabeth*
> *will bear you a son, and you shall call his name John. And you will*
> *have joy and gladness, and many will rejoice at his birth. For he will be*
> *great before the Lord, and he shall drink no wine nor strong drink, and*
> *he will be filled with the Holy Spirit, even from his mother's womb.*[3]

Zechariah, being an old man, wondered how Elizabeth could
conceive. The angel assured him that he was sent by God to speak
to him, and that he should keep it a secret. The same angel
presumably impregnated Mary while she was staying at the house
of Zechariah. This angel informed Mary that her cousin Elizabeth
had conceived a son also, six months earlier. At the request of
Elizabeth, Mary stayed three months longer (presumably until the
birth of John), after which she married Joseph.

At his birth, John praised God, and all were amazed – this is
reminiscent of the stories of Tibetan *tulkus* or reincarnated lamas,
who have been said sometimes to speak or teach at birth. John was
educated in the priestly trade by his parents, and later was admitted
with Jesus to the Order of the Essenes at Jutha near Masada[4]. He
grew, waxed strong in spirit, and was in the desert until he started
preaching[5].

He started his mission from Jordan, preaching the baptism of
repentance for the remission of sins[6]. To the people he asked them
to share their belongings, to the publicans (tax-farmers) he wished
that they should exact no more than what was authorised, and to
soldiers he admonished them to do no violence to anyone, neither
accuse anyone of false charges, and to be content with their sal-
aries[7]. John thus demanded repentance (recognition of errors) from
all, high or low, in the name of God. The people had to mend their
ways and wash their sins through baptism.

> *I baptise you with water; but one mightier than I comes, the thong of*
> *whose sandals I am not worthy to untie; he will baptise you with the*
> *Holy Spirit and with fire.*[8]

When many people had been baptised, Jesus himself went to John. When John saw Jesus coming, he told the gathering:

Behold, the Lamb of God, who takes away the sin of the world! This is he of whom I said, 'After me comes a man who ranks before me, for he was before me'. I myself did not know him; but for this I came baptising with water, that he might be revealed to Israel.[9].

Jesus the teacher

Jesus, being filled with the Holy Spirit, returned from Jordan and was led by the Spirit into the wilderness. As in the case of the Buddha, he fasted, hungered, and met temptations. When he returned to Nazareth, he declared:

The Spirit of the Lord is upon me, because he has anointed me to preach good news to the poor. He has sent me to proclaim release to the captives, and recovering of sight to the blind, to set at liberty those who are oppressed, to proclaim the acceptable year of the Lord.[10]

Jesus boldly announced that the fulfilment of what he had said was not in some remote future, but then and there[11].

Jesus preached in many towns and villages and his sermons created a furore among the people. Wherever he went, he was surrounded by men and women who sought his blessings. They ran after him and struggled to touch his feet. To them, he was the Messiah destined to deliver them from misrule, misery and oppression. The whole atmosphere became tense, and there also occurred a demonstration against the Romans. Pilate ordered general punishments of the masses. Some approached Jesus telling him about these atrocities and implored heavenly intervention. He advised them to repent so as to save themselves from destruction.

The whole country was in an agitated mood. On the whole, people were divided in their opinion about Jesus. While the common people considered him to be the Messiah, the upper classes rejected him. The priests became jealous of Jesus for he had become very popular among the masses. Here was a teacher who did not care for ceremonies but mixed with ordinary people, much to the dislike of the priests!

The preaching of Jesus antagonised the orthodox Pharisees, who demanded strict adherence to the Commandments according to *Torah*, and who quoted his claims to heavenly descent. To them he said that he was sent by God to be their teacher. The aristocratic Sadducees also opposed him, seeing in his teachings the seeds of their ruin, and pronouncing that a demon had possessed him. They encouraged people to disrupt his meetings, and accused him of blasphemy.

An enquiry was instituted to establish his guilt, but they could not find a single witness to prove the allegation. Thus his fame spread far and wide, and his name became a legend[12]. Then the priests asserted that Jesus had political motives in claiming to be King of the Jews. Pontius Pilate, who tried the case, found no fault in Jesus or his sermons.

An interesting report about the activities of Jesus in the year 32 AD has been brought to my notice by Andreas Faber-Kaiser, a friend of mine who was helped by me to write a book on Jesus. According to him, the original letter, written by Pilate to Tiberius Caesar, is preserved in the Vatican Library, and it is possible to acquire copies from the Library of Congress in Washington. When reports about Jesus had reached Pilate, he sent his spies to bring intelligence about him. After receiving a report, Pilate called Jesus for an interview. He felt satisfied that Jesus was not an agitator. Here is a summary of the letter:

A young man appeared in Galilee and preached a new law, humility. At first I thought that his intention was to stir up a revolt among the people against the Romans. My suspicions were soon dispelled. Jesus spoke more as a friend of Rome than as a friend of the Jews.

One day I observed a young man amongst a group of people, leaning against the trunk of a tree and speaking quietly to the crowd that surrounded him. They told me that he was Jesus. This was obvious because of the great difference between him and those around him. His fair hair and beard gave him a divine appearance. He was about thirty years old, and never before had I seen such a pleasant, kind face. What a vast difference there was between him, with his fair complexion, and those with black beards who were listening to him. As I did not want to disturb him I went on my way, telling my secretary to join the group and listen.

My secretary told me that he had never read anything in the works of the philosophers that could be compared with the teachings of Jesus, and that he was neither leading people astray nor was he an agitator. That was why we decided to protect him. He was free to act, to talk, and to call a gathering of people. This unlimited liberty provoked the Jews, who were indignant – it did not upset the poor but it irritated the rich and powerful.

When I asked for an interview at the Forum, he came. Looking at him I was transfixed. My feet seemed fettered with iron chains to the marble floor. I was trembling all over as a guilty person would, although he was calm. Without moving, I appraised this exceptional man for some time. There was nothing unpleasant about his appearance or character. In his presence I felt a profound respect for him.

I told him that he had an aura around him, and his personality had an infectious simplicity that set him above the present-day philosophers and masters. He made a deep impression on all of us, owing to his pleasant manner, simplicity, humility and love.

These, worthy sovereign, are the deeds that concern Jesus of Nazareth, and I have taken time to inform you in detail about this affair. [13]

Pontius Pilate exercised power as the Procurator of Judaea from 26 to 36 AD. It is recorded by Josephus that he hated Jews – perhaps he appreciated the stirring of the Jews by Jesus. It is possible that he may have felt that Jesus had stern enemies among the Pharisees[14]. The above letter may be genuine or not, but it fixes 32 AD as a year of active Ministry by Jesus.

Capernaum

Capernaum, now known as *Kafar Nahum*, stood on the shores of the Sea of Galilee, linking the lands beyond Jordan with the Mediterranean. Besides being a trade centre, it was a town of fishermen. According to the Gospels, these fishermen were the first people to accept the teaching of Jesus. They would often invite him to speak and had become his devotees. As such, Capernaum had a special significance for Jesus, and in the course of time became a centre of his activities. He would visit various towns and villages, and after each journey, would return to Capernaum[15]. Andrew, John and James would always prevail on him and his mother to rest in Peter's home on the seashore.

Once when he had gone there, the news of his arrival spread along the shore, and many people came to see him. They would come along with their children and seek his blessings. Some would touch his feet and others would press his hand. He would walk by the seashore and people would follow him[16]. Many people brought with them the sick and ailing, and some would bring those who were possessed by devils. Jesus would touch them and they would be healed. In this manner, he went about Galilee, healing sick and diseased people. His fame as a healer spread throughout Syria[17].

Martha and Mary Magdalene

Bethany is a small village on the far side of the Mount of Olives near Jerusalem. There lived a family consisting of Martha, Mary Magdalene, and their brother Lazarus. They had always taken a deep, loving and personal interest in Jesus. Once, during his wanderings, Jesus reached Bethany and visited this family. Martha complained that Mary Magdalene would abandon her and not help her in the work. Jesus said:

> *Martha! You are anxious and troubled about many things; one thing is needful. Mary has chosen the good part, which shall not be taken away from her.*[18]

Martha engaged herself in preparing food for Jesus and his disciples, and Mary Magdalene stayed with him. When all sat down to dine, Jesus said:

> *My little flock! Fear not. It is your Father's will that you shall rule the kingdom of the soul. A ruler in the house of God is a servant of the Lord, and man cannot serve God except by serving humankind. A servant in the house of God cannot be a servant in the house of wealth nor in the synagogue of the senses!*
>
> *Dispose of all your wealth, distribute it among the poor and put your trust in God. Neither you nor yours will ever come to want. This*

*is a test of faith and God will not accept the services of faithless ones.
The time is ripe: your master comes upon the clouds – the eastern sky is
glowing with his presence now.*

*Put on reception robes, gird up your loins, trim up your lamps and
fill them well with oil. Be prepared to meet your Lord: when you are
ready, he will come. Thrice blessed are the servants who are ready to
receive their Lord.* [19]

The above sermon of Jesus is not recorded by the four Gospels.
The four Gospels are also silent on the question of Jesus' marriage
to any woman. According to the Jewish scriptures Jesus was
bound to marry at the age of thirteen because celibacy was considered repugnant to God. Moreover, an unmarried man could not
claim to be a teacher. The Buddhist Scrolls of Hemis tell us that at
the age of thirteen many rich people were eager to have him as
their son-in-law[20]. But he was unwilling to marry, and at the
proposal of marriage, he decided to leave his father's house in
secret[21].

A close study of the Gospels reveal that Mary Magdalene, of
all the women in his following, loved Jesus more than any. He
would often visit her house in Bethany and she would accompany
him during his travels. There are other hints in the Gospels which
indicate that Mary considered herself consort to Jesus. A time came
when the other disciples of Jesus looked to her as the beloved of the
Master. In the *Gospel of Mary*, Simon Peter addresses her as follows:

*Sister. We know that the Saviour loved you more than the rest of
women. Tell us the words of the Saviour which you remember – which
you know but we do not, nor have we heard them.* [22]

In the same context, let me quote from the *Gospel of Philip*, which
informs that Mary Magdalene received more attention from him.

*And the companion of the Saviour is Mary Magdalene. He loved her
more than all the disciples. He used to kiss her often on the mouth*[23].

In Indian mythology, every Hindu God has a consort which represents his creative energy, termed as *shakti*. These wives of the gods are looked on as the source and support of all things. Both the God and the Goddess represent the active and passive poles of universal manifestation and each is incomplete without the other. The Hindu Tantric way of looking at this matter is helpful. I feel inclined to use the same symbols of the Indian mythology on Jesus Christ, for he came to the East and had studied the occultism of India during his first visit.

He knew that every Hindu God has his *shakti* in the form of one or more consorts. I am inclined to believe that Jesus did have a consort in the person of Mary Magdalene. However, there were other women such as Martha, Susanna, Philippi, Jehanna and Rachel who also loved him and took much interest in him.

In the *Gospel of John* there is an account of a marriage which puzzled me most, because the groom has not been pinpointed clearly. Nor is the name of the bride given, thus creating more confusion. We are told that there is a marriage at Cana, a town in Galilee. Not only is Jesus present, but also Mary the mother, and all the disciples. There are many guests and Mary asks Jesus to procure more wine for them. He miraculously produces up to 180 gallons of wine for these guests[24].

The question arises: who is the guest and who is the host? I would suggest Mary is the host for she orders the procuring of wine for the guests, which Jesus deals with. One wonders whether it is *his own* marriage with Mary Magdalene, and whether the whole episode has been kept under camouflage. Maybe the compiler of the Gospel wanted to tell the whole story in a way which could avoid all suspicion.

I believe that Mary Magdalene behaved as the chief consort of Jesus, and he also took her as his spouse. In confirmation of my view, I found from an Essene source that at a later stage they made him separate from her. I will quote:

> But, according to the rules of our Order, an Essene is not allowed to take unto himself a wife, lest the sacred work be thereby retarded. And so it was that Jesus overcame his love for this woman by his dutiful devotion to the brotherhood. [25]

There is a legend that Mary Magdalene and a child of hers went in exile to France after the crucifixion. She is supposed to have died at Saint Baume in France and her son is said to have founded the Grail family. But according to my researches, Mary Magdalene died at Kashgar, central Asia – more about this later.

I think it was Martha who migrated to France in the company of some devotees of Jesus, and lived there until her death. It was her son who preserved the lineage of Jesus in Europe. It was during this period that Joseph of Arimathaea and other supporters of Jesus Christ left for Glastonbury in England. All of them believed that the Roman masters or the Jewish priests would implicate them in criminal conspiracies connected with Jesus.

Go to the Lost Sheep

Jesus travelled the country and spoke in parables. His message of peace was well received. Now he wanted to select a band of trusted disciples who could heal the sick and preach. He went out to a mountain and continued all night in prayer to God. Maybe he met and consulted his Essene brothers.

When he came back from the mountain, he called his disciples and selected twelve from among them, whom he named apostles – Simon Peter, Andrew, James, John, Philip, Bartholomew, Thomas the Publican, Matthew, James the son of Alpheus, Lebbeus Thaddeus, Simon the Canaanite and Judas Iscariot. He also selected a further seventy, and sent them in twos to other cities and places. He expected to visit all these in times to come[26]. He assigned different duties to all of these, and commanded them to go to the lost sheep of the house of Israel:[27]

> Go nowhere among the Gentiles, and enter no town of the Samaritans. But go rather to the lost sheep of the house of Israel. And as you go, preach, saying: 'The kingdom of heaven is at hand'.

To the seventy disciples he said:

> The harvest is plentiful, but the labourers are few; pray therefore the Lord of the harvest to send out labourers into this harvest. Go your way; behold, I send you out as lambs in the midst of wolves. Carry no

*purse, no bag, no sandals, and salute no one on the road. Whatever
house you enter, first say, 'Peace be to this house!'*[28].

The Gospel of Barnabas

It is unfortunate that while western scholars have undertaken researches into the religion and beliefs of the eastern nations, they
have not gone beyond the four authorised Gospels of Christianity.
The accounts given in them are similar in nature and mostly cover
the few years of the ministry of Jesus. Jesus had come back to
Palestine in about 29-30 AD. He started preaching in about 23-24
AD and continued his activities up to 30-31 AD. After this year, his
activity gains momentum up to 35 AD, when he is put on the cross.
The Gospels inform us only about the last three years of his
ministry.

Fortunately, I found a copy of the *Gospel of Barnabas*, translated into English and published by the Oxford University Press in
1907. It appeared that the translation had been done by Lonsdale
Ragg from an Italian manuscript, preserved in the Hofbibliothek,
Vienna. I learned that Barnabas was a disciple of Jesus, an uncle of
Mark and a companion of Paul, travelling throughout Palestine
preaching from his Gospel. It further came to light that the *Gospel
of Barnabas* had been accepted as a canonical gospel in the churches
of Alexandria until 325 AD, when the Nicene Council of that year
ordered that all copies of this Gospel be destroyed and anyone in
possession of this Gospel be put to death. The net result was that
his Gospel was almost lost to posterity.

However, in the fifth century a copy of this Gospel, written in
Barnabas' own hand, was found lying on his breast in his tomb in
Cyprus. This manuscript found its way into the library of Pope
Sixtus V (1585-1590). It was made public by a monk named Frater
Marino. It does not differ from the authorised Gospels, but the
original manuscript is on an Italian paper with marginal notes
made in bad Arabic. It is unfortunate that the translators have also
included the translation of the Arabic notes, made on the margin of
each folio, as part of their translation. This has created controversy
about some passages purporting to Islamic doctrines in this Gospel. However, we need not lay emphasis on controversies but

adhere to the incidents given in the authorised Gospels.

One day Jesus called together his disciples and said:

Blessed are they that mourn this earthly life, for they shall be comforted. Blessed are the poor who truly hate the delights of the world, for they shall abound in the delights of the kingdom of God. Blessed are they that eat at the table of God, for the angels shall minister unto them.[29]

Comparing this sermon with that given in the *Gospel of Matthew*, it appears that this sermon, given in the *Gospel of Barnabas*, is simple and straight. It appears that the sermon given in Matthew and Luke has been compiled and polished by scholars so that it appears a masterpiece of oratory. One of the difficulties with the New Testament is that it has been improved upon from time to time by the Christian theologians.

Faith and prayer

Jesus went to Galilee, fearing that the Jews might kill him. Some told him to go into Judaea but he did not agree. He departed to the coast of Tyre and Sidon and healed the sick. The Pharisees challenged his authority to interpret the scriptures. He felt unhappy about these people, who had become his enemies. He felt restless and thought of going back to Galilee. He went up onto a mountain and sat there in meditation. After that he took a ship and came into the coasts of Magdala. The Pharisees shadowed him, asking him to prove his credentials and show a divine sign. He sighed and felt sorry for these wicked people.

One day, when Jesus and his disciples sat around the table, a courtesan came uninvited to the feast. She came forward and kissed his feet. Her tears fell fast and she dried them with her hair. Simon Peter did not like a sinner to touch the feet of Jesus. But Jesus told Simon that sin is a monster of iniquity and it may be small or it may be big. A person who leads a life of sin and repents is redeemed. But another person who is in careless mood, does not reform himself. A sinner who seeks forgiveness is forgiven. Then he said to the courtesan: *Your sins are all forgiven. Your faith has saved you.*[30]

Once, Jesus told his disciples that anyone who does not pray is hardly better than Satan. He said: *Make prayer unceasingly, my disciples, in order that you may receive. For he who seeks finds, and he who knocks, to him is opened. He who asks receives an answer from God.*[31]

He told them that hypocrites make much prayer in every part of the city in order to be seen and held as saints by the people. It is only a show and their hearts are full of wickedness. He told them that in reality very few people make true prayer.

Transfiguration

One day, Jesus took Simon Peter and other disciples up to a high mountain and showed them a miracle. He meditated and was transfigured before their very eyes: his raiment became shining white as snow and it was difficult to recognise him. Two men came and talked with him. In the *Gospel of Matthew*, these two men were identified as Moses and Elijah.

I have taken up this event to examine it in the light of eastern esoteric tradition. It is recorded by western visitors to Tibet that transfiguration, a Tantric feat, has been witnessed in Tibet and Ladakh. Calling of spirits and souls is a common practice, with *yogis* of India. Change of countenance and disappearance from sight is a Tantric manifestation mentioned by many travellers to the Himalayan region[32]. As such, I feel that Jesus, who had been to this region during his first journey, may have acquired such powers.

Who were these two men who came to talk with him? Moses and Elijah had died centuries before. Maybe they were their spirits! Another view could be that these two men were Essene brothers with whom Jesus worked whenever he went into the wilderness. At the time of transfiguration, Simon Peter, James and John were 'heavy with sleep' and Jesus advised them to keep this vision a close secret! From the point of view of the mystics and yogis of the East, it was a practice of *trance* which Jesus showed to his disciples. It was a high secret of meditation which was to be kept secret.

(1) Keller, Werner, *The Bible as History*, p323.

(2) *Matthew*, 3, 2-3. By 'the kingdom of heaven' is meant a state of bliss, happiness and righteousness.

(3) *Luke*, 1, 13-20.

(4) *The Crucifixion by an Eye-Witness*, pp47-48.

(5) *Luke*, 1, 80. The deserts mentioned by *Luke* point to the western shores of the Dead Sea and the Jordan, where Jesus was told by John the Baptist to undergo some sort of mystical experiences. But, according to another scholar, the words 'in the desert' "indicate that Jesus was neither in his own land nor in Judaea". In other words, it can imply that Jesus began his journey to a far-off land – see Nazir Ahmad, Khwaja, *Jesus in Heaven on Earth*, p338.

(6) *Luke*, 3, 2-3.

(7) *Luke*, 3, 10-14.

(8) *Luke*, 3, 16. Baptising with water means renunciation of sin and consecration to righteousness. Baptising with the Holy Spirit and 'with fire' means the perpetual but invisible operation of the Holy Spirit – *Peloubet's Select Notes on the International Lessons*, Boston, 1918, p21.

(9) *John*, 1, 29-33.

(10) *Luke*, 4, 18-19.

(11) Muggeridge, Malcolm, *Jesus, the Man Who Lives*, Collins, 1975, p60.

(12) Schonfield, Hugh, *The Passover Plot*, Bantam Books, New York, 1966, p70.

(13) Faber-Kaiser, Andreas, *Jesus Died in Kashmir*, Gordon & Cremonesi, 1977, pp22-24.

(14) Keller, Werner, *The Bible as History*, p355. "Jesus spoke with the scribes concerning holy things, and his doctrines gave deep offence to the Pharisees in Jerusalem, in that they considered them dangerous and incredible" – *The Crucifixion by an Eye-Witness*, p44.

(15) Keller, Werner, *The Bible as History*, p350.

(16) Levi, *The Aquarian Gospel*, pp112-113.

(17) *Matthew*, 4, 23-25. "They brought unto him all sick people that were taken with divers diseases and torments, and those which were possessed with devils, and those which were lunatic, and those that had the palsy; and he healed them". Speaking about the Essenes, Josephus, in his work *De Bello Judaico*, says: "They have profound knowledge of the art of healing, and study it arduously; they examine and are acquainted with medicinal herbs and plants, that they prepare as medicine for men and beasts" – *The Crucifixion by an Eye-Witness*, p178-179.

(18) *Luke*, 10, 41-42.

(19) Levi, *The Aquarian Gospel*, p161.

(20) "When Issa had attained the age of thirteen, when an Israelite should take a wife, the house in which his parents dwelt and earned their livelihood in

modest labour, became a meeting place for rich and noble, who desired to have for a son-in-law the young Issa, who had been celebrated for his edifying discourses in the name of the Almighty". This passage from chapter IV, recorded by Swami Abhedananda in 1922, during his visit to Tibet, is reproduced by Yehoshua Benjamin in his *Mystery of the Lost Tribes*, New Delhi, 1989, p102.

(21) Prophet, Elizabeth Clare, *The Lost Years of Jesus*, p235.

(22) Robinson, James M, ed, *The Nag Hammadi Library*, E J Brill, Leiden, Netherlands, 1977, p427. Forsström, Johan, *The King of the Jews*, p128.

(23) *Gospel of Philip*, 63, 31, found in *The Nag Hammadi Library*, ed James M Robinson, E J Brill, Leiden, 1977, 1984, p138.

(24) *John*, 2, 1-10. Jesus speaks on marriage: "There is no tie more sacred than the marriage tie. The chain that binds two souls in love is made in heaven, and man can never sever it in twain" – Levi, *The Aquarian Gospel*, p111.

(25) *The Crucifixion by an Eye-Witness*, p53. With reference to the Essenes, Josephus says, "They do not absolutely deny the fitness of marriage, and the succession of mankind thereby continued; but they guard against the lascivious behaviour of women, and are persuaded that none of them preserve their fidelity to one man". Josephus, *The Wars of the Jews*, Book II, viii; Loeb Classical Library, Harvard Univ Press, Cambridge MA, USA.

(26) *Luke*, 10, 1.

(27) *Matthew*, 10, 5-7.

(28) *Luke*, 10, 2-6.

(29) Ragg, Lonsdale and Laura, tr, *The Gospel of Barnabas*, Oxford Univ Press, 1907, p16. Walker, Alexander, tr, *Acts of Barnabas*, Ante-Nicene Christian Library, Vol XVI, T & T Clark, Edinburgh, 1970.

(30) Levi, *The Aquarian Gospel*, p151. The Jews of Palestine never believed in human sacrifice, nor in the crucifixion of the Messiah for the sins of the world. The pagans believed that their gods, Adonis, Attis, Osiris and Mithra had died for the sins of mankind. It was Paul who borrowed the idea of a scapegoat and laid stress on the crucified Jesus. The theory of 'original sin' and redemption by the death of the Son of God was an invention by Paul. For clarification, see Shamas, J D, *Where Did Jesus Die?*, London Mosque, London, ch 10, titled 'Redemption'.

(31) Ragg, Lonsdale, *The Gospel of Barnabas*, p47. "Prayer is the heart of Christian life. The greatest argument for prayer is in the nature of God, his nearness, sympathy, love and power. Jesus taught us how to pray, and the results of prayer. *Luke*, 11, 1-13, was spoken by Jesus near the end of his ministry" – *Peloubet's Select Notes on the International Lessons*, Boston, 1918, pp212-219.

(32) See, for example: Govinda, A, *The Way of the White Clouds*, Rider, London, 1966; Evans-Wentz, W Y, *Tibetan Yoga and Secret Doctrines*, Oxford Univ Press, 1958; David-Neel, A, *Initiations and Initiates in Tibet*, London, 1958.

10

The Essenes and Early Christianity

Canaanites and Hebrews

Canaan is the narrow mountainous strip of land west of the river Jordan, which, during ancient times, served as a link between Egypt and Asia. After its conquest by the Hebrews, the northern part was redesignated as Israel and the southern part as Judah. Due to its strategic position on an important trade route, it was occupied by several powers at different times, such as Egypt, Assyria, Babylon, Persia and Greece. The Romans, who subjugated this country in about 63 BC, changed its name to Palestine.

During its ancient period, Canaan was not only occupied by different tribes but also ruled over by a variety of tribal lords and princes. Most prominent amongst them were the Indo-Aryan (Kurgan) princes who ruled over this country in about 15th and 14th centuries BC. Some of these Indo-Aryan princes, whose names are preserved in the tablets found at Tell el-Amarna in Egypt, are Suwar-datta, Inda-rutta, Birash-sinha, Birya-vaza and Biri-diya[1].

It appears that the Canaanites followed the same religions as were followed by the Indo-Aryans. These tribes worshipped many gods and goddesses. They followed the Tantric rituals of the Hindu *Shaktas* in honour of goddess Astarte. All sexual manifestations of life were under her patronage. Like the Aryans, the tribes in Canaan believed in the sun, moon and other light deities, and their temples contained altars and statues of many gods and goddesses. In each temple stood a stone pillar as found in every Hindu

91

temple, called a *Lingam* or the phallus of *Shiva*. Like the Hindu votaries of *Durga*, they also indulged in animal and human sacrifices.

Jacob, who was also known as Israel, had twelve sons, eight born to legal wives: Reuben, Simeon, Levi, Judah, Issachar, Zebulun, Joseph and Benjamin claimed a superior lineage. Those born to concubines, Gad, Asher, Dan and Nephtali were considered of inferior lineage[2]. These two groups comprising twelve sons of Israel are known as *Bani Israel* in the East. The became the chiefs of the Twelve Tribes of Israel.

Both groups fought among themselves with the result that their kingdoms of Israel and Judaea were gradually destroyed by invaders. However, the Judaeans re-established themselves and played an important role in the history of Bani Israel. It is for this reason that their religion became known as *Judaism* and its followers as *Jews*[3].

The Jews are the last remnants of the Hebrews and are mentioned as *Judaeus* in Latin, *Loudaios* in Greek, *Yhudai* in Aramaic, *Yhudi* in Hebrew, *Yahud* in Persian, Arabic and Kashmiri.

The Sects of Israel

There were many religious sects among the people of Palestine at the time when Jesus returned from his first journey. Among the Jews, the *Pharisees* were very prominent – they observed all ceremonies and rituals of the Mosaic law in a very rigid way. They laid emphasis on outward forms but did not care about real purification of the heart. It was a sect full of hypocrisy and egotism. At public meetings they always endeavoured to be the principal ones, and aspired to esteem and dignity among the people. Jesus reprimanded them severely and rebuked them, for he considered them the most vicious, cunning and dangerous among the Jews.

The *Sadducees* were philosophers of a sort who denied the immortality of the soul and a life hereafter. They asked people to lead a virtuous and good life, to be more contented or accepting in their mind. They were the keepers of the Temple in Jerusalem. Being active and energetic, they desired to be wealthy and influential. As such, they belonged to an aristocratic priestly class[4].

The Essenes

Then there were the *Essenes* or *Essees*, a distinct class of mystics among the Jews. Josephus wrote that the Essenes were the most esteemed philosophers among the Jews. "They show great virtue. They show great kindness to children and teach them all kinds of knowledge and science. They despise riches and worldly gains and live in communes."[5]. Josephus writes elsewhere that the Essenes "are the most honest people in the world and are as good as their word, very industrious and enterprising, and they show great skill and concern for agriculture. They exercise justice and equality in their dealings with all people. They never marry, and they keep no servants. They all live the same simple, industrious and frugal life."[6].

The Christian Church teaches that Jesus was the sole creator of Christianity, denying any relevant prior tradition – the facts, however, seem somewhat different.

Sources on the Essenes

There are quite a few ancient historical works which mention the Essenes. Among these, mention may be made of:
- *Quod Omnis Probus Liber*[7], written by Philo of Alexandria in 20 AD, provides us with detailed information about the Essenes in Palestine and Syria;
- *Historia Naturalis*[8] by Pliny the Elder, written in 70 AD, tells us about the Essenes, and tells us that they had lived on the shores of the Dead Sea for a very long time;
- *Wars of the Jews*[9], written by Josephus in 94 AD, provides us with information about the Jewish people and their sects. It also tells us about the Essenes, including many of their beliefs.
- *Antiquities of the Jews* by Josephus[10] provides the following general information about Jesus:

> *And there lived Jesus, a holy man if he may be called, for he performed wonderful works and taught men, and they joyfully received the truth. And he was followed by many Jews and many Greeks. He was the Messiah. And our leaders denounced him. But when Pilate had condemned him to the cross, those who had loved him did not at first deny*

him. For he appeared to them after having risen from death on the third day. The holy prophets had, moreover, predicted of him those and many other wonders. The race of the Christians takes its name from him and still exists at this present time. [11']

The Dead Sea Scrolls

In 1947 AD a number of manuscripts were discovered in a cave of *Wadi Qumran*, by the north of the Dead Sea. In 1949 fragments of the Old Testament were recovered in the Qumran cave, and in 1952 a considerable number of coins and fragments of scriptures were discovered in the caves of *Wadi Marabbaat*, as a result of an expedition. The manuscripts, which are popularly known as the Dead Sea Scrolls, are the compilations of the Essenes, whose monastery, known as the *Khirber Qumran*, was destroyed by the Romans in about 70 AD. The *Lamech* scrolls, written in Aramaic, contain chapters from the *Book of Genesis*.

By 1956 two copper scrolls were deciphered. In 1956, Millar Burrows' translation of some of scrolls was published as *The Dead Sea Scrolls*[12]. In 1956, too, the fascinating story of the discovery of the Dead Sea Scrolls was published, *The Meaning of the Dead Sea Scrolls*[13] by A. Powell Davis, also giving interesting material on the content of the teachings. In recent years, much new work has been emerging, including translations of material concealed by various authorities, for a variety of political and religious reasons[14].

The Essenes believed in a Teacher of Righteousness, who was to come and explain the wisdom of all previous prophets. He would be the Anointed One, who would inaugurate a new order. The Dead Sea Scrolls, therefore, give us a great deal of insight into the background of the New Testament. There are many parallels between the doctrines of the Essenes, formulated long before Jesus was born, and the early Christian doctrines. In the Dead Sea Scrolls there exist many teachings which in the Gospels are attributed to Jesus, but there is evidence that they stem from an ancient tradition.

In 1928 Edmond Szekely published a manuscript which was originally written in Aramaic, and is known as *The Gospel of the Essenes*[15]. Szekely declared that he had found this ancient work in a

Qumran, Cave 4, discovered in 1954 *(Beth Davis)*

secret repository of the Vatican. It is now preserved in the Royal Archives of the Habsburgs, Austria. In it Jesus is shown as a Teacher of Righteousness who preaches renunciation, austerity, a simple life, high ideas and mental purification[16]. I will quote a passage from this Gospel:

> One day, Jesus sat amidst people who listened to his words with amazement. He said: "Seek not the Law in your scriptures, for the Law is life, whereas the scripture is dead. The Law is the living word of the living God to living prophets for living men. In everything that is life, is the Law written. You find it in the grass, in the trees, in the river, in the mountain, in the birds of heaven, in the fishes of the sea, but seek it chiefly in yourselves. God did not write the Law in books, but in your heart and in your spirit[17]."

In 1881 an ancient *Aramaic Gospel* was found by Ouseley in a Tibetan *gompa* (monastery). This text tells us, amongst other things, that Jesus went into a small village, where he found a kitten which was not cared for. Jesus picked her up and put her inside his garment. He gave food and drink to the cat, which was hungry. Some of the villagers were surprised that he cared so for all creatures and asked him if they were his brothers and sisters. Jesus said:

> Verily, these are your fellow creatures of the great household of the Eternal Being. They, indeed are thy brethren and sisters and have the same breath of life in Eternal God, and are breathing the same Spirit[18].

In this Gospel, there is also an interesting story of temptation, mentioning that Satan appeared before Jesus with a woman of overwhelming beauty and grace. Satan told Jesus to take her because it is not good for a man that he should be alone. Jesus replied:

> Get thee behind me Satan, for it is also written: be not led away by the mere beauty of a woman, for all flesh is as grass and the flowers of the field, the grass withereth and the flower fadeth away, but the Law endureth forever[19].

A close study of the available Essene works provide ample information about his teachings which we do not find in the official Gospels. In the *Book of Thomas*, Jesus speaks against sensuality in these words:

> *Woe to you with the fire of sensuality raging within you, for it is unquenchable. The fire will devour your flesh visibly and tear at your soul secretly*[20].

In the *Gospel of the Hebrews*, Jesus pronounced on the torture and torment of animals:

> *Let all know that God giveth grains and the fruits of the earth for food, both to man and best. Those whose hands are stained with blood, and whose mouths are defiled with the flesh of innocent creatures are not worthy of life in this world nor in the world to come*[21].

When Jesus was instructing his disciples at the Temple, one of them asked, "Can blood sacrifices wash away sins?", to which Jesus answered:

> *No bloody sacrifices of animals or humans can ever wash away sins, and for [but] few could a fault become eradicated through the shedding of innocent blood. He who kills kills himself, and whoso eats the flesh of slain beasts eats of the body of death*[22].

Testament of the Twelve Patriarchs
This was one of the scriptures considered authentic by the early Christians. Even Paul seems to have used these Testaments and copied some portions from them, while compiling his letters. Matthew, while composing his Gospels, was also indebted to the *Testament of the Twelve Patriarchs*. These Testaments were later on left out of the Bible[23].

The Dead Sea Scrolls were written before Jesus was born. The *First Book of Enoch* was written in 170-164 BC, and the *Testament of the Twelve Patriarchs* was compiled between 109-107 BC. During the lifetime of Jesus all these scrolls, including the *Psalms of Solomon*, the *Testament of God*, and the *Book of Jubilees* were available for study. The famous Sermon on the Mount, now included in the New Testament, was known to Jesus, for he had already become familiar with it as a body of Essene teaching.

The Crucifixion by an Eye-Witness

The *Crucifixion by an Eye-Witness*[24] was published in Chicago in 1907. The introduction states that the substance of the book was first published in 1873 but withdrawn from circulation, and almost all its copies and the plates were destroyed. One copy, however, found its way into the possession of a prominent Mason in Massachusetts and remained with him until 1907. The book was a translation of a Latin manuscript then in the possession of the Masonic Fraternity in Germany. This work contains what is claimed to be a translation of a letter, written by a member of the Essene Order to another member in Alexandria just seven years after the crucifixion. It narrates the story of the crucifixion, Jesus' removal from the cross, and his resuscitation. Many key quotations from this source are found within this book.

The Aquarian Gospel of Jesus the Christ

This was compiled by Levi H. Dowling before 1907[25], after many years of study and silent meditation. The *Aquarian Gospel* tells us the story of Jesus, giving a complete account of the period Jesus spent in Tibet, India, Persia, Egypt and Greece. Levi was a student of world religions and it is possible that he obtained much inspiration for his gospel from *The Crucifixion by an Eye-Witness*, and Notovitch's *The Life of Saint Issa* and *The Unknown Life of Christ*.

The book, however, also contains much that is not to be found in these sources, and though he may have access to other sources which we are not familiar with, some believe that his additional knowledge was achieved somehow through his meditation, whether this be through 'channelling' or some other means. This has to remain conjecture, of course, until we discover definitively the historical sources he had access to and until further research confirms or disconfirms his story. So far, anyway, the information he offers fits the picture emerging from other sources, so his book deserves attention.

One of the most interesting passages in this book tells of Jesus meeting again with the Essenes on his return from the East at the age of thirty or so. According to this account, Jesus was received with great honour by the Brotherhood and the aged teachers praised his wisdom. However, he told them that he wished to undertake further tests, and his request was accepted. The story of his tests was quoted in Chapter Eight[26].

---

(1) Keller, Werner, *The Bible as History*, pp144–145. "In the table of nations (Genesis) Canaan is not included among the Semites. In Amarna time there are Indo-Aryan names among the rulers of Canaan. Palestine derives its name as the home of the Philistines (Egyptian *Pulesati*, which threatened Egypt in about 1194 BC" – Chakraberti, *Classical Studies in Ancient Races and Myths*, Puja Publications, New Delhi, 1979.

(2) Margolis, Max, & Marx, Alexander, *A History of the Jewish People*, Temple Books, Massachusetts, 1969 & 1978, p9.

(3) Benjamin, Yehoshua, *Mystery of the Lost Tribes*, New Delhi, 1989, p8.

(4) *The Crucifixion by an Eye-Witness*, pp160–161.

(5) Quotation from *De Bello Judaico* (*The Wars of the Jews*), ch 8, by Josephus, given in *The Crucifixion by an Eye-Witness*, p173.

(6) Whiston, W, ed, *Historia Antiqua Judaico* or *The Antiquities of the Jews* by Josephus, London, 1872; or Loeb, ed, *Antiquities of the Jews*, London & Cambridge MA, 1924ff; Josephus, Flavius, *War of the Jews*, T Nelson, London, 1873.

(7) Philo, Judaeus, *Every Good Man is Free*, tr F H Colson, London & Cambridge MA, 1962, 1967.

(8) Pliny the Elder, *Natural History*, tr H Rackham & W H S Jones, 10 vols, London, 1938–42; Pliny the Elder, *Natural History*, Loeb Classical Library, Heinemann and Harvard Univ Press.

(9) Josephus Flavius, *The Jewish Wars*, tr W Whiston, William, London, 1872, Josephus Flavius, *The Jewish Wars*, tr G A Williamson, Harmondsworth, 1978.

(10) Josephus Flavius, *Antiquities of the Jews: A History of the Jewish Wars and Life of Flavius Josephus, Written by Himself*, tr W Whiston, London; Josephus Flavius, *Antiquities of the Jews*, Loeb Classical Library, London & Cambridge MA, 1924ff.

(11) Josephus, quoted by Nazir Ahmad in *Jesus in Heaven on Earth*, Lahore, 1952 & 1972, p2. He is of the opinion that Josephus, being a Jew, could not have written this sentence, based on the following passage: "The holy prophets had, moreover, predicted of him those and many other wonders". Khwaja Nazir Ahmad formed his opinion on the basis of a similar idea expressed in Moore, G F, *Judaism in the First Century of the Christian Era*,

Cambridge, 1930, Vol 1, p20.

(12) Burrows, M, *The Dead Sea Scrolls*, Viking Press, London, 1956; Burrows, M, *More Light on the Dead Sea Scrolls*, London, 1958; Davies, Powell, *The Meaning of the Dead Sea Scrolls*, Mentor Books, New York, 1956; Allegro, John, *The People of the Dead Sea Scrolls*, New York, 1958; Allegro, John, *The Dead Sea Scrolls – A Reappraisal*, Penguin, Middlesex, 1956; Vermes, G, *The Dead Sea Scrolls in English*, Pelican, Middlesex, 1962; Milik, J T, *Ten Years of Discovery in the Wilderness of Judaea*, tr from French by J Strugnell, London, 1959. The total number of books and articles on the Dead Sea Scrolls approaches 2000.

(13) Davis, A Powell, *The Meaning of the Dead Sea Scrolls*, Mentor Books, New York, 1956.

(14) Schonfield, Hugh, *The Secret of the Dead Sea Scrolls*, New York, 1960; Allegro, John, *The Dead Sea Scrolls and Christian Myth*, New York, 1984; Baigent, Michael and Leigh, Richard, *The Dead Sea Scrolls Deception*, Jonathan Cape, London, 1991.

(15) Szekely, E B, tr, *The Gospel of the Essenes*, C W Daniel, Saffron Walden, 1978. Szekely, E B, *The Gospel of Peace of Jesus Christ by the Disciple John*, C W Daniel, London, 1937 & 1973; Szekely, E B, *The Teachings of the Essenes from Enoch to the Dead Sea Scrolls*, C W Daniel, London, 1978.

(16) Forsström, Johan, *The King of the Jews*, p347, p355. "The sect's own leader was called the *Teacher of Righteousness*, or the *Righteous Teacher*. Themselves they called the *Sons of Zadok*, thinking doubtless of Ezekiel, XI, 46, or the *Children of Light* in contradistinction to their religious opponents, the *Children of Darkness*" – John Allegro's *The Dead Sea Scrolls*, Pelican, 1956, p104.

(17) Forsström, Johan, *The King of the Jews*, pp347, 355, quoting Szekely's *Essene Gospel of Peace 1a (San Diego, 1981)*.

(18) Szekely, Edmond Bordeaux, *The Essene Humane Gospel of Jesus*, Santa Monica, 1978, quoted in Forsström, Johan, *The King of the Jews*, p334. The Essene Humane Gospel of Jesus is also known as the ancient Aramaic Gospel, found in 1881 by Rev G J R Ouseley in Tibet.

(19) Szekely, E B, *The Essene Gospel of Jesus*, 1978. While the *Gospel of John* has no reference to the Temptation of Jesus, *Luke*, *Matthew* and *Mark* describe briefly when the temptation came to him. But an exhaustive account of the temptation can be seen in Levi, *The Aquarian Gospel*, ch 48-65, pp88-107.

(20) *The Book of Thomas*, quoted in Forsström, Johan, *King of the Jews*, p315. In his work *De Bello Judaico* or *The Jewish Wars*, ch 8, vs 2-13, Josephus makes the following remarks about the moral life of the Essenes: "They shun and despise sensuality as a great sin, but consider a moral and temperate life a great virtue, and pride highly the strength of mind and the power to overcome the passions and desires of their nature".

(21) Forsström, Johan, *King of the Jews*, p322.

(22) Forsström, Johan, *King of the Jews*, p325.

(23) Davies, A Powell, *The Meaning of the Dead Sea Scrolls*, New York, 1956,

p104; *Testament of the Twelve Patriarchs*, tr R H Charles, A & C Black, London, 1908.

(24) *The Crucifixion by an Eye-Witness*, Supplemental Harmonic Series, vol 2, Indo-American Book Co, Chicago, 1907. This book is in two parts, the first dealing with the life of Jesus and his connection with the Essenes, the second pertaining to the order of the Essenes.

(25) Levi (H Dowling), *The Aquarian Gospel of Jesus the Christ*, London, 1908ff, DeVorss & Co, California, 1972.

(26) Levi, *The Aquarian Gospel*, pp87-97. "Issa – whom the Creator had selected to recall to the worship of the true God men sunk in sin, was twenty-nine years old when he arrived in the land of Israel" – Notovitch, N, *The Life of St Issa*, IX, 1.

11

The Crucifixion

Jerusalem

The chief priests and the scribes now decided that Jesus must be killed. However, they feared that there could be an uproar among the people. Jesus was informed about the plot. He told his disciples about the trouble ahead. He also informed them that he would be denied by Simon Peter and betrayed by one of his apostles. When they came to a place known as Gethsemane, he asked his disciples to wait for him while he made a prayer. He was sad and gloomy. He kneeled down on the ground and prayed:

> *Abba, Father, all things are possible unto Thee: take away this cup from me. Nevertheless, not what I will, but what Thou wilt*[1].

While he made this moving prayer, he felt agony and his sweat was as if it were drops of blood falling down to the ground. As he prayed to God, an angel from heaven appeared before him, strengthening him[2].

Why did Jesus pray? He had made an earnest prayer to God asking that the cup of death be taken from his lips. Earlier, in a sermon, he had declared that if a sincere request is made of God to show his mercy, his prayers are answered, and he makes and strengthens his faith. Once, on an earlier occasion where he was faced with the challenge of raising Lazarus from the dead, he had declared that God hears him:

> *Father, I thank you that you have heard me. I know that you hear me*

always, but I have said this on account of the people standing by, that they may believe that you did send me.[3].

When Jesus learnt that he would be betrayed by *Judas*, he made a special prayer to God to save him from death. Was he afraid of death? If he was not afraid of death, why should he pray *"Abba, take away this cup from me"*? This issue perplexed me, and an answer came to me from the observations made by Mirza Ghulam Ahmad in his treatise on the missing years of Jesus. I will quote from his work.

> *It was necessary that he should escape death on the cross, for it was stated in the Holy Book that whoever was hanged on the wood was accursed. It is a cruel and unjust blasphemy to attribute a curse to an eminent person like Jesus, the Messiah, for, according to the agreed view of all who know the language, lanat, or curse, refers to the state of one's heart. Can we say that Jesus' heart was ever really estranged from God? Then, how can we say that he was, God forbid, accursed?*
>
> *Look through the Bible, wherein Jesus clearly claims that he is the beloved Son of God. How then, in spite of these holy relations, can a curse be attributed to Jesus? Therefore, there is no doubt that Jesus was not crucified, for his personality did not deserve the underlying consequence of death on the cross*[4].

The Pharisees wished to put Jesus on the cross and cause him to die an accursed death. According to the Mosaic Law, only the *accursed* are hanged – and an accursed person cannot be a Messiah. It is laid down that a sinner is to be put to death by hanging, for one who is hanged is accursed of God[5]. Jesus was aware of the Mosaic Law and this made him make a passionate prayer to God to save him.

Trial and Crucifixion

It is not my intention to go through the details leading to the trial and crucifixion of Jesus Christ, for these events are given in the Gospels. My aim is to find any information, however scanty, from other sources so that a new light be thrown on this fateful event.

Jesus was staying at Capernaum when the angel Gabriel came

to him and said: *"Arise and go to Jerusalem"*. Accordingly he departed[6]. He took a long way round because the Samaritans refused to allow him to pass through their territory. After his arrival in Jerusalem, Jesus taught daily in the Temple. Fearing that Jesus was planning a revolt against them at the coming Passover, the priests convened a council under the chairmanship of Joseph ben Caiaphas, the chief priest. They decided that Jesus must be killed, for he had assumed the role of the promised Messiah, and wanted to be the king of the Jews.

At this juncture, Nicodemus defended Jesus saying that it was not legal to punish a man without hearing him first. The priests and the Pharisees refused to admit his plea[7]. Nicodemus met Joseph of Arimathaea and other Essene friends to inform them of the danger to Jesus. While the Pharisees wished to kill Jesus as early as possible, the Essenes decided to save him from the vengeance of his enemies[8]. After his arrest, Jesus was brought before Pontius Pilate in the castle of Antonia. While the disciples of Jesus held council with Joseph of Arimathaea, Pilate was pressurised by the priests to issue the death warrant for Jesus.

While excavating in the ancient city of Aquila, Naples, a copper plate was found in an antique marble vase. It was discovered by the Commissioner of Arts in the French Army. Written originally in Hebrew, it was translated into French in 1810. On the reverse side of the copper plate, the following sentence is engraved: "A similar plate is sent to each tribe." At the same time of its discovery, the copper plate was preserved in the sacristy of the Chartem (Certosa)[9]:

> *In the year seventeen of the Emperor Tiberius Caesar and the 27th day of March, in the city of the holy Jerusalem – Annas and Caiaphas being priests, sacrificators of the people of God – Pontius Pilate, Governor of Lower Galilee, sitting in the presidential chair of the praetory, condemns Jesus of Nazareth to die on the cross between two thieves, the great and notorious evidence of the people saying:*

i.   Jesus is seducer.
ii. He is seditious.

iii. He is the enemy of the law.
iv. He calls himself falsely the Son of God.
v. He calls himself falsely the King of Israel.
vi. He entered into the Temple followed by a
multitude bearing palm-branches in their
hands.

Orders the first Centurion, Quilius Cornelius, to lead him, the prisoner, to the place of execution. Forbids any person whomsoever, either poor or rich, to oppose the death of Jesus Christ. The witnesses who signed the condemnation of Jesus are:

Daniel Robani, a Pharisee; Joannus Robani; Raphael Robani; Capet, a citizen.

When was the Crucifixion?

Without entering into the controversy about the genuineness of the copper plate, I feel that the information contained in it deserves serious consideration. For the first time, we learn the names of the witnesses who have condemned Jesus. Secondly, the death warrant gives a definite date when Jesus was sentenced. The date is 27th March in the 17th year of Tiberius Caesar. Thus, according to the account given in this copper plate, Jesus was crucified in 30-31 AD.

This date requires thorough examination. It was Pontius Pilate who imposed the death penalty on Jesus, but his verdict was recommended by Joseph ben Caiaphas, the chief priest. Both of these men were removed from their posts by the Romans in about 36 AD. We can deduce therefore that Jesus was put on the cross prior to 36 AD, and very likely within one or two years of this date, since both of them were removed in connection with the crucifixion of Jesus Christ. In view of the above, I am inclined to fix 35 AD as the most probable year of crucifixion. This question remains to be firmly answered.

Golgotha

Jesus was taken in a procession to Golgotha for crucifixion. In this peculiar kind of execution, the victim was fastened to the cross with ropes or nails through the hands and feet. On the vertical beam there would be a small support called a *sedile*, or seat, on which the victim sat, as on a saddle. In some cases, there was attached a foot rest besides the sedile. In order to ease his misery, the victim could support himself on the sedile and the foot-rest. The "victims of crucifixion did not die for two days or even longer"[10]. It was possible for the victim to ease his misery from time to time by supporting himself on the saddle.

It was customary on the part of Jewish women to bring and administer *toska* to the sufferers. This drink was made from sour wine mixed with wormwood, and it had the effect of making the victim unconscious[11]. The original idea behind this punishment was not to kill the victim directly, but to expose him to agony for many days. Finally, the victim could not be kept on the cross on the Sabbath day, and, if the victim had not already died, his knees and legs would be broken with blows from a club. After this the victim was not able to ease himself on the saddle or the foot-rest. He would faint due to insufficient blood circulation and ultimately die of exhaustion and hunger.

Hanna Williams, who has witnessed crucifixion during modern times, asserts that the victim on the cross generally lingers three days before death[12]. I also discovered that in the present-day Philippines, young boys and girls, each year, for fulfilment of a wish, carry crosses on their back to a selected spot and are put on the cross by priests. This ritual of crucifixion is done at Easter. Some are bound with rope to the stake and some prefer to be nailed. In the evening of the same day they are brought down alive and treated. This ritual is performed every year by Philippine Christians[13]. In Africa, when the condemned are crucified, they also usually live for three days on the cross[14].

The cross used to crucify Jesus differed from the usual ones used. This may be connected with the fact that he and his father were carpenters. While the cross in general was constructed in such a manner that the perpendicular beam did not reach above the cross beam, the cross made for Jesus had a perpendicular beam which reached far above it. Furthermore, in front of the cross, a short stake was attached in such a way that he could rest there while being tied[15]. After putting him on this cross, the executioners nailed his wrists and feet – a common practice.

It is stated that this special type of cross was made for Jesus at the request of the servants of the Sanhedrin. Why should they make this special request if not in an attempt to save his life?! That Joseph of Arimathaea had returned to Palestine from his various journeys is certain, and that he was in council with Pilate is also sure[16]. He was a rich and influential man, said to be a good and just man, a disciple of Jesus, and, with Nicodemus, a member of the Essene order[17]. It seems that he was aware of the fate of Jesus and felt that he could serve him best by remaining in the background. Nicodemus, a Pharisee and a secret disciple of Jesus, had earlier protested against the condemnation of Jesus without a hearing. He and his other Essene friends were also in secret council devising ways to save Jesus.

Passion

Jesus suffered quietly, directing his gaze to the sky. Then he said: *Father! Forgive them. For they know not what they do*[18].
Jesus was consumed by thirst. His lips were parched and dry. At that time, a soldier put a sponge dipped in vinegar on a long cane of hyssop, and from this Jesus drank[19].

Jesus remained on the cross from the sixth hour to the ninth hour and there was darkness all over the earth[20]. When this darkness descended, many of the people present smote their chests and started returning to their homes – people were seized by a great fear, thinking that they might be punished by evil spirits[21]. However, some people did not move: Jesus' enemies, the priests and soldiers, and his friends, amongst whom were Mary the mother, his mother's sister, Mary the wife of Cleophas, Mary Magdalene[22], Joseph of Arimathaea[23], Mary the mother of James, Salome and other women[24], the mother of Zebedee's children[25], various disciples and devotees, and the Essenes of Golgotha[26].

At the ninth hour, he sank upon his breast and before sinking he cried with a loud voice, saying: *Elo-i, Elo-i, Lama sabach-thani!*

Out of the four Gospels, only *Matthew* and *Mark* have included this sentence[27]. *Luke* says that Jesus cried: *"Father unto Thy hands I commend my spirit"*. *John* says that before Jesus bowed his head, he said: *"It is finished"*. The other two Gospels have retained this cry in its original language, and added: "That is to say, '*My God, my God, why hast thou forsaken me?*'". All this, despite Jesus having preached, in the Sermon on the Mount:

> *Ask and it shall be given you,*
> *Seek, and you will find,*
> *Knock, and it will be opened to you.*
> *For every one that asks receives,*
> *And he who seeks finds,*
> *And to him who knocks it will be opened*[28].

According to *Luke*, Jesus' prayer was heard, and an angel of God visited him forthwith, strengthening him[29] It is thus a strange logic to say that God was forsaking him, especially in the light of the quote at the beginning of this chapter, wherein Jesus thanks his Father for hearing him.

The question arises, why have the words of Jesus' cry been changed by the compilers of the Gospels? When all the Gospels are translated versions from the Greek, why was this sentence retained in its original Hebrew and Aramaic? In the original Hebrew, the words *"Eli, Eli, Lamah shavahhtani"* actually mean *"God, God, how Thou hast glorified me!"* What is the correct translation? Was Jesus truly *forsaken* by God?

I discovered that the sentence: *"My God, my God, why hast thou forsaken me?"* occurs also in the *Psalms*. But the question arises as to why God should forsake Jesus? This confusion can be removed if we obtain another translation of the sentence. The Sumerian version shows that Jesus spoke in Hebrew and Aramaic. The first two words, *"Elo-i, Elo-i"*, usually translated as "God, O God", would more correctly be, in Hebrew, *Elauia*, which means *"There is no God save Elohim"*. The next words are in Aramaic and are to be rendered as: *"Li-mas-ba (la) g-ants"*, which means *"No God except God, glorious and praised One sent forth"*[30].

The Sumerian rendering makes sense and gives clear meaning. It is interesting to note that the phrase is similar to the Islamic witness: "*There is no God save God, and Muhammad is sent forth by God*". In Arabic, *Muhammad* means 'praised one' or 'glorious'. *Eloi* or *Eli* has some other examples: this word was also used by Krishna, during the war between the Kauravas and Pandavas, when he cried: "*Elia, Elia!*"[31]; Buddha also recited the word "*Elia*" in his prayers, at the time he was being opposed by his people[32].

At that time, if a person was considered nearly dead it was common practice to thrust a lance into the lungs in order to bring this about. The Roman soldier who thrust his spear into the side of Jesus may have undertaken this task halfheartedly, for he seems to have believed that Jesus was already dead. In those days little was known about circulation of blood and what we now know medically about death.

Jesus was put on the cross on the day before the Sabbath and also the day of preparation for the Passover. By evening all activities had to be stopped and the bodies of the victims brought down[33]. *Mark* says that Jesus was put on the cross at the third hour. Both *Mark* and *Matthew* say that Jesus 'yielded up his ghost' at the ninth hour. This would mean that Jesus Christ remained on the cross for at least six hours. But *Luke* says that Jesus gave up his ghost at the sixth hour. So, according to the version in *Luke*, Jesus Christ remained on the cross for three hours only. *Luke* informs us, however, that a strange darkness lasted from the sixth to the ninth hour. *John* says that Pilate sat in judgment over Jesus at the sixth hour.

During ancient times, among the Jews, a day was counted from sunrise, so the third hour could be 9 am, the sixth hour 12 noon and the ninth hour 3 pm. Taking together the information given in the Gospels, I would be inclined to chalk out the events of the day as follows:

- 9 am (third hour): the case against Jesus presented before Pilate. Discussions until the sixth hour (12 noon) when final orders were given;
- 12 noon (sixth hour): Jesus was put on the cross at Golgotha;
- 3 pm (ninth hour): Jesus Christ was taken for dead and was allowed to be taken down from the cross.

Thus it seems probable that Jesus remained on the cross for three hours only, because it was both the day before the Sabbath and also the day of preparation for the Passover.

According to *The Crucifixion by an Eye-witness*, it was the ninth hour (6 pm), and Jesus had been on the cross for three hours. A reddish fog rose from the Dead Sea, the mountain ridges shook violently and there was an unnerving darkness as Jesus' head sank down upon his breast[34]. The Sabbath had begun and no victim could be kept on the cross. When the priests had heard that Joseph had been permitted to take away the body of Jesus, they went to Pilate and besought that, as the victims were not to be kept on the crosses on the Sabbath, their legs should be broken[35]. The soldiers came and broke the legs of the two thieves, thus bringing them quickly to their end. But, when the soldiers approached Jesus, he seemed to be already dead. They did not break his legs[36], but one soldier pierced his right side and, according to the *Gospel of John*, drew forth blood and water[37]. The soldier ignored this and left the scene, permitting the mourners to take down their victims.

It is strange that while the other two victims were administered the punishment of the breaking of legs, Jesus was spared – was this because of negligence, ignorance, bribery or complicity? It appears that Jesus could have been in a state of coma at the time[38]. It could also be that he was feigning death by putting himself in a cataleptic trance. The existence of blood and water coming from his body would demonstrate on medical grounds that he was still alive. Was Jesus in a coma or was he actually dead?

---

(1) *Mark*, 14, 36.
(2) *Luke*, 22, 43.
(3) *John*, 11, 42.
(4) Ahmad, Mirza Ghulam, *Jesus in India*, Qadian, India, 1944, pp23-24. This is an English version of *Masih Hindustan Mein*, from Urdu, translated by Qazi Abdul Hamid, editor of *The Sunrise*, Lahore. The original Urdu version was published in 1908.
(5) *Deuteronomy*, 21, 22. According to the scriptures, death by hanging is accursed: "for a hanged man is accursed of God". The Pharisees believed that they caused Jesus to die an accursed death, to prove that he was a false prophet.

(6) Ragg, tr. *The Gospel of Barnabas*, p59.

(7) Levi, *The Aquarian Gospel*, p194.

(8) *The Crucifixion by an Eye-witness*, p57. The writer of the letter, who was an Essene, informs: "We might indeed have saved our beloved brother from the vengeance of his enemies, if everything had not come to pass so quickly. Nevertheless, we have saved him in secret, as he fulfilled his divine mission in the sight of all the universe".

(9) This death warrant, engraved on copper plate, written in Hebrew, is quoted in *The Crucifixion by an Eye-Witness*, pp29-30.

(10) Keller, Werner, *The Bible as History*, p359.

(11) *The Crucifixion by an Eye-Witness*, p58. Also, Dummelow, Rev J R, *Commentary on the Holy Bible*, Macmillan, London, 1917. Why was this *toska* administered to Jesus only, and not to the two robbers?

(12) Williams, Hanna, *The Life of Christ*, viii, New York, 1928, p328.

(13) The *Times of India*, New Delhi, 10 April 1993. "Over 80% of Filipinos are Roman Catholic, but there is also a flourishing indigenous Christian church, the *Iglesia ni Kristo*. Twice a year about a million worshippers push and jostle each other when a life-size image of the Black Nazarene is borne in procession from the Quiapo Church in Manila. During Easter, religious rites are performed in all churches from Holy Wednesday to Easter Sunday every year. During these days can be witnessed in Manila and the provinces folk observances of these penitents, who not only wound and lash themselves, but even carry their crosses, on the analogy of Jesus Christ, and are nailed on these crosses and brought down alive, after intervals". The *Golden Guide to South & East Asia*, Tokyo, 1969, p362: "Most of those who endure crucifixions say they are fulfilling religious vows, atoning for sins or demonstrating the depth of their faith".

(14) Stroud, William, *On the Physical Cause of Death of Christ*, London, 1965, p55.

(15) *The Crucifixion by an Eye-Witness*, pp59-60.

(16) "Moreover, two of our brethren, influential and experienced, did use all their influence with Pilate and the Jewish Council on behalf of Jesus" – *The Crucifixion by an Eye-Witness*, p66.

(17) *Jewish Encyclopaedia*, Funk & Wagnalls, London, 1905, Vol 8, p250. Very little information is available in the Gospels about Joseph of Arimathaea. He comes at the time of the crucifixion, obtains the body of Jesus from the cross, and hurries to his garden to put it in a newly-constructed tomb. Why did he rush to Pilate and ask for the *body*, not the *corpse* of Jesus? Why had he constructed a new tomb in his garden? Why did he and Nicodemus bring a heavy load of ointments, linen and spices? There is no plausible explanation, except in the context of Jesus' survival of crucifixion, achieved with Essene help.

(18) *Luke*, 23, 34. In some translations, it simply says "...*forgive them, for they know not*." This is the first utterance of Jesus on the cross, demonstrating Jesus' love for his enemies.

(19) *The Crucifixion By An Eye-Witness*, p64. When Jesus was in an agony of thirst, a sponge was dipped in the common sour wine, and put to his mouth on a stalk of hyssop. Immediately after the alleviation of his thirst, Jesus spoke the sixth utterance from the cross: "It is finished!" – *John*, 19, 28.

(20) *Matthew*, 27, 45. It is supposed that the trial of Jesus before the Sanhedrin lasted from 1am to 6am on Friday, and the trial before Pilate continued from 6am to 9am. The crucifixion is supposed to have lasted from 9am to 3pm – a mater of six hours, which I believe is incorrect.

(21) *The Crucifixion by an Eye-Witness*, pp64–65. The *Gospel of Peter* states that "Many went about with lamps, supposing it was night, and darkness lasted until Jesus was taken from the cross, when the earthquake took place".

(22) *John*, 19, 25.

(23) *Luke*, 23, 50.

(24) *Mark*, 15, 40.

(25) *Matthew*, 27, 56.

(26) *The Crucifixion by an Eye-Witness*, p62.

(27) *Mark*, 15, 34; *Matthew*, 27, 46.

(28) *Matthew*, 7, 7-8.

(29) *Luke*, 22, 43.

(30) Allegro, John M, *The Sacred Mushroom and the Cross*, Hodder & Stoughton, London, 1970, pp158, 199, 234, 305.

(31) Ram Dhan, *Krishen Bainti*, (Hindi), Sagri Pustakaliya, Delhi, 1931, p72.

(32) Bhatnagar, K L, *Buddha Chamitkar, Ram Narayan*, (Hindi), Onkar Pustakaliya, Kanpur, 1927, p54.

(33) Keller, Werner, *The Bible as History*, p359. Jesus remained on the cross for about three hours, and his 'death' occurred at about 3pm on Friday. He was brought down at about 4pm, because all normal activities were to be stopped for preparation of the Sabbath, and none could remain hanging overnight, according to Mosaic Law. In computing the time, it must be kept in mind that while the Jewish Saturday started at 6pm on Friday, our Saturday started at midnight at the end of Friday 7th April, in the year of the crucifixion.

(34) *The Crucifixion by an Eye-witness*, p64. *Mark*, *Matthew* and *Luke* testify that on the day of the crucifixion, darkness, the like of which could not be visualised, occurred from the sixth hour to the ninth hour. Nothing was visible to the naked eye when the body of Jesus was carried over to the kitchen garden of Joseph of Arimathaea.

(35) *Luke*, 23, 44; and *The Crucifixion by an Eye-Witness*, p68.

(36) *John*, 19, 32-33.

(37) *The Crucifixion by an Eye-Witness*, p71; *John*, 19, 32-34: "One of the soldiers stuck his spear into the body in such a manner that it passed over the hip and into the side. But from the insignificant wound flowed blood and water, at which John wondered".

(38) Ferrar, Dean F W, *The Life of Christ*, Cassell, Peter & Galpin, London, 1874, p421. "They who saw me marvelled at me, because I was persecuted,

and they supposed that I was swallowed up: for I seemed to them as one of the lost. And I did not perish, for I was not their brother, nor my birth like theirs. And they sought for my death and did not find it" – *The Odes of Solomon*, ode 28, in *The Lost Books of the Bible*, New York, 1944, part 2, p120.

Crucifixion Scene, 1st Century AD Hinidan, Sind. This unique slab depicts spear wounds on palms, an arrow and a cross *(Archeol. Survey of India)*

113

12

The Turin Shroud

History of the Shroud
Whether or not Jesus did die could only be solved by a medical view. I exchanged many letters with members of the medical profession. My friend, Dr Kittermaster, who is a consultant pathologist at Tunbridge Wells, England, took a great interest in the question. He was of the opinion that "dead or alive, the flow of water is difficult to explain; but blood does not flow from a stab wound which is inflicted after death. Blood flowing from a stab wound is very much suggestive of life rather than death". The learned consultant has now published a paper on the subject[1].

The crux of the matter lies with a vital piece of evidence, the *Turin Shroud*. The Holy Shroud, said to have covered the body of Jesus while he lay in the sepulchre, has created great controversy over its authenticity. Let me outline its history. At the time of Christ, Edessa was a state in Syria, with trade connections stretching as far as India, through Babylon[2]. Its king, Abgar Ukkama, at one stage, was ill with arthritis and black leprosy. His attendant, Ananias, told him of Jesus, a miracle-worker in Jerusalem, who might heal him. Ananias was sent, and was told by Thomas that Jesus had been killed, and that after the crucifixion, the Master had disappeared.

However, Thomas gave Ananias the Shroud, telling him that the cloth had covered the body of Jesus after his crucifixion, and that it would have miraculous healing powers. Ananias, with Andreas, took it back to Edessa, and the king was duly cured[3].

114

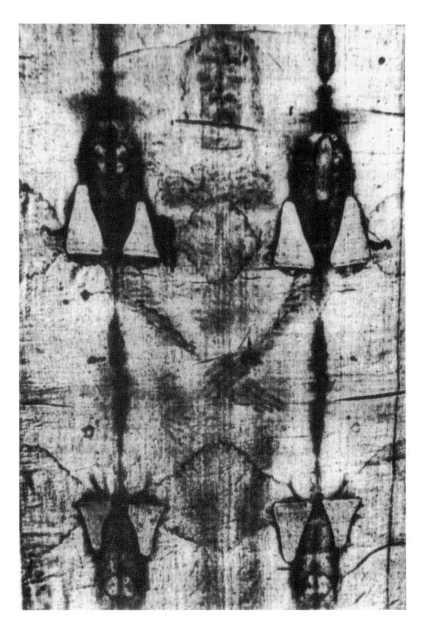

The Turin Shroud figure of Jesus *(Enrie, Turin)*

After this, Abgar Ukkama encouraged the spread of Christian teachings amongst his subjects, who were mostly Jews. Numerous Jews accepted the teaching, and several became early bishops, though they did not change their Jewish names.

The Shroud had been carried to Edessa in about 30 AD. It was discovered in a niche in 525 AD, and preserved in the cathedral of Hagia Sophia, Edessa. After the city was taken by Muslims, it was handed by them to the Bishop of Samossata around 944 AD, then to be taken to Constantinople. It was seen there in the cathedral by Abu Nasr Yahya, a Christian Arab writer, in 1058, and by the French Crusader Robert de Clari in 1203. In the following year, when the city was sacked by the Crusaders, it disappeared, but found refuge in France, where it was shown to the public for the first time, in the presence of the royal family of the House of Savoy[4].

The Shroud was first photographed by the Italian Secondo Pia, in 1898, during an exhibition for the public. When he developed the glass plates in his darkroom, he discovered the imprinted face of a person with a close likeness to pictures of Jesus. The photograph showed the body with wound marks made by the crown of thorns, the spear mark in the right side and the bloodstains caused by nails.

Doctors and Scientists

There are different views on the causes of the image on the Shroud. In 1902, Yves Delage, a professor of anatomy, declared that the image of Christ was created by a physio-chemical process which took place while he was wrapped in it. In 1924, Paul Vignon, a biologist, declared that the colourations and imprints were caused by Jesus' sweating body, with a mixture of aloe and oil tincture. Some are of the opinion that the image is a faint scorch. Scientific tests have revealed that marks of the wounds are made of blood rather than pigment, since the deposits have the correct proportion of iron in them to demonstrate the presence of blood[5].

In Jewish ritual, a dead body is washed before burial. In the case of Jesus, there is no evidence that his body was washed. Instead, the gospels state that Joseph of Arimathaea, Nicodemus and others applied ointment to his body. If he were dead, they would have washed the corpse.

My German friends drew my attention to a book entitled *Jesus nicht am Kreuz Gestorben* (*Jesus did not die on the Cross*), by Kurt Berna. In his book, the learned scholar produced scientific evidence that the heart of Jesus was still beating after he was taken down. When Jesus was wrapped in the Shroud, blood continued to flow from many wounds in his body. His argument was that dead bodies stop bleeding. Kurt Berna believes that Jesus survived crucifixion and considers the Turin Shroud inescapable proof of this matter. I began to correspond with Kurt Berna over this issue and had many discussions with him. Berna had written to Pope John XXIII about the Turin Shroud in 1959 concerning his findings, and claimed:

> During the past twenty-four months different specialists from German universities have tried to refute my discoveries, but to no avail. They now recognise and admit the validity of my investigation and its importance for both the Christian and the Jewish religions.
>
> It has been proven without doubt that Jesus Christ was laid to rest in this Shroud after the crucifixion and the removal of the crown of thorns. The tests carried out so far have established that the body of the crucified person was wrapped in this cloth and left for some time.
>
> From a medical point of view, it has been proved that the body that lay in the Shroud was not dead, as the heart was then still beating. The traces of blood fluid, its position and nature, give positive scientific proof that the so-called execution was not legally complete. This discovery suggests that the present and past teachings of Christianity are incorrect.[6]

The whole issue concerning 'blood and water' had not only become controversial but sensational. I studied, amongst other material, the report prepared by Dr Primrose of the Royal Society of Edinburgh, Scotland. Let me quote some portions of this testament of this Senior Anaesthetist:

> In the case of Christ, vitality was reduced to such a low level that even active breathing was not the metabolic exchange prevailing after the

collapse. Respiration had not actually failed, as seemed to be so obvious from the absence of respiratory movement, as sufficient respiration was being effected by the beat of the heart against lungs which to a great extent surround it. Of this we have practical experience in anaesthesia. The breathing bag of the conventional apparatus will, in such conditions, show movement, the chest and diaphragm being quite at rest.

Combined with this feeble respiration in the case of Christ is the concentration of the circulating blood owing to the loss of so much fluid into the abdominal haemorrhage cavity. As there has not been any severe haemorrhage, and as so little oxygen was being used for maintaining the very low metabolism, more active breathing was not physiologically called for. It is entirely owing to this very reduced physiology that no sign of breathing betrayed to those carrying out the crucifixion the fact that life was still present in our Lord, even after two hours of collapse[7].

Paul had presented Jesus' crucifixion as an atonement for the sins of the world. The Shroud was becoming a perplexing matter for the Church, because of the scientists' findings. The Church permitted a secret scientific evaluation of the Shroud by ten specialists, who started work on 16th June 1969. They were directed to study and report confidentially. A report was prepared and submitted to Cardinal Pellegrino. All information was kept secret, even the names of the specialists.

However, it was reported in the newspapers that scientific analysis demonstrated the genuineness of the blood. "No post-mortem bleedings are on the Shroud because the position of the marks and the blood serum borders around the identified human blood prove active bleeding as a result of heart activity. The existence of serum borders requires the existence and activity of fibrin in blood outflow. Post-mortem blood does not have this active fibrin"[8].

Owing to the leak of information about the blood, the Church adopted a defensive attitude. In 1973, another secret examination of samples of blood-stained threads was permitted. The ensuing report stated that, after tests, no blood was detected on the Shroud. In 1976, when this result was published, the Church succeeded in re-establishing its doctrines concerning the crucified Christ, and the Shroud was declared a forgery. After the flames had subsided, the Church was asked to answer what chemical compounds the stains were made of, and why, if the Shroud is fake, the Church was preserving it as a venerable relic.

Yet again, in 1978, the Shroud was examined by two groups of scientists equipped with highly sophisticated instruments. The data obtained created many other problems and riddles. However, some observations were startling. The team succeeded in reconstructing a life-size, three-dimensional relief of the body wrapped in the Shroud. Also, it was shown that the impression, with such fine detail, could not be the work of any artist – thus the Shroud was not an outright forgery. The next observation was that the image was not produced by any identifiable substance. However, the blood stains showed iron, the characteristic component of blood[9]. The American scientists came to the following conclusion: "Nearly all of us now believe that the Shroud is not a painting. Except for a small amount of iron oxide, we find no pigment. And we do not think that either liquid or water vapour could have produced the image we see"[10].

In 1973, Max Frei, a Swiss botanist, noticed minute dust particles on the Shroud. He obtained samples at twelve different points, and, by 1978, had identified 49 species of plant pollens found mixed with the dust. The main groups were: 1. Halophyte plants typical to Palestine and the Dead Sea region, including desert varieties of Tamarix, Suaeda and Artemisia; 2. Steppic plants characteristic of the Anatolian steppe, a dry zone where no natural pollen can grow; 3. a few plants characteristic of the area around Istanbul; and, 4. a few plants belonging to France and Italy[11].

In March 1977, the Church granted special permission for a team of NASA scientists to make an examination. However, they had to work under strict instructions, being permitted to test the thread only at one or two points along the margin. Their conclusions were:

1.   the antiquity of the linen is confirmed through its herring-

bone weave, of a kind fashionable in the first century AD;

2.   the image on the Shroud is three-dimensional, not flat, and is not the work of a human hand;

3.   pollen is of the type found in Palestine in the first century AD;

4.   blots and stains show the presence of myrrh from the ointment used on the wound marks of Jesus;

5.   one nail was struck into the crossed feet between the second and third toes, and no bone was damaged;

6.   both palms were nailed above the fleshy side of the palms;

7. the spear thrust was aimed between the second and third rib, about six inches from the mesial line, in an upward angle from the heart;

8.   positive photos of the facial features show the person to be of Jewish origin, with a long nose, long hair and beard. [12]

The linen shroud is preserved in the cathedral at Turin, Italy, measuring 4.35 metres long and 1.1 metres broad. The body was 1.62 metres, with bloodstains and blots located on the head, hands and right side of the chest.

The most recent examination was announced on October 1988, by the Archbishop of Turin, Anastasio Cardinal Ballestrero: according to him, it had been found by radio-carbon dating that the linen is no older than 728 years. On the face of it, this dating seems concocted, for it is impossible to give an exact year using this technique – only a range of years. Secondly, it is impossible to obtain radio-carbon dating of the blood on the linen because dried blood clots do not absorb carbon – only living organisms absorb radiant carbon and non-radiant isotopes $C12$. Thirdly, the examination was carried out under the sole guidance of Professor Luigi Gonella, scientific advisor to the Church, whose involvement cannot be claimed to be unbiased. Fourthly, the team did not carry out examinations of traces of pollen, ointments and dust particles on the Shroud. The examination was incomplete.

Leading from all this, I felt sure that Jesus did not die on the cross but survived. I knew that this view ran contrary to the religious belief of Christians, and later found out that Kurt Berna had suffered imprisonment leading out of his open discussion of this issue, despite being Roman Catholic. I, being a Muslim, also suffered, as a result of my own work. It convinced me that there is no freedom in faith.

Sai Baba's impression

I would like to tell you an anecdote, involving the present-day teacher Sathya Sai Baba, or Prashanti Niliyam, Bangalore, India. In August 1988, Carol Bruce visited me in my home in Kashmir, having read in the books on Christ by Andreas Faber-Kaiser and Helger Kersten that I was the source of information for them concerning Jesus' life in the East. She brought me a special photograph of the risen Christ, which the Baba had manifested miraculously. (see plate 15) The story, as told by Barbara McMalley of New Zealand, goes as follows:

I had gone to Puttaparti with a friend from New Zealand. We both supported and encouraged each other, since it was our first visit to India. While I was happy with everything, my friend had been very much caught up in the suffering of Christ. She had with her two items she hoped the Baba would bless for her, a crucifix and a black-and-white photo of the image of Christ from the Turin Shroud. Daily we would attend darshan (audience with the master), and on one occasion, Sri Sathya Sai Baba stopped before us. He looked at the items held out to him for his blessing, and refused to accept the crucifix.

As I watched, spellbound, Sai Baba, with a lift and wave of his hand, drew the black-and-white image of Christ from that photo until there was nothing but a blank sheet of gloss photo paper. By the same token, he then drew up and through that blank sheet – just as if it were laid in a darkroom developing tray – the image to be seen today on the photograph: that of the risen Jesus Christ, in colour. A Christ whose eyes are haunting, so full of love and compassion are they.

With a blessing for the two women from New Zealand, the Baba went on his way.

(1) *Faith and Freedom*, Volume 32: Number 96, Summer 1979, pp131-136. For medical theories, see *The Guardian*, Manchester, 27 Oct 1972, 'Jesus only

fainted'; *Time Magazine*, 10 Dec 1965, 'Did Christ die on the Cross?';*Sunday Times*, London, 24 Jan 1965, 'The Resurrection of Christ'Stroud, *On the Physical Death of Christ*, London 1905;*Encyclopaedia Biblica*, Art Cross, London, 1903; Wilson, Ian, *The Turin Shroud*, Penguin Books, Middlesex, 1978; Willis, Dr David, 'Did He die on the Cross?', in *Ampleforth Journal*, LXXIV, 1969, pp27–39.

(2) Segal, J B, *Edessa, the Blessed City*, Oxford, 1970, pp67–69.

(3) Wilson, Ian, *The Turin Shroud*, pp313–331.

(4) Wilson, Ian, *The Turin Shroud*, pp287–305.

(5) *National Geographic Magazine*, vol 157, no 6, June 1980, p752.

(6) Faber-Kaiser, Andreas, *Jesus Died in Kashmir*, Gordon & Cremonesi, London, 1977, pp30–33. This work, for which I provided an introduction, material and photographs, was originally published in Spanish, under the title of *Jesus Vivo Y Murio en Cashemira* (A T E, Barcelona, 1976). See also: Berna, Kurt, *Christ did not Perish on the Cross*, Expositions Press, New York, 1975, and *Inquest of Jesus Christ: Did He die on the Cross?*, Leslie Frewin, London, 1967.

(7) *Sunday Express*, London, January 1970. Report of Dr W B Primrose, Senior Anaesthetist, Glasgow Royal Infirmary, headed 'St John reports the Life after the Cross, not the Death'. Also, report read at the Royal Society of Edinburgh. Summary in Berna, Kurt, *Christ did not Perish on the Cross*, pp195–196.

(8) Bruknaer, N T, and Berna, Kurt, media release. *The Second Life of Jesus Christ*, Exposition Press, New York, 1978, p59. This statement was based on an AP, UPI and Reuters report that: "From June 1969 to January 1970, a team consisting of ten specialists conducted a proper scientific analysis of the blood marks on the Turin Shroud. It was found that all the really important blood marks on the Shroud flowed, without doubt, directly from open wounds. Marks of such blood cannot have serum borders, because fibrin does not exist in dried blood, being chemically destroyed".

(9) Kersten, Holger, *Jesus Lived in India*, Element Books, Dorset, 1986, pp147–148. This book was originally published in 1983 in Munich, under the title *Jesus lebte in Indien*. Kersten's study rests on the work of Kurt Berna.

(10) *National Geographic*, vol 157, no 6, June 1980, p751.

(11) Wilson, Ian, *The Turin Shroud*, pp91–92; see also Wilcox, R K, *Shroud*, Macmillan, New York, 1977.

(12) Berna, Kurt, *Jesus ist Nicht am Kreuz Gestorben*, Hans Naber, Stuttgart, 1957, pp102–142.

13

Resurrection

I once received some books written by the Ahmadiyya Muslims, denouncing the beliefs of Christianity. The founder of this sect, Mirza Ghulam Ahmad had claimed that he was a prophet, reformer, messiah and a Mahdi among the Muslims. He claimed that Jesus died a natural death in Kashmir, and that the belief in atonement through the blood of Jesus is an erroneous doctrine. Finally, he added that the renaissance of Islam was certain and that there was no need to wait for the promised Messiah, for he had come in the person of Mirza Ghulam Ahmad. My contact with the Ahmadis provided me with much information on the subject of my research, despite the fact that their literature had been produced zealously for missionary purposes.

The Hindu version of the Crucifixion
There are *yogis* who can slow their heartbeat almost to vanishing point, reducing their respiration to no more than one breath every few minutes[1]. An ancient Hindu *sutra*, known as *Natha-nama-vali*, a holy Sutra of the Nath Yogis, has given a different version about the crucifixion of Jesus, whom they call *Isha Natha*. Let me quote:

> *Isha Natha came to India at the age of fourteen. After this he returned to his own country and began preaching. Soon after, his brutish and materialistic countrymen conspired against him and had him crucified. After crucifixion, or perhaps even before it, Isha Natha entered samadhi or profound trance, by means of yoga.*

123

Seeing him thus, the Jews presumed he was dead, and buried him in a tomb. At that very moment however, one of his gurus or teachers, the great Chetan Natha, happened to be in profound meditation, in the lower reaches of the Himalayas, and he saw in a vision the tortures which Isha Natha was undergoing. He therefore made his body lighter than air and passed over to the land of Israel.

The day of his arrival was marked with thunder and lightning, for the gods were angry with the Jews, and the whole world trembled. When Chetan Natha arrived, he took the body of Isha Natha from the tomb, woke him (Jesus) from his samadhi, and later led him off to the sacred land of the Aryans. Isha Natha then established an ashram in the lower regions of the Himalayas and he established the cult of the lingam and the yoni there².

The cult of the *lingam* and the *yoni* relates to the early eastern fertility cults which were prominent in the region between Tigris and Euphrates, in Mesopotamia³. The legends of the Natha *yogis* cannot be dismissed as wholly irrelevant: Jesus belonged to the East, and Eastern traditions and legends about him are as historically important as the theological tales of the Gospels. The Natha *yogis* exist in India today, and some of their hymns contain references to John the Baptist. As such, the legends about Jesus in the Hindu *sutras* deserve consideration.

The Essene version

The *Gospel of John* tells us that Joseph of Arimathaea besought Pontius Pilate that he be allowed to take away the body of Jesus from the cross. As hardly a few hours had elapsed, Pilate wondered if Jesus was already dead. He called one of his guards who informed him that Jesus was already dead. He then commanded that the body of Jesus be delivered to Joseph. Here is given a clear hint about the role of Essenes in providing assistance to Jesus. Here is the Essene version:

Two of our brethren, influential and experienced, used all their influence with Pilate and the Jewish council on behalf of Jesus, but their efforts were frustrated in that Jesus himself requested that he might be permitted to suffer death for his faith — and thus fulfil the Law; for, as you know, to die for truth and virtue is the greatest sacrifice.

Now it so happened that after the earthquake, when many people had gone away, Joseph and Nicodemus arrived at the cross. Although they loudly lamented his fate, it nevertheless appeared strange to them that Jesus, having hung less than seven hours, should already be dead. They could not believe it and hastily went up to the place. Joseph and Nicodemus examined the body of Jesus and Nicodemus, greatly moved, drew Joseph aside and said to him: "As sure as is my knowledge of life and nature, so sure is it possible to save him".

After this, according to the prescriptions of medical art, they slowly untied his bonds, drew the spikes out and with great care laid him on the ground. Thereupon, Nicodemus spread strong spices and healing salves on long pieces of byssus, which he had brought. These he wound about Jesus' body. These spices and salves had great healing powers and were used by our Essene brothers. Joseph and Nicodemus were bending over his face and their tears fell upon him, and they blew into him their own breath [artificial resuscitation] and warmed his temples.

Nicodemus spread balsam in both the nail-pierced hands, but he believed it was not best to close up the wound in Jesus' side, because he considered the flow of blood and water therefrom helpful to respiration and beneficial in the renewing of life.

The body was then laid in the rock sepulchre which belonged to Joseph. They then smoked the grotto with aloe and other herbs and placed a large stone in front of the entrance that the vapours might better fill the grotto.

Thirty hours had now passed since the assumed death of Jesus. Our brother, having heard a slight noise within the grotto, went to observe what had happened. He observed with inexpressible joy that the lips of the body moved and that it breathed. He at once hastened to Jesus to assist him. Twenty-four brethren of our Order arrived at the Grotto along with Joseph and Nicodemus. But Jesus was not yet strong enough to walk far, wherefore he was conducted to the house belonging to our Order, that is close by Calvary in the garden.[4]

Though the authorised Gospels tell us that Jesus lost his life on the cross, the Essene version is similar to the Hindu version in that they imply Jesus survived crucifixion and was saved – according to the Hindu version, in a miraculous way, and in the Essene version, in a way which is credible in the light of medical science. Moreover, the efforts of Joseph and Nicodemus in helping Jesus out of difficulty are mentioned in the authorised Gospels.

We are informed by the *Gospel of John* that they brought fine linen and a mixture of myrrh and aloes of about a hundred pounds weight with them[5]. The *Gospel of Luke* tells us that Joseph of Arimathaea brought spices and ointments for Jesus. Why should they do this if we are to disbelieve the Essene version of this event? These questions certainly need to be investigated.

It would seem that the Essenes had the necessary experience to provide medical relief to Jesus and save his life because 'they had investigated, to good purpose, in the interests of medicine, the healing virtues of roots and stones'[6]. We know that myrrh and aloes were reduced to powder and inserted between the bandages which were wound fold upon fold[7].

According to Essene texts[8], Nicodemus gave him wine to drink, after which Jesus was greatly refreshed. The Essenes kept Jesus in concealment for safety and in order for him to recover his strength. He was clothed in the Essene working–garb to look like a gardener. He ate dates and bread dipped in honey. Nicodemus again bandaged his wounds, gave him a medical draught, and asked him to rest quietly. As he was not safe in the country, he later went in secret to another Essene centre.

Jesus healed

It was Mirza Ghulam Ahmad, the founder of the Ahmadiyya sect, who drew the attention of scholars towards the ointment used for healing the wounds of Jesus. Let me quote:

> *A piece of evidence of great value has come to us regarding Jesus and his recovery after crucifixion. It is a prescription of an ointment, known as 'Marham-i-Issa', which is recorded in hundreds of medical books. Some of these books were compiled by Christians, some by the Magi, or by Jews and some by Muslims. Most of these works pertain to old times.*

Researches have shown that its preparation was known to millions of people through oral tradition. It was recorded a little after the crucifixion of Jesus Christ in Latin pharmacopoeia. It was also mentioned there that it had been prepared for healing the wounds of Jesus Christ[9].

The learned scholar also mentions the titles of 23 medical treatises which mention this ointment. Abu-bakr Mohammad Zakariya Razi (864–932 AD), known in Europe as Rhazes, wrote several medical treatises, some of which have been translated into Latin. He mentioned this ointment in a treatise published in 1489 in Latin under the title *Liber Almansoris-Continens*, and an English translation was published in 1848. His original medical encyclopaedia was called *Havi-Kabir*[10].

A treatise published in Arabic under the title *Kamil-us-Sanaah*, by Ali bin Abbas al-Majusi (d.994) who was known in Europe as *Haly Abbas*, is an important medical source. It was published in Latin under the title *Liber Regius* in 1492. This treatise was also published in French under the title *Trois Traites de Anatomie Arabs* in 1504[11].

Another world-famous medical treatise, *Al-Qanun-fi-al-Tibb*, by Abu Ali Hussain bin Abdullah bin Sena (980–1037). Its Latin translation by Gerard of Cremona was published in 1544 and is known in English as the *Canon of Medicine* by Avicenna[12]. Another important medical treatise, known in Europe as *Hesagps* by Jarjani, mentions the ointment[13].

The ointment of Jesus is known as *Marham-i-Havarin*, the ointment of the apostles, or *Marham-i-Rusul*, the ointment of the prophets, or *Marham-i-Shalikha*, the ointment of Sheliakh. Avicenna records that this ointment has miraculous powers to heal wounds[14]. Its use can eliminate puss and restore damaged flesh in a few days[15]. This ointment not only encourages the formation of fresh tissue but also helps the circulation of blood and recovery from numbness[16].

The twelve ingredients of the ointment of Jesus were: 1. white wax; 2. gum *gugal*, also known as *balsamo dendron mukul*; 3. *plumbi oxidum*; 4. myrrh, also known as *balsamo dendron myrrh*; 5. *galbanum*; 6. *aristoelchia longa*; 7. sub-acetate of copper; 8. gum *ammonicum*; 9. resin of *pinus longifolia*; 10. *olibanum*; 11. aloes; 12. olive oil.

I first discovered the twelve ingredients of this ointment through Syed Abdul Hai, a researcher of the Dead Sea Scrolls in Pakistan, but the ingredients of the ointment were, in fact, first recorded in the Greek *Pharmacopoeia*.

The great Abbasid emperor Mamun al-Rashid (913-83) established a library and a school of translation in Baghdad, in which the translators made Arabic versions of Greek works on medicine, science and mathematics. It was during this golden age of Islamic medicine that the Greek *Pharmacopoeia* was translated into Arabic and named *Qarabadin-i-Rumi* or the *Pharmacopoeia of the Romans*. This treatise was also translated into Persian, entitled, *Qarabadin-i-Unani* or the *Pharmacopoeia of the Greeks*. These medical treatises all mention the ointment of Jesus and its ingredients[17].

The scientists who have so far made investigations into the Holy Shroud of Turin have had no knowledge of the ointment's true ingredients. Their researches were limited to finding traces of myrrh and aloes only. Now, with the complete pharmacopoeia exposed, further examination of the Shroud may prove interesting.

Life after death

Many treatises have been written on the question of whether or not Christ triumphed over death on the cross. Jesus made a prophecy that he would rise again, and I believe that he did indeed rise again, alive out of the jaws of death. Here is another version about the events that took place after crucifixion.

Master Yessu, although maltreated beyond the meaning of brutal, and wounded with great loss of blood, recovered more rapidly than his best friends had expected. Once down from the cross and his wounds given the necessary attention, it became only a question of nature doing the rest.

His inner circle of friends had determined to save him at any cost and their understanding of the higher sciences, obtained from him, were now brought to a test. Thus, as soon as the body had been taken down from the cross, it was interned in the private sepulchre, and after the stone door had been carefully sealed, the Master's friends entered the secret passageway leading thereto. Here they set to work at once.

When he was taken from the cross they knew that he was not dead, but merely in an unconscious condition, super-induced by an opiate which had been so ingeniously administered under the cover of night. Once the body was brought to the sepulchre and away from public gaze, Yousef [Joseph of Arimathaea], Nicodemus, Mathaeli and others set to work to do all within their power to revive their beloved Master. It was nearly midnight when the body of their Lord had been sufficiently revived to warrant his removal to the house of Joseph[18].

It is becoming clear that Jesus Christ triumphed over death on the cross through a combination of planned and unforeseen circumstances. Leaving aside the possibility of supernatural causes, let me reiterate some major blunders committed by the prosecutors:

a) Jesus was provided with a special type of cross, which had a *sedile* to sit on, and a foot-rest;

b) Jesus was put on the cross on Friday at the sixth hour, and the Sabbath had to start on that very day at sunset, only three hours later;

c) his legs were not broken;

d) Pilate allowed Joseph to carry away the body of Jesus.

It is astonishing that in the *Gospel of Matthew*, we are told that Pilate himself hints at having made a mistake:

The chief priests and the Pharisees gathered before Pilate and said, 'Sir, we remember how that impostor said, while he was still alive, "After three days I will rise again". Therefore, order the sepulchre to be made secure until the third day, lest his disciples go and steal him away, and tell the people, "He has risen from the dead", and the last fraud will be worse than the first.' Pilate said to them,
You have a guard of soldiers; go, make as secure as you can.'[19]

The first error to which they refer was that Joseph of Arimathaea had been permitted to bring down the body of Jesus, when it was not certain that he was fully dead.

It is interesting that the body of Jesus was never found and buried. The Gospels inform us that the body of Jesus was taken by Joseph and placed in a new tomb which was hewn out of a rock, and by the next day it had disappeared.

In 326 AD the emperor Constantine erected a basilica in Jerusalem, in honour of Jesus Christ[20]. It is said that he had discovered this site under divine inspiration[21]. However, only graves are found in the site and no rock-cut tombs are there. This could be because Constantine had ordered the cutting away of rocks for the building project. No archaeologist has found any relic pertaining to Jesus at the site.

Information has, however, come out about a slab, mentioning that Jesus was not killed on the cross, having been on it for only a few hours, but was saved, nursed and protected by the Essenes. This engraved stone slab is in the possession of the Freemasonry Society of Germany and out of the reach of the Christian Church[22].

The Bible tells us that after the crucifixion, Mary Magdalene, together with Mary the mother of James and Salome, visited the sepulchre of Jesus. They brought sweet spices with them, with which to anoint Jesus. There were other devotees with them[23]. They saw that the stone had been rolled away and there was no body there[24].

They were perplexed and inquired of a young man who was sitting there, clothed in a long white garment[25]. The *Gospel of Mark* tells us that the young man told them not to feel frightened but to inform everyone that Jesus had left for Galilee and that they could see him there[26]. Accordingly, they went to bring disciples to Galilee to meet him, keeping the whole incident a secret[27].

It seems probable that the young man was an Essene, because it was binding for them to wear long white garments. It seems Mary Magdalene informed Simon Peter that Jesus had been taken from the sepulchre: he and some other disciples ran there, and Simon Peter went into the tomb and saw linen clothes laid on the floor, and the napkin that had been around Jesus' head was in another corner[28]. But Jesus was not there. From the Gospels we understand that Jesus had disappeared. There was no sign either of

Joseph or Nicodemus.

The Essenes have provided further information about Jesus in the days and weeks that followed. Two Essenes carried Jesus between them to the house of an elder near the Mount of Olives. He was still weak and faint from fatigue. In this house, Jesus was placed on a soft bed of moss where he soon fell into a profound slumber. A youth was sent to bring Joseph of Arimathaea, Nicodemus and others.

Next day, a council was held by the Essene Order that they might further protect Jesus. Both Joseph and Nicodemus told Jesus to save himself and never again permit himself to fall into the hands of the priests. He was advised to take further rest because 'even if the wounds in his hands were beginning to heal and the wound in his side emitted no more humour, his body was still weak.'[29].

Jesus was eager to meet his disciples, but his Essene protectors would not allow him to undertake such a venture. They decided to take him to Masada in the valley of Rephaim. One night, they conducted him to this place, along a narrow path which was known to them. Here, in the wild valley, he was provided with shelter. Jesus was told to remain there until he was called. He gave his word that he would do so.

After this, Joseph of Arimathaea, Nicodemus and others left for Jerusalem. Jesus remained there for a number of days, and each day they inquired about his health through a messenger. Jesus felt sad and sorely afflicted with melancholy thoughts. He and John the Baptist (now dead) had often wandered in this very valley. Every day, Jesus went to a selected spot to refresh his body. From this spot he could view the splendours of nature as well as the high tower of Masada and the valley of Sittim[30].

The Resurrection story

The *Gospel of Peter*, written around 150 AD, provides details about the resurrection of Jesus:

> *Now in the night whereon the Lord's day dawned, as the soldiers were keeping guard two by two in every watch, there came a great sound in*

the heaven, and they saw the heavens open and two men descend thence, shining with a great light, and drawing near unto the sepulchre. And that stone which had been set on the door rolled away of itself and went back to the side, and the sepulchre was opened, and both the young men entered in.

When therefore those soldiers saw that, they woke up the centurion and the elders, and while they were yet telling them the things which they had seen, they saw three men come out of the sepulchre, and two of them sustaining the one, and a cross following after them. And of the two they saw that their heads reached unto heaven, but of him that was led by them, that it overpassed the heavens.[31]

I believe it is no coincidence that at the time of transfiguration, Jesus was seen talking to two men, and here again, he is seen with two men clothed in white, taking him out of the sepulchre[32]. Were these two Joseph and Nicodemus?

Later, when he was healed, Jesus went to a village called Emmaus, where two villagers met him. One of them, whose name was Cleopas, asked Jesus whether he had not heard that Jesus of Nazareth had been condemned to death and crucified by the priests. Jesus said to them:

O foolish men, and slow of heart, to believe all that the prophets have spoken! Was it not necessary that the Christ should suffer these things and enter into his glory?[33]

As they drew near the village, Jesus was in a hurry and wanted to go further, but the villagers constrained him and invited him to stay for dinner. He accepted their hospitality.

When he was at table with them, he took the bread and blessed, and broke it, and gave it to them. And their eyes were opened and they recognised him; and then he vanished out of their sight.[34]

The various disappearances of Jesus created many misgivings among his disciples. Some thought he had resurrected while others believed that he had died. They would discuss his whereabouts secretly and also get news about him. Thomas thought that it was not possible for any man to rise from the grave. During one such meeting, Jesus came to them:

> Jesus himself stood among them. But they were startled and frightened, and supposed that they saw a spirit.
>
> And he said to them, 'Why are you troubled? Why do questionings arise in your hearts? See my hands and feet, that it is I myself; handle me and see; for a spirit has not flesh and bones, as you see that I have.'[35]

The orthodox interpretation of all this is, of course, that he had actually died and then miraculously come to life again. But the passage could equally be read as a denial of the rumour that he had died. The passage continues:

> And while they still disbelieved for joy, and wondered, he said to them, 'Have you anything here to eat?' They gave him a piece of broiled fish, and he took it, and ate it before them.[36]

Again we could see this as an attempt to reassure his disciples that he was truly alive and still human. One day, Jesus, along with his Essene friends and protectors, met Thomas ('the Contender') because he would not believe that Jesus was still alive. When Jesus saw Thomas, he told him:

> Reach hither thy finger and behold my hands; and reach hither thy hand and thrust it into my side and be not faithless but believing.[37]

In this passage Jesus clearly wanted to convince Thomas that he was truly alive as a human being. Many superstitions had been woven about him by his disciples, and they were talking of miracles. Jesus and many of his Essene friends possessed profound knowledge in the secret powers and processes of nature. He was alive thanks not to a miracle but to the laws of nature, plus skill, and he wanted to convince his disciples that they could understand his presence there without recourse to such superstitions.[38]

If Jesus was physically alive soon after the crucifixion, it does not require much of a leap of imagination to believe that he could continue teaching for many years following these events which the

Bible documents.

The Essene story continues: Jesus Christ travelled each day from place to place and stopped only with Essene friends. In Bethany, he stayed in the house of Lazarus. He also met Mary the mother and some disciples. On the same day Nicodemus came with the sad news that Joseph of Arimathaea had been arrested. Great anxiety arose from all the Essenes. Jesus prayed to God for the protection of Joseph. As no case could be proven against Joseph, he was set free. Jesus now wanted to travel alone. He reached Bethsaida and stayed with Simon Peter.[39]

Jesus reached the Sea of Galilee and stayed in a hut built by Simon Peter. There he found Thomas, Nathanial, the sons of Zebedee, and two other disciples. They had gone there to fish. Jesus told them to bring the fish which they had caught, and they roasted this fish on a fire. Jesus and his disciples then ate bread and fish[40]. Next day, Jesus continued on his journey.

Having rested and refreshed himself for some days at the foot of Mount Carmel, he again went to Bethany, where he comforted his mother before going on to Kedron. He stayed there for a little while and wept for Jerusalem. He went to the summit of the Mount of Olives. From this spot, he saw the country where he had lived and worked. Then he rose and hastily went away through the gathering mist[41]. His disciples knew that he would return no more, and that they themselves were to proclaim the word of Jesus.

Jesus had once said:

I am the good shepherd; I know my own and my own know me, as the Father knows me and I know the Father; and I lay down my life for the sheep. And I have other sheep, that are not of this fold. I must bring them also, and they will heed my voice. So there shall be one flock, and one shepherd.

For this reason the Father loves me, because I lay down my life, that I may take it again. No one takes it from me, but I lay it down of my own accord. I have power to lay it down, I have power to take it again; this charge I have received from my Father.[42]

---

(1) Serrano, Miguel, *The Serpent of Paradise*, Rider & Co, London, p140."My

far-reaching memories are not unique. Many yogis are known to have retained their self-consciousness without interruption by the dramatic transition to and from life and death", Paramahansa Yogananda, *Autobiography of a Yogi*, Los Angeles, 1952. See also: Ajaya, Swami, *Living with the Himalayan Masters*, Himalayan Inst of Yoga, Honesdale PA, USA.

(2) Serrano, Miguel, *The Serpent of Paradise*, p143.

(3) Concerning fertility cults, see Allegro, John M, *The Sacred Mushroom and The Cross*, pp 72, 84, 91, 128. See also *Linga Purana*, published by Gurumandala Grathamala, Calcutta, 1960.

(4) *The Crucifixion by an Eye-Witness*, pp65-75.

(5) *John*, 19, 39. "Joseph of Arimathaea, being a disciple of Jesus, took the body of Jesus. Thereafter came also Nicodemus by night and brought a mixture of myrrh and aloes, about a hundred pound weight".

(6) *Encyclopaedia Biblica*, Col, 1938. London, 1903. See also: Dupont-Sommer, *The Jewish Sect of Qumran and the Essenes*, Macmillan, 1956.

(7) Dummelov, *Commentary on the Holy Bible*, p808. *The Crucifixion by an Eye-Witness*, pp 73-81. "According to the prescription of the medical art, they slowly untied his bonds, drew the spikes out from his hands, and Nicodemus spread strong spices and healing salves on long pieces of byssus; these he wound about Jesus' body. Nicodemus spread balsam in both the nail-pierced hands. Then they smoked the grotto with aloe and other strengthening herbs".

(8) *The Crucifixion by an Eye-Witness*, p81. "Then Nicodemus urged him to take some refreshments, and he ate some dates and some bread dipped in honey. And Nicodemus gave wine to drink, after which Jesus was greatly refreshed, so that he raised himself up".

(9) Ahmed, Mirza Ghulam, *Massih Hindustan Mein*, (Urdu), Qadian, 1908, p101.

(10) The *Havi-Kabir* was translated into English by Green Hill and published in 1848. E G Brown, in his *Arabian Medicine*, and D Campble, in his own *Arabian Medicine*, vol 2, p235, inform that scattered folios of this medical treatise are deposited in the British Museum, and libraries in Munich, Berlin and St Petersburg.

(11) *Ansar Allah*, monthly magazine, Rabbwah, Pakistan, March 1978, p43.

(12) Campble, D, *Arabian Medicine*, vol 1, p78; see also Brown, E G, *Arabian Medicine*. "Today the students of the faculty of medicine at Rue de Saint Peres in Paris go past the statue of Avicenna – this to express our indebtedness for his contribution to medical science" – talk by Maurice Bucaille, author of *The Origin of Man*, at the 20th annual convention of the Islamic Medical Association of America, 26-28 Nov 1987.

(13) *Ansar Allah*, monthly magazine, Rabbwah, Pakistan, March 1978.

(14) Abu Ali Hussain bin Abdullah bin Sena, *Al-Qanun-fi-al-Tibb*, (Urdu), Vol 3, p133. See also: Abu-bakr Muhammad Zakariya Razi, *Havi-Kabir* (Persian); Khan, Hakim, & Hussain, Muhammad, *Qarab-ud-din-Kabir*, vol 2, p576. The above works have been published by the famous Oriental publisher

Munshi Newal Kishore & Co, Lucknow, India.

(15) Khan, Syed Muhammad Hussain, *Majma-al-Jawamah, wa Zakhir-al-Tarakeeb, Qarab-ud-din Kabir*, (Urdu), Newal Kishore & Co, Lucknow, India, vol 2, p575.

(16) Minhaj-ul-Bayan quoted in *Qarab-ud-din Kabir*, Vol 2, p576.

(17) Ahmad, Mirza Ghulam, *Massih Hundustan Mein*, (Urdu) p103–10.

(18) *The Life of Christ*, Revised Edition, the Mazdaznan Elector Corp., Los Angeles, 1960, printed by Stockton Doty Press, Whittier, California, 1969, p79. It is significant that nowhere in the Gospels has the word 'corpse' been used in the case of Jesus (*Luke*, 23, 52), while it was used in the case of John the Baptist (*Mark*, 6, 29).

(19) *Matthew*, 27, 62–65.

(20) Keller, Werner, *The Bible as History*, p359.

(21) Eusebius, *Vita Const.*, 111, 26, as mentioned in *Jesus in Heaven on Earth*, by Khwaja Nazir Ahmad, p199. "Today the Church of the Holy Sepulchre is a chaotic jumble of dim chapels. In the Chapel of the Holy Sepulchre a well-worn flight of steps leads down to a grotto where a 6-ft long tomb is hewn out of the rock" – Keller, W, *The Bible as History*.

(22) Inayat Allah Khan al-Mashriqi, *Tazkirah*, (Urdu), Khaksar Publications, Lahore, 1976, pp16–17.

(23) *Luke*, 24, 1–2. Why was a stone rolled across the entrance to the sepulchre, instead of proper sealing? It would suggest temporary sealing which allowed air to pass in, and the possibility of removing Jesus and taking him elsewhere. See *The Crucifixion by an Eye-Witness*, p81.

(24) *John*, 20, 1.

(25) *Mark*, 16, 5. A Coptic manuscript from Egypt, preserved in the British Museum, called *The Book of Resurrection according to Bartholomew*, informs that it was a gardener named Philogenes who had gone to the sepulchre with the purpose of giving Jesus spices, sweet-swelling unguents and scents, and carrying Jesus away. See Schonfield, Hugh, *The Passover Plot*, p164. *The Book of Resurrection* was translated by E A Wallis Budge from Oriental Manuscripts no 6804 in the British Museum.

(26) *Mark*, 16, 7.

(27) *Mark*, 16, 8.

(28) *John*, 20, 7.

(29) *The Crucifixion by an Eye-witness*, pp98–101.

(30) *The Crucifixion by an Eye-witness*, pp102–104. According to the Canonical Gospels, Jesus appeared eleven times to his disciples and devotees, between Sunday 9th April and Thursday 18th May. He appeared to Paul about six years later, near Damascus, in about 35 AD. This means that Jesus was seen by people for six years and forty days after crucifixion. For his appearances during this period, see *Peloubet's Select Notes on the International Lessons*, Boston, 1918, pp190–193.

(31) *Gospel of Peter*, 9, 35–40, from *The Apocryphal New Testament*, tr M R

James, Oxford, 1926.,

(32) *Mark*, 16, 5. Mary Magdalene's statement (*John*, 20, 13), "They have taken away my Lord..." is significant in that it shows that there was not only one man but many who took Jesus from the sepulchre.

(33) *Luke*, 24, 25-26.

(34) *Luke*, 24, 30-31.

(35) *Luke*, 24, 36-40.

(36) *Luke*, 24, 36-42, *John*, 21, 13.

(37) *John*, 20, 27. "Behold my hands and my feet, that it is myself; handle me and see; for a spirit hath not flesh and bones, as you see me have". This statement by Jesus, mentioned in *Luke*, 24, 39, clears the controversy regarding the spiritual Ascension of the Master – Jesus himself was demonstrating that he was physically alive. I would also draw attention to the *Odes of Solomon* from the first century. In one Ode, Jesus says: "And I rose up and am with them; I will speak by their mouth. I did not perish, though they devised it against me. And I made a congregation of living men amongst his dead men, and I spoke with them by living lips" – Ode 42, v 6, 14, 18, in *The Lost Books of the Bible*, World Publishing Co, New York, 1944, second part.

(38) *John*, 20, 27. Jesus made his first appearance on Sunday 9th April, in the early morning, to Mary Magdalene. His second appearance was near Jerusalem on Sunday, to the women returning from the sepulchre (*Matthew*, 28, 9-10). His third appearance also happened on Sunday near Jerusalem, to Simon Peter alone (*Luke*, 24, 34). His fourth appearance happened on Sunday to two disciples going to Emmaus (*Mark*, 16, 12-13). His fifth appearance was on Sunday evening, to the apostles, except Thomas, near Jerusalem (*Mark*, 16, 14). He appeared for the sixth time to Thomas and other disciples near Jerusalem on Sunday evening, 16th April, to impress him and the disciples that he was alive.

(39) *The Crucifixion by an Eye-witness*, pp108-115.

(40) *John*, 21, 9-13; *Luke*, 24, 42. "He said unto them, *Have ye here any meat?* They gave him a piece of broiled fish, and of a honeycomb, and he took it and did eat before them". *John* provides additional information: "Jesus came and ate bread and fish". This was his seventh appearance after resurrection, to seven disciples on the Sea of Galilee, on 1st May.

(41) *The Crucifixion by an Eye-witness*, pp118-124. Jesus made his eighth appearance to eleven disciples on a mountain near Galilee in 1st May (*Mark*, 16, 15-18). His ninth appearance occurred on 1st May to over five hundred devotees near Galilee – this information was provided by Paul in 56 AD (*I Corinthians*, 15, 6). Jesus appears for the tenth time to James only, in May, probably in Jerusalem (*I Cor*, 15, 7). He makes his eleventh appearance to all his disciples on Thursday, 18th May, near Bethany, forty days after his resurrection (*Mark*, 16, 19-20).

(42) *John*, 10, 14-18.

14

Parthia

If Jesus did not die on the accursed cross, where did he go? The story of his life after crucifixion has become a mystery. The Church tells the world that Jesus Christ ascended into heaven. Now, in the modern age, growing numbers of people have began to take the story of ascension as improbable. Jesus was a human being and he had to die *somewhere* as a human being. If he died in Jerusalem, where can we find his grave?

We have seen earlier that there is a good case to show that Jesus did not die on the cross. We have also seen that he met his disciples, ate food and showed his wounds to them, after the crucifixion. Jesus had foretold that he would go in search of the lost tribes of Israel: had he died his mission would have remained incomplete. As such, he told his disciples in clear terms that "*other sheep I have which are not of his fold, them also I must bring and they shall heed my voice*"[1].

Jesus kept his destination a well-guarded secret: he would not even tell his disciples where he would go. They felt that he had been taken up by clouds. Maybe it was a mythological tale woven by his disciples to strengthen the idea that Jesus was a man of miracles[2].

Paul
It transpires that Jesus escaped alive towards the East and was seen at Damascus by Paul, in around 35 AD. Paul had been sent by the Romans to apprehend him for a second crucifixion[3]. We are also

informed that Jesus had a faithful disciple named Ananias, who met Paul at the behest of Jesus. This is the story given in the *Acts of the Apostles*.

The question arises as to why the story of Paul's meeting with Jesus was written. Is it visionary, a work of disinformation, or does it resemble reality? Paul was nearing Damascus when he heard a voice saying, "*Saul, Saul, why do you persecute me?*". It was Jesus who had spoken. Later when Ananias went to see Paul, he told him that he had been directed by Jesus to inform him that Paul was the chosen vessel and he was to preach in the name of Jesus in Israel[4].

Accordingly, Paul went to spend some time with other disciples at Damascus. After that he preached in the synagogues and made many converts[5]. He went to Jerusalem and Tarsus, and continued missionary activities in collaboration with Barnabas and John[6]. The account of Paul and Jesus' meeting has been called a vision by the compilers of the *Acts of the Apostles*, yet I would propose that this was a bending of the truth to protect Jesus.

We know that Paul, formerly Saul, was born in Tarsus and received his education in Jerusalem as a Pharisee. At first he was against Christ, but after conversion he eventually took the faith to Europe – a momentous step. While doing so he invented beliefs and dogma which he thought were near to the teachings of Jesus. But in doing so, did he invent a new religion?

We are told by Church historians that Christianity was preached by Paul all over the Roman empire between 50 and 100 AD, but Greek and Roman historians of the time do not mention anything about it – yet, a century after this, at least 10% of the population of the Roman empire had embraced Christianity. They do not even make mention of Paul, neither do they take note of any such works as the *Gospels* or the *Epistles*. In the *Antiquities of the Jews*, Josephus is supposed to have made a report about Jesus, but a minute examination will show that it is an interpolation by Church apologists. We are also informed that Paul was later condemned and executed in Rome. What was the cause of this execution?

The Apostolate

Before we proceed, it is worth noting what happened after Jesus left his followers. We do not have much information about them, except hints that they dispersed to various lands, but it is clear that the Jews hated them. James, a brother of Jesus, was chosen as the leader of the Christian community in Jerusalem, but Herod Agrippa took savage measures against him, and had him executed. Simon Peter was imprisoned by Herod Agrippa also. Accordingly, the early Apostolate was shifted to Antioch in Syria, where Paul met Simon Peter, and was enlisted as a disciple[7].

The Apostles gradually carried the teachings of Jesus along the major trade routes to the various cities of Arabia, Syria, Rome, Egypt, Persia and Armenia, and early Christianity became very popular amongst the common people. Seeing this, the antagonism of the Jewish hierarchy became acute.

The Pharisees saw it to be absolutely necessary to revive the Jewish people and establish an independent theocratic kingdom. They raised the banner of revolt against the Romans, who proceeded to subjugate and ravage Israel. The Romans stormed Jerusalem and burnt down the Temple in 70 AD. Thousands perished, and more were taken away as slaves. According to one estimate, nearly 11,000 prisoners died of starvation[8]. Jesus had already predicted the destruction of Jerusalem:

> O Jerusalem, Jerusalem, killing the prophets and stoning those who are sent to you! How often would I have gathered your children together as a hen gathers her brood under her wings, and you would not! Behold, your house is forsaken and desolate. For I tell you, you will not see me again until you say 'Blessed is he who comes in the name of the Lord'[9].

The Romans devastated settlements by killing all capable of bearing arms. Josephus described the destruction of the Jews:

> One could see the whole lake red with blood and covered with corpses, for not a man escaped.[10]

All this took place some 35 years after Jesus' departure from his homeland, but it forms an aftermath to the story of Jesus' ministry and crucifixion.

Jesus' Journey to Kashmir after 36 AD

Necessary exile

Jesus lived in hiding at the house of Ananias around the time of his meeting with Paul. After about eighteen months there, the Jews sent a commission to Damascus to seek him out, and he left the place and headed towards Babylon. He appointed James as his successor[11]. Thomas had already been deputed to Parthia and India by Jesus[12]. Jesus, having travelled that way earlier in his life, will have felt relatively safe as soon as he reached Parthia, out of the reach of the Romans – the Parthian empire stretched from Antioch and Palmyra in the west to Kabul in the east, the Caspian Sea in the north and the Arabian Sea in the south.

From Damascus he went to Nisibis, which had a colony of exile Jews[13]. The city was the meeting-place of many caravan routes, and was filled with people from many nations, engaged in commerce[14]. Jesus sought to hide his identity, and at this place he came to be known as *Yuzu Asaph*. Mir Khwand, in his classical work in Persian, titled *Rauzat-us-Safa*, has described the journey of Jesus to Nisibis in these words:

> *Hazrat Issa was called the Messiah because he was a great traveller. He wore a woollen scarf on his head and wrapped his body with a woollen cloak. He also held a staff in his hand and roamed from one country to another in disguise. He ate fruit and vegetables during his travels. He journeyed on bare feet until his companions bought a horse for him.*
>
> *At last he reached Nisibis, which was known as Nasibain in those days. A mysterious report about him and his mother Mary had spread in the city. As such, he was summoned by the Governor, who received him with much honour and reverence. All of them became his disciples[15].*

Mir Khwand wrote his *Rauzat-us-Safa* in the Hijra year 836, which corresponds to 1417 AD. It is mentioned in this book that Jesus concealed his identity in Nisibis and came to be known as *Yuzu-Asaph*. We are also informed that Jesus preached his doctrines in Nisibis, and many believed in his teachings, but some became his enemies, and tried to kill him[16]. Early evidence of the existence of Christianity in Nisibis is provided by an inscription on a grave:

*I saw the Syrian plain, and all the cities, even Nisibis, having crossed
the Euphrates. Everywhere I found people with whom to speak.*[17]

Nisibis lay on the Silk Road from Damascus to Mosul and
Babylon. Jesus had gone there because it was relatively safe.
Nisibis was ruled on behalf of the Parthians by Ezad, ruler of the
small principality of Adiabene, between Tabriz and Mosul. Ezad
had been converted by Ananias. Abgar, who had received the
Holy Shroud, was a contemporary and neighbour of Ezad.

However, Nisibis had become unsafe for Jesus, so it was time
to continue. He moved east to Mosul, then to Babylon, then to
Ur, and from there to Kharax, capital of the kingdom of Mesene.
It was the main port to which ships brought products from India
and the Far East. It was possible for Jesus to take the sea route, but
instead he crossed into Persia.

Persia

Jesus delivered many sermons in Persia, and he was welcomed by
people. At one stage, a high priest had him arrested, however, and
he was asked whether he was preaching about a new God, and told
not to sow doubt in the hearts of Zoroastran believers. In Persia it
was held that only Zoroaster had the privilege of communion with
the Supreme Being, and that the Laws had been given to Zoroaster
alone. Jesus said to them:

*It is not of a new God that I speak, but of our Heavenly Father who
has existed since all time, and who will still be, after the end of all
things. It is of him that I have discoursed to the people, who, like unto
innocent children, are not capable of comprehending God by the simple
strength of their intelligence, or of penetrating into his divine and
spiritual sublimity.*[18]

Jesus paused in many of the hamlets, villages and towns of Persia,
preaching and healing amongst the people, who apparently followed him in throngs. He spoke to the priests in these words:

There is a silence where the soul may meet its God, and where the fount

*of wisdom is. All who enter are immersed in light and filled with
wisdom, love and power. The silence is not circumscribed: it is not a
place enclosed within a wall, or rocky steeps, nor guarded with the
swords of men!*

*Men carry with them the secret place where they may meet their
God. It matters not where people abide, on mountaintop, in deepest
vale or in the quiet home; they may at once, at any time, fling wide the
door and find the silence, find the house of God. It is within the soul[19].*

During his sojourn in Persia, Jesus sat in silence in the prayer hall
of the Magi for seven days. Then he spoke on the origin of good
and evil. He told them not to worship the sun, for it was but a part
of the cosmos. It was to God and God alone that people owed all
they possessed in this world. On hearing him, the priests asked
how people could live according to the rules of justice without a
preceptor. Jesus replied that as long as the people had no priests,
natural law governed them, and they preserved the candour of
their souls. And when their souls were with God, they could
commune with their Father without the medium of any idol,
animal, the sun or the fire. He said:

*You contend that one must worship the sun, the spirit of good and evil.
Well, I say unto you, your doctrine is incorrect – the sun acting not
spontaneously but according to the will of the invisible Creator, Who
gave it birth.*

*The Eternal Spirit is the soul of all that is animate. You commit a
great sin in dividing it into a spirit of evil and a spirit of good: for there
is no God outside the good. Who, like unto the father of a family, does
but good unto his children, forgiving all their faults, if they repent.*

*Wherefore I say unto you, beware of the day of judgment, for God
will inflict a terrible chastisement upon all those who have led his
children astray from the right path[20].*

I found an interesting explanation of the name *Yuzu Asaph* in a
Persian dictionary. Let me quote this:

*Hazrat Issa, who cured many lepers, came to be known as Asaph. He
was known as Yuzu, and as he had cured lepers, he came to be known*

as Yuzu Asaph, for he not only cured them but gathered them under his merciful protection.[21]

It appears that the term *Asaph* can also denote 'healed leper' as well as 'gatherer' – Jesus got them admitted among the healthy, a veritable miracle for a leper to receive.

A Persian scholar, Agha Mustafa, in his *History of Persian Saints*[22], makes mention of Jesus. He says that the sayings and teachings of Hazrat Issa or Yuzu Asaph were much the same as those recorded in the Gospels. Jesus' teachings did not affect too wide a public, though a small minority of his followers did exist when Islam came to dominate the region seven centuries later. With the advent of Islam both Jews and Zoroastrans were wiped out and no traces of the *Asaph* lepers of Jesus Christ are seen anywhere in the region.

Another important historical source in Persian, *Kamal-u-Din*, was written by the historian Al Shaikh Said–us–Saddiq, who died in 912 AD. This book is also known as *Kashful Hairat* or *Ikmal-ud-Din*, and is considered by orientalists to be of great value. The text was first printed in Iran in 1881 and translated into German by Professor Muller of Heidelberg University[23]. Al Shaikh Said–us–Saddiq was a learned scholar from Khorasan, who travelled a good deal during his lifetime and collected material, mostly from Hindu sources, for this and his other works. The book mentions the journeys of Yuzu Asaph to Sholabeth, or Ceylon, and other places, terminating finally in Kashmir. Teachings and parables are given, with many parallels with the Gospels.

No information is available about the route taken by Jesus and his companions on their onward march. Jesus is said to have stayed at Mashag, where he visited the grave of Shem, Noah's son[24]. Maybe they visited Hamadan, or Nishapur, the meeting-point of three roads, one from Kashgar in central Asia, the others from Kabul and Herat in Afghanistan. As the possible tomb of Mary Magdalene has been located six miles from Kashgar, by Nicolai Roerich[25], I presume that Jesus took the route leading to that famous city, from Nishapur to Bokhara, Samarkand and then Kashgar. It was here that Mary Magdalene, who had loved Jesus more than any other disciple, apparently passed away.

Sources

It took me many years to locate and examine oriental sources, in Sanskrit, Tibetan, Arabic, Persian and Urdu dealing, with the lost years of Jesus. The material was rich, and, unlike much of the historical material to which the Church had had access, on the whole, untouched since ancient times. These ancient documents, recording as they did a little-known connection between Christianity and the East, were of immense fascination to me – each new discovery further fuelling my passion for the quest. As my research progressed, it became possible to reconstruct, piece by piece, some of this second and final journey of Jesus in the East.

Yet there were also disappointments and sad discoveries. Central Asia has been the home of several exotic civilisations and a seat of vast empires. Many cultures, including Greek, Buddhist and Islamic, flourished at various times in this region. It is the birthplace of many prophets, philosophers and great men.

The vastness and richness of its various cultures can be seen from the treasures from this region which are now housed in the great museums of the world. Westerners have stolen caravan-loads of priceless treasures from the temples, mosques, tombs, caves and historical sites of Central Asia. Among the chief culprits, mention may be made of Aurel Stein of England, Albert von Le Coq of Germany, Seven Hedin of Sweden, Paul Pelliot of France, Langdon Warner of the United States and Otani of Japan.

In 1907, for example, Stein ravaged thousands of manuscripts and documents from the Tun-huang caves. These manuscripts were written in several Semitic alphabets. It is certain that some manuscripts written in Aramaic pertained to Jesus. Stein intentionally concealed this information from the world for the sake of the Church. He declared that these manuscripts embodied the teachings of Mani, which are similar to those of Jesus[26]. His statement, though half-true, served as a warning to the Church, who then deployed special missions to search out for destruction, documents relating to Jesus. In this way, a great deal of invaluable information about Jesus has been destroyed.

(1) *John*, 10, 16.

(2) *The Crucifixion by an Eye-Witness*, p124-125. "There arose a rumour that Jesus was taken up in a cloud and had gone to heaven. This was invented by the people who had not been present when Jesus departed".

(3) Graves, Robertson, and Podro, Joshua, *Jesus in Rome*, London, 1957. Jesus appeared to Paul near Damascus in about 35 AD, six years and forty days after resurrection. There is no better and fuller evidence than the Gospels to find that Jesus did not die, but lived for at least these six years and forty days, in and around Palestine, after crucifixion.

(4) *Acts of the Apostles*, 9, 10-15.

(5) *Acts*, 9, 20-22.

(6) *Acts*, 12, 25. "Chief among the makers of Christian doctrines was St Paul. He was a man of great intellectual vigour and deeply and dispassionately interested in the religious movements of the time. He was well-versed in Judaism, and in Mithraism and the Alexandrian faiths of the day. He carried over many of their ideas and terms of expression into Christianity" – Wells, H G, *A Short History of the World*, Pelican, p129.

(7) Pareti, Luigi, *History of Mankind*, Vol II, p850; Margolis, Max, & Marx, Alexander, *A History of the Jewish People*, p228; Kamal-ud-Din, Khwaja, *The Sources of Christianity*, Woking, 1924; Scott, C A, *Christianity According to St Paul*, Cambridge, 1927; Wilkinson, Rev J R, *Jesus or Paul*, Harper, London, 1909.

(8) Schonfield, Hugh, *Saints against Caesar*, Macdonald, London, 1948, p142.

(9) *Matthew*, 23, 37.

(10) Josephus, *The Jewish Wars*, tr W Whiston, Loeb Classical Library, London, vol III, iv, I; X, p9.

(11) *Acts*, 9, 10-19; *James*, 1, 1-9; Schonfield, *The Passover Plot*, p204; Eusebius, Pamphili, *Historica Ecclesiastica*, 2, 23, tr Krisopp Lake, New York, 1926; Eusebius, *Ecclesiastical History*, tr C F Cruse, London, 1874; Kersten, Holger, *Jesus Lived in India*, Element, Dorset, 1986, pp176-177;"The disciples said to Jesus, *Who shall be chief over us?* Jesus said to them, *Wherever you have come, you shall go to James, the righteous one*" – *The Theology of the Gospel of Thomas*, Bertil Gartner, pp56-57, quoted by Shaikh Abdul Qadir, *The Truth about the Crucifixion*, London, 1978, p136.

(12) *The Acts of Thomas*, tr A F J Klijin, E J Brill, Leiden, 1962; Farquhar, J N, *The Apostle Thomas in North India*, Manchester, 1926; Brown, L W, *The Indian Christians of St Thomas*, Cambridge, 1956; Buchanan, C, *Christian Researches in Asia*, Cambridge, 1811.

(13) Josephus, *Antiquities*, xviii, 9, 1-8.Pratten, tr, *Syrian Documents attributes to the First Three Centuries*, Ante-Nicene Christian Library, vol XX, Edinburgh, 1871, pp5-35; Cureton, *Ancient Syriac Documents*, London, 1864, vol XXII, p141; Khwand, Mir Muhammad, *Rauzat-us-Safa* (Persian), 7 vols, translated in *The Garden of purity*, tr E Rehatsek, 5 vols, Royal Asiatic Soc, London,

1892, vol 1, pp165-169.

(14) MacMunn, Townsend, *The Holy Land*, vol II, p61; Fraser, David, *The Short Cut to India*, p121; Nisibis (Nusaybin or Nasibain among Arab geographers) is on the caravan route between Mosul and Damascus. Travellers en route to Persia passed through this important commercial centre. The Persian Gulf is about 150 miles away. Urfa, known earlier as Edessa, is the next proximate town, from which one can reach Aleppo. Mir Muhammad Khwand, in his famous historical work *Rauzat-us-Safa*, informs that Issa travelled to Nisibain, accompanied by some apostles and his mother Mary. In response to some adverse reports against Issa and his mother, the city chief arrested some apostles. Issa cured some ailing people in Nisibin, and performed some miracles. Even though people were against him in the beginning, all of them, including the ruler of Nisibain came to understand the greatness of Issa and accepted him as a saviour. Other sources on this are *Tafsir – Ibn-i-Jarir at-Tibri*, *Jamia-ut-Tawarikh* of Faqi Muhammad, and *Majma-ul-Buldan*.

(15) Mir Khwand; *Rauzat-us-Safa*, Vol I, p134, trans by E Rehatsek, in *The Garden of Purity*, 5 vols, Royal Asiatic Soc, London, 1892, vol 1, p134.

(16) Mumtaz Ahmad Faruqi, *The Crumbling of the Cross*, p67, quoting Jarir, Imam Abu Jaffar Muhammad, *Tafsir Ibn-i-Jarir at-Tabri* (Arabic), 30 vols, Kubr-ul-Mara Press, Cairo, 1921, vol 3, p197.

(17) Segal, J B, *Edessa – the Blessed City*, Oxford, 1970, p69.

(18) Notovitch, Nicolas, *The Life of St Issa*, VIII, 15-20. "The countries around about were filled with the renown of Issa's preachings, and when he came into Persia, the priests grew afraid and forbade the people hearing him". See also: Mustafa, Agha, *Ahwal-i-Ahalian-i-Paras* (Persian), Teheran, 1909, p219.

(19) Levi, *The Aquarian Gospel*, p79.

(20) Notovitch, Nicholas, *The Life of St Issa*, VIII, 6-7.

(21) *Farhang-i-Asafiyah*, Persian dictionary, Vol I, p91. ed Syed Ahmad Dehlvi, Hyderabad, 1908.

(22) Agha Mustafa, *Ahwal-i-Ahaliyan-i-Paras* or *History of the Persian Saints*, (Persian), Teheran, 1909.

(23) Al Shaikh Said-us-Saddiq, *Kamal-ud-Din*, Sayyid-us-Sanad Press, Iran, 1881. Translated into German by H Muller, Heidelberg Univ, Germany, 1901.

(24) Faqi Muhammad Qazi Muhammad Raza, *Jami-uf-Tawarik*, (Persian) Vol II, p81.

(25) Roerich, Nicolai, *The Heart of Asia*, New York, 1929. Here is another viewpoint about the tomb of Mary, provided by Below, who accompanied the British Embassy to Kashgar in 1874: "This is a shrine over the grave of Alanor Turkan in Artosh. The history of Alanor resembles that of Miryam, the mother of Jesus. One night the Angel Gabriel appeared and poured a drop of light into her mouth. It pervaded her whole body with a sense of ecstasy. Finally, after some months and days, Alanor gave birth to a son – an infant

with ruddy complexion, gazelle eyes and angelic voice. While the people were amazed, the king ordered an assembly to investigate. She was fully questioned, and later was pronounced a chaste lady. When her son was slain by the Chinese, she was so incensed with grief that she and her maidens entered the battlefield. Having sent 25 infidel souls to hell, she was put to flight. The ground miraculously opened and received her and other fugitives in the shelter of its caverns. But their pursuers slew them all in their hiding. The shrine which stands on the bank of a deep ravine is called *Mazar Bibi Miryam* or the Shrine of the Lady Mary. The legend attached to her name resembles that of Allan Coa, the mother of the great ancestor of the Mughal, as given in the *Rauzat-us-Safa* of Mir Khwand. Her case is comparable to that of the mother of the Lord Jesus. The existence of these legends in this area at the present day is a remarkably interesting circumstance. Whether they are to be viewed as outgrowths of the Christianity which formerly flourished here, or merely as grafts from the Islam which took its place, I will not pretend to consider". H W Bellow, *Kashmir and Kashgar*, Trubner & Co, London, 1875, pp333–336.

(26) Stein, Aurel, *On Central Asian Tracks*, Macmillan, 1935, pp214–216.

15

India

From Kashgar Jesus and his companions will probably have had to bear many hardships on their journey to Kabul and then to Taxila. It was in 326 BC that Buddhists had migrated from Taxila to Khotan in central Asia due to the Graeco-Bactrian invasion[1], spearheaded by Alexander the Great – Jesus will have followed the same path back. Taxila was swept away by the invasion of the Sakas (75 BC), who were soon after overcome by the Parthians. After the death of the Saka Azes II, the kingdom of Taxila passed to the rule of Gondapharos, a Parthian who figures in the early Christian writings as the king to whose court Thomas was sent as an Apostle of Jesus Christ[2].

Thomas, the Apostle of India

Thomas had been reluctant to go to India. He had met up with Jesus at a marriage ceremony at Andrapolis in Anatolia, and Jesus had asked him to go to India:

> But he did not want to go, and said he could not travel because of weakness of the flesh, and moreover: "How can I, a Hebrew, travel and preach the truth to the Indians?" And after he had considered and said this, the Messiah appeared to him in the night and spoke to him. "Do not be afraid, Thomas, go to India and preach the word there, for my grace is with you". But he would not obey, and said: "Send me anywhere you want, but somewhere else! For I shall not go to India."[3]

150

Thomas, the apostle who built a palace for the King at Taxila, 1st century AD
(Archeol. Survey of India)

According to the *Acta Thomae*, Jesus then sold Thomas 'the Contender' as a slave to an Indian merchant, Abban, who had been commissioned to find a carpenter by King Gondapharos in Taxila. However, this could be interpreted as an elevation from being a brother of the Essenes to a Nazarene of higher authority – *Abba* meaning 'Father', and the sentence symbolising a consecration of Thomas to his work.

Thomas, also known as Didymos, held seventh position among the chief disciples of Jesus. His real name was Judas and the *Acta Thomae* provides information about his missionary activities in the East. It is curious that the *Acta Thomae* refers to him as *Didymos*, the twin of Jesus: "Twin brother of Christ, apostle of the Highest who shares in the knowledge of the hidden word of Christ, recipient of his secret pronouncements"[4]. This requires more research – the Mother Mary did have other children besides Jesus, or it could relate to Thomas' special relationship with Jesus as his confidant. When the disciples of Jesus divided the world for missionary activities, Parthia and India fell to the lot of Thomas.

At that time, the Parthian empire included the north-western region of India, extending from the Euphrates river to the Indus. It is for this reason that Thomas is known as *the Evangelist of Parthia and India*[5]. He preached among the Parthians, Medes, Persians, Bactrians, Indians and Hyrecaneans[6].

After enslavement, a proportion of members of the lost tribes of Israel had scattered themselves in North-west India. Arguably, Thomas thus went to this region in search of his people. An Indian merchant named Habban or Abban, who had gone to Jerusalem, took Thomas along with him to India. They sailed together from Chaldea and reached Sindh after touching Hormuz and Makran[7].

Taxila

This information roused my interest in going more and more into the life and work of Thomas in India. It came to light that Thomas had reached India during the period when Gondapharos ruled over his kingdom, with Taxila as his capital – Gondapharos had merged the territories held by the Parthians and the Sakas, ruling all of North-west India. His coins have been found in Kashmir and north India, and inscriptions at Takht Bhai[8]. According to historical writings[9], Gondapharos ruled over his kingdom from 21 to 50 AD – one of a series of Graeco-Bactrian rulers, including Euthydemus (220 BC), Eucratides (180 BC), Hippostratus (140 BC), Menender the Great (110 BC), Antimajus II (100 BC), Azilises (20 BC), Spalagadames, Vonoes, Spalyrises (10 AD), Gondapharos (21-50 AD) and Abdagases (60-100 AD)[10]. Taxila, during that period, occupied an important place on the trade routes between India, central Asia and the Middle East. Alexander the Great had halted there in 326 BC as the guest of its ruler.

Thomas was introduced to Gondapharos by Abdagases at Attock[11], and it was Thomas who supervised the construction of a palace for the king in the year 48 AD. At Char Sadah near Taxila, archaeological excavations have revealed many Christian antiquities, such as the statues of Thomas and Simon Peter, together with slabs bearing images of crucifixion. These archeological excavations have established that Taxila was a centre of Christianity during the first century AD.

It was Sir John Marshall who conducted excavations at Taxila around 1924 in his capacity as the Director of the Archeological Survey of India. He describes his findings in his two works entitled *Taxila* (two volumes)[12] and *A Guide to Taxila*. While describing the statues found in the cell 29, he says that the dress and bearded heads of these statues are of a particular style suggesting not Indians but foreigners[13]. All the figures in this group are shown barefoot, except the central figure, who has sandals. This figure is peculiar because it wears the peaked cap of a Syrian traveller, a tunic to the knees, as worn in Syria at the time, and boots. The figure has definite Jewish features[14].

These figures of foreigners were found at Julian in Taxila, where an Assyrian-type monastery was built by Julian, who accompanied Thomas during his travels in India[15]. Near this monastery king Gondapharos ordered the construction of his palace, in which an Aramaic inscription has been excavated, which reads:

A highly regarded foreign carpenter, who is a pious devotee of the Son of God, built this palace of cedar and ivory for the great king.[16]

The palace was built within six months and all remuneration received by Thomas was spent in providing alms to the poor and needy. It is also mentioned in historical works that during his stay in Taxila, Thomas won many devotees. The brother of King Gondapharos became a Christian. It is also mentioned that Thomas showed many signs and miracles[17]. When the king asked him to account for his giving away funds given to him for building the palace, Thomas explained that he was also building an everlasting palace for the king in heaven.

He preached with such zeal and grace that the king, his brother Gad, and multitudes of people embraced the faith. Many signs and wonders were wrought by this holy apostle.[18]

Thomas arrived in Taxila in the year 40 AD[19]. He is said to have supervised the construction of the royal palace in 48, and he met Jesus in the year 49 at Taxila. The *Acta Thomae* mentions Thomas thanking Jesus for the opportunity to do such good works:

"I thank thee, Lord, in every respect, for dying for a short while in order that I might live in you eternally; and for selling me, in order to emancipate many others through me". And he did not cease to teach and give peace to the troubled, saying, "The Lord gives you this, and assures everyone of nourishment. For he is the nourisher of the orphans and the provider of the widows, and offers the troubled recovery and peace.[20]"

Klijn's version of the *Acts of Thomas*[21] provides very interesting information about an occurrence at the time of this meeting, during a royal marriage ceremony at Taxila:

And the King requested the groom's man to go out of the bridal chamber, and when all the people had gone out, and the door of the bridal chamber was closed, the bridegroom raised up the curtain, that he might bring the bride to himself.
And he saw our Lord in the likeness of Judas [Thomas] standing and talking with the bride. The bridegroom said: "Lo, thou didst go out at first, then how art thou still here?" Our Lord said to him: "I am not

Thomas *(Dir. of Historial Archives and Archeology, Goa)*

Judas, but I am the brother of Judas." And our Lord sat down on the bed, and let the young people sit down on the chairs, and began to speak to them.

The Christians of St Thomas

Thomas came to India to fulfil a duty asked of him by Jesus saying *"Go rather to the lost sheep of Israel"*. The *Acta Thomae* reveal that Thomas reached the coast of Malabar in 52 AD, establishing his first church there, after having lived at the court of Gondapharos for a number of years. Around this time, north India was disrupted by the conquest of the Kushanas, under Kanishka, from central Asia.

Twenty years later he went to Mylapore, near Madras, in south India. He suffered martyrdom there and his relics were preserved in the cathedral dedicated to him[22]. Another source said that Thomas visited Travancore in south India and baptised the first Indian Christian in the year 59 AD[23]. The tomb of Thomas is situated near Fort St George in Tamil Nadu, India[24].

The Christians of St Thomas are also known as the Syrian Christians, because of their links, up to 325 AD, with the Church of Edessa in Syria. They were also simply called 'Nazarenes'. This Christian community founded by Thomas in the first century has continued up to present times. Later, Hsiung-Nu (Hun) invasions of north India, around 430 AD, drove non-Hindu minorities in all directions, the Buddhists towards Ladakh, Tibet and the east, and the Jews and Christians to the south, especially Malabar. The Shaivite Hindus of the north were prepared to adapt their faith to the needs of the times, but these minorities were not prepared to do so – thus, the Christian communities in Taxila and Kashmir died out.

Simon Peter in India

Back in Israel, shortly before the crucifixion, Jesus had predicted that he would be denied thrice by Simon Peter. He had asked his disciples to love one another as he had loved them. Then Simon Peter asked him:

"Lord, where are you going"? Jesus answered him, "Where I am going you cannot follow me now; but you shall follow afterward.[25]*"*

What happened to Simon Peter after Jesus' crucifixion? Soon after, the disciples met together, and Simon Peter addressed them[26], later going forth to preach, adding some three thousand converts to the early Christian fold[27]. Peter and John both preached in Jerusalem, with the result that the number of Christians rose to some five thousand[28]. Both were arrested and brought before the Jewish Council: the priests admonished them and warned them not to speak in the name of Jesus. Meanwhile, many, including Barnabas and Ananias, gave them moral and financial support. The apostles were jailed, but set free by angels (Essenes?) during the night.

They again started preaching, and again were brought before the Council, and this time told to stop their activities. However, Simon Peter and the other apostles replied that they would obey God, but not men. They were saved from slaughter only by the intercession of Gamaliel[29]. Simon Peter went to Lydda, Joppa and Caesarea, healing and teaching. Then James was killed, and Simon Peter was imprisoned, under orders of Herod[30]. Again, an angel rescued him, and he went to Caesarea, where he lived for some time. After this we hear of him at Antioch, where Paul rebuked him for not eating with the Gentiles[31].

While Paul preached amongst the Romans and the Greeks, Simon Peter looked north and east, communicating with the Jewish exile communities in Anatolia – Pontus, Galatia, Cappadocia, Asia and Bithynia[32], writing:

You are a chosen race, a royal priesthood, a holy nation, God's own people, that you may declare the wonderful deeds of him who called you out of darkness into his marvellous light. Once you were no people but now you are God's people; once you had not received mercy, but now you have received mercy.[33]

It is possible that Peter was addressing the Anatolians from Babylon, or somewhere *en route* from Babylon to Anatolia[34]. After this, nothing is known about the whereabouts of Simon Peter.

Tomb of Mary at Muree

However, later findings have revealed that Simon Peter followed Thomas to Taxila[35]. In his researches, Shaikh Abdul Qadir drew attention to a bronze statue found by the Archaeological Survey of India at Char-saddha, a photo of which had been published without identification[36]. This bronze statue was an early specimen of Christian antiquities in India, identified by orientalists to be Simon Peter[37], sitting on a chair, wearing royal attire. His beard and hair are thick and curly. He holds a key in one hand, the other hand being held up in a blessing gesture. Skeletal features, thick and heavy hair on face and head, and the facial index demonstrate that the statue is of a person belonging to the Mediterranean area.

Mother Mary lies at Muree

Mary the mother presumably followed with Jesus and Mary Magdalene to India, according to the *Gospel of Philip*:[38]

> *There were three who always walked with the Lord: Mary his mother and her sister and Magdalene, the one who was called his companion. His sister and his mother and his companion were each a Mary.*

Mary the mother enjoys great respect amongst Christians: she agreed to conceive Jesus, nourished him as a mother would, went to great pains to protect and educate him, and went through worrisome times, such as when Jesus was inadvertently left in Jerusalem after the feast of the Passover when he was twelve. After the resurrection, she accompanied Jesus to the East. She was presumably with him at Taxila. Shortly afterwards, when the

Kushans attacked the region, they had to flee towards the hills. Mary, the mother, died on the way, and was buried at a place which became called *Mari* until 1875, after which spellings were changed to *Murree*[39]. The tomb is called *Mai-Mari-de-Asthan*, or the 'resting place of mother Mary'[40].

Mumtaz Ahmad Farouqui, who has conducted researches on the Tomb of Mary, says the following:

> *Mary belonged to the priestly class of the Israelites and it was befitting her honour that she be buried on a higher place like the Hill of Muree. According to local tradition, the tomb is known as the resting place of the mother Mary. This tomb has been a place of pilgrimage by Hindus and Muslims alike, who make their offerings by putting oil in earthen lamps to be lit by the devotees.*
>
> *In 1898, the garrison engineer ordered this tomb to be demolished so as to construct a military observation tower. But, shortly afterwards, he died in an accident. The locals connected this incident with his evil intentions towards this holy tomb. Since then no one, to date, has done any harm to this grave, which faces east. Memorial flags decorate the grave now.*[41]

Murree, 45 miles east of Taxila, is an idyllic mountain resort on the border of Kashmir. When Jesus was in this region, Mary must have been at least seventy years old. No other tombs to Mary exist in the world. The tomb, oriented east–west in the Jewish fashion, is located on Pindi Point outside the town, now sealed off by the military, because of its proximity to the Kashmiri border. The area, Hindu in Jesus' time, contains no Hindu graves, because Hindus are cremated, and ashes are scattered. When the region was conquered by the Muslims in the seventh century AD, all monuments of 'infidels' were destroyed. Mary's grave was spared, however, presumably because she was one of the 'People of the Book', honoured in Islam.

Later Indian Christianity

Marco Polo told people in the West about the Indian Christians in 1295. He visited India from China, and reported Christians wor-

Inscription on the Victory Gate, Fateh puṛ Sikri, the Moghal capital translates "Issa says – the World is like a bridge". 1596 AD

shipping at the grave of the apostle Thomas at Mylapore on the east coast of south India. There had also been Christians on the west coast, around Malabar. Earlier records exist too[42]. Tertullian listed India among those lands influenced by Christianity – and known back in Rome to be so. Ephraem (c306-373 AD) wrote of Thomas' missions in India, and Anorbius (around 305 AD) listed India as Christian-influenced. Then, one of the participants in the Council of Nicaea was a person called 'Bishop John of all Persia and Greater India'[43].

The Aramaic *Gospel according to Matthew*, which originated around 180 AD, tells of a missionary voyage by Pantaenus of Alexandria. Around 300 AD, David, Bishop of Basra (Parthia) went to India and preached there with great success. In around 335, Emperor Constantine sent Bishop Theophilos to India to reform the churches there, according to Philostorgius. Around the end of the 300s, Symeon of Mesopotamia mentions the martyrdom of Indian 'barbarians' from Christ. Cosmas Indicopleusta gave quite

160

full details of his voyage to India around 525. He found Christians in Sri Lanka and on the Indian west coast "in Male [Malabar], and in the place called Kalliana [Kalyan, near Bombay]", where he mentions the seat of a bishop who had once lived in Persia[44].

Finally, there are the dated inscriptions on the mosque at the ruined city of Fatehpur Sikri, built by Akbar the Great (1542-1605) around 1569, stating:

> *Jesus (peace be with him) has said, 'The world is a bridge. Pass over it, but do not settle down on it! He who hopes for an hour may hope for eternity! The world is but an hour: spend it in devotion, for the rest is of no worth.'*

Another inscription in another part of the mosque says:

> *Jesus (peace be with him) has said, 'The world is a proud house, take this as a warning and do not build on it!'*

Pacifist by nature, Akbar was kind to the followers of all faiths, and his court included Portuguese Jesuit missionaries, though they will not have had a source for these statements. The *Gospel of Thomas*, a collection of 114 sayings of Jesus, begins each saying with the introduction '*Jesus has said...*', but this Gospel was unavailable for some 1600 years until this century. Thus, the only other plausible answer is that the statements came from the Indian Christians of Thomas.

---

(1) Stein, Aurel, *Sand-buried Ruins of Khotan*, Fisher Unwin, 1903, Vol 1, p156.

(2) Marshall, John, *A Guide to Taxila*, Delhi, 1936, p14. See also: Marshall, John, and others, *Taxila*, 3 vols, Cambridge, 1951.

(3) *Acta Thomae*, I, p101, in Hennecke, E, and Schneemelcher, W, *New Testament Apocrypha*, Philadelphia, 1963-66; *The Acts of Thomas*, ed A F J Klijn, Brill, Leiden, 1962, pp6-66. "Thomas was not initially happy over his lot to go to India, and possibly murmured dissent, but Jesus appeared to him by night and reassured him of his continued blessing and presence with him" – Matthew, P V, *Acta Indica*, Cochin, 1986, p35.

(4) *Acta Thomae*, ch 39, in Hennecke, E, and Schneemelcher, *The New Testament Apocrypha*, Philadelphia, 1963-66. Speaking about the real teachings of Jesus, my good friend Sir George Trevelyan, says: "This apocryphal *Gospel*

of Thomas is an extraordinary document. It consists of 120 aphorisms of holism, and is quite simply the Oneness doctrine. We usually write off 'Doubting Thomas' as one who wouldn't believe his Lord had risen, but the truth is that he was the only one who had grasped who his Lord was. He knew that Christ was the Oneness" – George Trevelyan, *Summons to a High Crusade*, Findhorn Press, Scotland, 1986, p93.

(5) Rapson, Prof E J, *Ancient India*, CUP, Cambridge, UK, 1911, p174; Cureton, *Ancient Syriac Documents*, London, 1864, vol XXII, p141; *The Acts of Thomas,* ed A F J Klijn, p65; Montague, James, *The Apocryphal New Testament*, Oxford, 1924.

(6) Salmond, S D F, *The Writings of Hippolytus*, Vol III, p131, quoted in Khwaja Nazir Ahmed, *Jesus in Heaven on Earth*, p349. See also, Klijn, *Acts of Thomas*, p65, and Ante-Nicene Christian Library, vol IV, p130-132.

(7) Smith, Arthur Vincent, *The Early History of India*, Clarendon Press, Oxford, 1904, pp204-205; Vaux, W S W, *Ancient History of Persia*, London, 1874, p121; Matthew, P V, *Acta Indica*, Cochin, 1986, pp33-41 – this discusses the three routes followed by Thomas during his three journeys to India. According to him, Thomas took the land route via Edessa, Media, Sandaruk and Sogdiana to Taxila, capital of Gandhara.

(8) *Imperial Gazateer of India*, Govt of India Press, Calcutta, Vol II, p288. Takt Bhai is a town in NW Pakistan, where a few inscriptions have been unearthed, referring to the year 47 AD, when Gondapharos ruled.

(9) Taran, W W, *The Greeks in Bactria and·India*, Cambridge, 1931; Mohan, Mehta Vasishta Dev, *Indo-Greek Coins*, Ludhiana, Punjab, 1967; Majumdar, R C, *Ancient India*, 1952; Cunningham, A, *Coins of Alexander's Successors in the East*, London, 1884; Rapson, E J, ed, *The Cambridge History of India*, Cambridge, 1935; Narain, A K, *The Indo-Greeks*, Oxford, 1957; Marshall, John, *Taxila*, 3 vols, Cambridge, 1951; *Imperial Gazatteer of India*, vol XXVI, Oxford, 1909, maps nos 30-47; Whitehead, R B, *Catalogue of Coins in the Punjab Museum*, Lahore & Oxford, 1914.

(10) Rapson, Prof E J, *Ancient India*, CUP, Cambridge, UK, 1911, p174; Smith, V A, *The Early History of India*, p217. Abdagases, nephew of Gondapharos, also known as Habban or Abanes, later succeeded Gondapharos after 50 AD.

(11) *The Acts of Thomas*, ed Klijn, p6.

(12) Marshall, Sir John, *Taxila*, Cambridge, 1951; *Guide to Taxila*, Delhi, 1936; *Annual Report of the Archaeological Survey of India*, 1920-21.

(13) Marshall, John, *Guide to Taxila*, pp15, 136, 138; Wheeler, Mortimer, *Five Thousand Years of Pakistan*, London, 1951, p42.

(14) Nazir Ahmad, *Jesus in Heaven on Earth*, addendum to p348. Taxila was known as *Takshila* during ancient times, and formed part of Gandhara country, lying on either side of the Indus. Ashoka, the great Buddhist ruler of India, died at Taxila in 236 BC. In about 190 BC the kingdom of Taxila came under the rule of Demetrius, Greek ruler of the Indus delta. Taxila is renowned as a centre for Buddhist and Greek culture, and it was here that the

image of the classical Buddha was first shaped, using Greek realistic human representation for the first time in Asia, where realistic representations were, up to that time, forbidden.

(15) Julian is an important site where the Archaeological Survey of India conducted excavations in 1913. Among antiquities found is a 'group of foreigners in front of cell 29', sculptures excavated in front of the monastery. No explanation is available about these sculptures, nor about the origin of the place name, Julian. "It is not an Indian name, and the village might have been names after Julian of Nisibis, who accompanied Thomas to Taxila".

(16) Qureshi, Molvi Muhammad Hamid, *Rahnuma-i-Taxila* (Urdu), Govt of India Press, Calcutta, 1924, p144. The learned scholar, who served as Assistant Superintendent to the Archaeological Survey of India in 1924, has correctly translated the ancient Aramaic inscription found at Julian in Taxila, referring to a devotee of the son-God who constructed a palace of deodar and ivory for the king. In the first place, an inscription in Aramaic is significant. Secondly, the site has been declared to belong to the first century. Thirdly, construction of the palace by a foreigner is confirmed. Fourthly, we are informed that the services of Thomas were requisitioned by Habban for this work, and, as in *Acta Thomae*, both of them departed for India together. It is evident that the inscription refers to Thomas, a devotee of the son-God, Jesus.

(17) Smith, Viscount Arthur, *The Early History of India*, p205; Klijn, A F J, *The Acts of Thomas*, Leiden, 1962, pp151-153.

(18) Smith, Vincent Arthur, *The Early History of India*, p205. William Hunter in *The Indian Empire*, and Dorothy Whitelock in *The Anglo-Saxon Chronicle* mention that King Alfred of England sent offerings to the tombs of Thomas and Bartholomew in 833 AD (Matthew, P V, *Acta Indica*, Cochin, 1986, pp45-46).

(19) Jesus was put on the cross in the year 36 AD. He appeared to Paul around 42 AD. The allocation of regions for the apostles was done some time earlier, maybe 40 AD. Thomas completed construction of the palace of cedar and ivory for Gondapharos at Taxila in about 46 AD. This is confirmed from the *Takthi-Bahi* plaque found in 1903. It mentioned King Gondapharos in the year 103 of the Bikrami era, from which date 57 years should be deducted to find the Christian era date. Both Jesus and Thomas, according to *Acta Thomae*, were present at the marriage of Abdagases in 49 AD. For details of this marriage, see *Ante-Nicene Christian Library*, Edinburgh, 1869, vol XX, p46.

(20) *Acta Thomae*, 19.

(21) Klijn, A F J, *The Acts of Thomas*, E J Brill, Leiden, 1962, p70. The *Acts of Thomas* are part of the *Syriac Documents*, collected by Epiphanius in 363 AD, translated into English by Wright in 1871, included in the *Ante-Nicene Christian Library* as apocrypha. See Wright, *Apocryphal Acts of the Apostles*, Society for the Publication of Oriental Texts, London, 1871, vol II. In order to belittle the value of *Acta Thomae*, it has been alleged that they were compiled by Bardaisan, Bishop of Edessa, who during his travels in India had come into contact with the followers of Jainism and Buddhism (Matthew, *Acta Indica*,

Cochin, 1986, p77). See also *Liturgical Books and Calendars of the Syrian Church*, and Panaji, Karan Joseph, *The Syrian Church in Malabar*, Trichinopoly, 1914.

(22) *Encyclopaedia Brittanica*, entry Acts Thomas, vol XXIII; Sadiq, Mufti Muhammad, *Qabr-i-Masih* (Urdu), Talif-o-Ishait, Qadian, 1936, pp114–126; Geddes, M, *History of the Christian Church of Malabar*, London, 1694; *Portuguese Discoveries, Dependencies and Missions*, London, 1893.

(23) Plattner, Flex Alferd, *Christian India*, New York, 1957, p29. "Modern research is inclined to accept as true the traditional claim of the Travancore Christians to have been evangelised by St Thomas". See also: Marshall, J W M, *Christianity in India*, London, 1885; Hugh, James, *History of Christians in India from the Commencement of the Christian Era*, London, 1839; D'Souza, Herman, *In the Steps of St Thomas*, Madras, 1972; Farquhar, J N, *The Apostle Thomas in South India*, Manchester, 1927.

(24) Buchanan, Claudius, *Christian Researches in India*, Cambridge, 1811, p229; Rae, George M, *The Syrian Church in India*, Edinburgh, 1892.

(25) *John*, 13, 36.

(26) *Acts of the Apostles*, 1, 12–15.

(27) *Acts*, 2, 41.

(28) *Acts*, 4, 4.

(29) *Acts*, 5, 17–40. "But if a man suffer as a Christian let him be not ashamed, but let him glorify God in this name". See also: *Gospel of Peter*, from *The Apocryphal New Testament*, tr M R James, Oxford, 1926.

(30) *Acts*, 12, 1–4.

(31) *Galatians*, 2, 11. A legend has been invented connecting the Basilica of St Peter with Simon Peter, but doubts have been cast regarding its identity. There are no documentary proofs except a casual mention by Pope Pius XII, in an address to students in 1949.

(32) *I Peter*, 1, 1.

(33) *I Peter*, 2, 9–10.

(34) *I Peter*, 5, 12–14.

(35) Shaikh Abdul Qadir, article in the weekly *Badar*, Qadian, India, 17 May 1979.

(36) *Annual Report of the Archaeological Survey of India*, Frontier Circle, Govt of India Pubs, Delhi, 1912. data?

(37) Roland, Benjamin, *St Peter in Gandhara*; see also the magazine *East and West*, Rome, vol IV, no 4, 1953.

(38) *Gospel of Philip*, 59. Found in *The Nag Hammadi Library*, ed, James M Robinson, New York, 1977, & E J Brill, Leiden, 1977; Eilson, R M, *The Gospel of Philip*, London, 1962.

(39) Farouqui, Mumtaz, *The Crumbling of the Cross*, p62; Sadiq, Mufti Muhammad, *Qabr-i-Masih*, Qadian, 1936, pp26–27.

(40) Nazir Ahmad, Khwaja, *Jesus in Heaven on Earth*, p361.

(41) Farouqui, Mumtaz Ahmad, *The Crumbling of the Cross*, pp62–65.

(42) Jeremias, Joachim, essay in *Nachrichten aus der Akademie der Wissenschaft*,

Gottingen, I.Phil-Hist. Kl 1953, p95; Bartholomew, D S, *A Voyage to the East Indies*, London, 1800; Geddes, Michael, *The History of the Church of Malabar*, London, 1694; Komroff, Manuel, *The Travels of Marco Polo*, New York, 1926.

(43) Kersten, Holger, *Jesus lived in India*, Element, Dorset, 1986; Sadiq, Mufti Muhammad, *Qabr-i-Masih* (Urdu), Qadian, 1936, p124. The learned scholar informs that Bishop Johanan participated in the Council of Nicaea in 325 AD. While endorsing his signature on the proceedings of the Council, he designated himself as the Bishop of India.

(44) Jeremias, Joachim, *ibid*, p99. See also: Cosmas, *The Christian Topography*, tr McCruidle, J W, Hakluyt Society Pubs, London, 1897; Raulin, *Historia Ecclesiae Malabartcae*, Rome, 1745.

16

Hazrat Issa the Prophet

Islamic historians

There are many Islamic traditions which deal with Jesus of
Nazareth. These come from the sixth century AD. According to
one tradition:

> *Jesus, son of Mary, was a ruddy man, inclined to white, with long hair,
> which he never anointed. He used to walk barefoot and could walk on
> the surface of the water.*

Abu Huraira says that after being saved from the cross, Jesus went
on a strange odyssey. Allah guided him throughout his travels and
saved him from further persecution[1].

Jesus and his mother had to migrate from Jerusalem to a far-
off country, traversing from one country to another[2]. According
to Islamic traditions, Jesus lived up to an age of one hundred and
twenty years. This tradition is ascribed to Hazrat Ayesha Siddiq,
the wife of the Prophet of Islam, Hazrat Muhammad. She says that
the Prophet once told her that Jesus, son of Mary, had lived to this
ripe old age[3].

Various sayings of Jesus are recorded by Muslims.

> *Jesus, son of Mary, may peace be upon him, said: "He who seeks after
> the world is like one who drinks sea water. The more he drinks, the
> more his thirst increases, until it kills him[4]."*
>
> *Jesus, son of Mary, may peace be upon him, said: "The world
> consists of three days: yesterday, which has passed, from which you*

have gained nothing; tomorrow, of which you do not know whether you will reach it or not; and today, in which you exist, so avail yourself of it![5]

When Jesus, son of Mary, may peace be upon him, was asked: "How are you this morning?" he replied: "Unable to forestall what I hope, or to put off what I fear, bound by my works, with all my good in another's hand. There is no poor man poorer than I".[6]

Before we look into Islamic references to Jesus' movements in the East, we need to settle whether Yuzu Asaph and Jesus of Nazareth are the same persons. Jesus came to be known by a number of names.

Jesus' names

At the time of his birth, he was to be given the name *Immanuel* – 'God with us'[7]. One of his earlier names was *Joshua*, but the Gospels refrained from naming him so, because he would then be known as *Joshua II*, since we already have one Joshua in the Old Testament. In Aramaic, Jesus was *Jesu*, and in Urdu language, he is called *Yuzu*. In Persian language he is called *Yuzu*, while in Arabic, he is *Issa*.

In Kashmir, Jesus was known as *Yuzu*, which derives from the Aramaic *Jesu*, as does *Yusu* in Urdu. It also derives from the original name of Jesus, *Joshua*. It is a strange coincidence that *Yuzu Asaph* is a Hebrew name, *Yuzu* standing for Jesu and *Asaph* standing for 'gatherer' – or this might have some connection with the Asaph who composed several Psalms in the Old Testament. How Jesus came to be known as *Yuzu Asaph* in Kashmir has been mentioned in the *Tarikh-i-Kashmir* of Mulla Nadri. He writes:

I have found in the ancient Hindu works that Issa, the Spirit of Allah, assumed the name of Yuzu Asaph in Kashmir[8].

This information is very important and significant. I also found archaeological evidence in support if this. It came to my knowledge that an inscription inside the *Takhat-i-Sulaiman* (the Throne of Solomon) informed: *In this year, Yuzu Asaph proclaimed his*

Ministry, in the year 54.

He was *Yusu*, the Prophet of the Children of Israel. By now, I had collected sufficient evidence that Yuzu Asaph was the same as Jesus. Further support came from the study of the Dead Sea Scrolls, wherein it has been revealed that *Asaph adn Ya Asaph* stands for the mystical name of Jesus[9].

The Holy Quran

My researches into Jesus' travels showed that Basilides of Alexandria, Mani of Persia and Julian (331-363) had declared openly that Jesus had not died, but had migrated to India. Maybe these voices were stopped by the Church: everyone was taught to believe that Jesus had given his life for our sins.

The position in the East was different, and all over Central Asia, Tibet, Ladakh, Kashmir and India, people continued to believe that Jesus had visited these places. This made me search out the sources connected with Islam. The Holy Quran is the primary source of Islamic knowledge about Jesus, who is respected by Muslims as one among the foremost prophets of God. Let me quote:

> *And we caused Jesus, son of Mary, to follow in their footsteps, confirming what was before him, and we bestowed on the Gospel wherein is guidance and a light, confirming that which was before it in the Torah – guidance and an admonition to those who are careful[10].*

The Holy Quran makes mention of the miraculous birth of Jesus in these words:

> *O Mary! Allah has chosen you and made you pure, and has preferred you above all women of creation.*
>
> *O Mary! Be obedient to your Lord, prostrate yourself and bow with those who bow in worship.*
>
> *O Mary! Allah gives you glad tidings of a word from him, whose name is the Messiah, Jesus, son of Mary, illustrious in the world and the hereafter, and one of those brought near unto Allah. He will speak to mankind in his cradle and in his manhood, and he is of the righteous. She said: "My Lord! How can I have a child when no mortal has*

touched me?" He said: "So it will be. Allah creates what he will".

The Holy Quran rejects the crucifixion of Jesus in these words:

And for their saying: we have killed the Messiah, Jesus, son of Mary, Messenger of Allah, and they killed him not, nor did they cause his death upon the cross, but he was made to appear to them as such. And certainly those who differ therein are in doubt about it. They have no [definite] knowledge about it but only follow a conjecture; and they did not kill him for certain: Nay, Allah exalted him in his presence. And Allah is ever mighty and wise[11].

This quote led me deeper into researching Jesus' survival. It seemed that Islam, with its variety of schools of thought, might possibly hold a key to knowledge of Jesus' survival. The Holy Quran questions the episode of the crucifixion, but also there exist many legends among the Muslims that some other was hanged instead of Jesus, and he was taken up bodily into heaven by God. But these legends are not supported by the Quran or the authentic traditions.

A verse in the Quran, which has become a source of heated controversy among various sects of Muslims reads:

O Jesus! I will cause thee to die and exalt thee in my presence and clear thee of those who disbelieve[12].

The expression that God 'exalted him unto himself' has created confusion, and some Muslims believe that Jesus was taken up by God or was raised up into heaven alive. On this issue, Muslims have reviled each other. The issue was referred to the Al Azhar University, Cairo, and its Rector gave the following *fatwa* or verdict.

a) There is nothing in the Holy Quran to endorse that Jesus was taken up bodily into heaven;
b) God caused him to die a natural death and then exalted him;
c) Any person who denies his bodily ascent is not an apostate. [13]

It was now clear that while the Quran reflected the story of crucifixion, many fanciful legends had established themselves not only among Christians but also among Muslims. Secondly, while Christians, under the influence of Mithraic dogma left over from Roman times, started believing that Jesus had died on the cross for the atonement of original sin, Muslims began to believe that Jesus, as a prophet of God, could not succumb to such an accursed death on the cross, and hence was raised up to heaven, bodily, by God.

To Jews, crucifixion is a heinous form of death reserved for criminals. To Muslims, crucifixion is an accursed death in a derogatory sense. As such, Muslims exalt and honour Jesus by declaring that he was elevated by God towards himself. However, there were two opinions among Muslims: one declaring that Jesus was alive and the other declaring that he had a natural death.

This controversy led me to discover Mirza Ghulam Ahmad, the founder of the Ahmadiyya sect. He had declared that Jesus had died a natural death and had not ascended into heaven as a living being. This created a furore among the Muslims. For this, Mirza Ahmad was not only criticised but was openly declared to be an apostate. Mirza Ahmad was born in 1835 at Qadian, India, and passed away in 1908. He wrote eighty books on Islam and established the Ahmadiyya Community.

He claimed to be a prophet of God, this being his second advent as Jesus Christ. His announcements profoundly disturbed his followers. However, all this made it clear that it was necessary to make a thorough search among Muslim works, particularly of the Ahmadiyya Community. I established contact with them and obtained relevant material on this issue. The most important among them was a research work by their founder.

Masih Hindustan Mein

Masih Hindustan Mein or *Jesus in India* by Mirza Ghulam Ahmad is a work of great research, and was published after his demise in 1908. In the year 1890, he had, in his work called *Izalah Auham*, advocated the view that according to the Holy Bible and the Holy Quran, Jesus had escaped the accursed death of crucifixion due to divine will, and that he had set out secretly from Palestine in search of the lost tribes of Israel. His work was read with interest by his followers.

In 1899, Khalifa Noor ud Din, who lived in Kashmir, informed Mirza Ghulam Ahmad that in the capital city of Srinagar there was a tomb said to be the tomb of the prophet Yuzu Asaph, who had come to Kashmir from a foreign country during ancient times. Further investigations revealed that Yuzu Asaph could be no other person than Jesus. With this evidence at his disposal, Mirza Ghulam Ahmad set out to compile a comprehensive work on the subject, but it remained incomplete. In spite of this, this research work is unique in many respects.

The main thesis expounded is that Jesus Christ escaped an accursed death on the cross, was treated and nursed by his disciples, and then went to Kashmir and eventually died there. Jesus made this journey in quest of the lost tribes of Israel.

---

(1) Abu Huraira, *Kanz-ul-Aimal*, vol II, p34. He also reports that God guided Jesus to depart from Jerusalem so that he could be saved from further persecution. *Kanz-ul-Aimal* is a collection of sayings and teachings of the Holy Prophet, compiled by Shaikh Ala-ud-Din, published in 1836 in Hyderabad.

(2) Ibn-i-Jarir; *Tafsir Ibn-i-Jarir-at-Tibri*, vol III, p197. *Tafsir-ul-Quran* is a world-famous commentary on the Quran in 30 volumes by Ibn-i-Jarir at-Tibri. Its original Arabic edition was published by Kubr-ul-Mara Press, Cairo, in 1921. Since then, its Persian and Urdu translations have been done, and are available in India.

(3) *Kanz-ul-Aimal*, vol VI, p120; Siddiq Hasan Khan, *Hujaj-ul-Kiramah*, (Urdu), p428; Ahmad, Mirza Ghulam, *Massih Hindustan Mein*, p98.

(4) Inayat Khan, *The Unity of Religious Ideals*, vol IX, Delhi, 1990, p181. There are numerous references to Jesus in the writings of Sufis such as Zhun Nun (861), Bayazid (875), Attar (1230), Ibn-al Arabi (1239), Rumi (1273), Shabistari (1317), Mohsin Fani (1670) and Prince Dara Shikoh (1659). In his celebrated work *Al-Futuhat-al-Makkiya*, the great Sufi master Ibn-al Arabi makes a unique declaration about Jesus: "The seal of universal holiness, above which there is no other holy, is our Lord Jesus". Another great Sufi master of India writes: "The soul who realised the truth even before he claimed to be Alpha and Omega, is Christ".

(5) Parables and events in the Gospels have been preserved by the Sufis in their Books of Tales. See Idries Shah, *Tales of the Dervishes*, London, 1967, and *Recollections*, London, 1969. Numerous sayings of Jesus are recorded by Shaikh-us-Sadiq (d 962) in his work *Kamal-ud-Din*, Syed-us-Sanad Press, Iran, 1782.

(6) Stoddart, William, *Sufism*, reprint, Delhi, 1983. In the *Holy Quran*, Jesus is spoken of as the incarnate Word of God; in the *Hadis*, he is exalted in these words: "Every son of Adam is touched at birth by Satan, save only the son of Mary and his mother".

(7) *Matthew*, 1, 23.

(8) Mulla Nadri, *Tarikh-i-Kashmir*, Folio 69. This rare historical manuscript by the first Muslim historian of Kashmir, compiled in 1454, has remained in the private possession of Sahibzada Ghulam Mohiyuddin as a family property. His son, Sahibzada Basharat Saleem, did not let me see this document. I have had to depend on the photograph of folio 69, made by Khwaja Nazir Ahmad for his book *Jesu in Heaven on Earth*, Lahore, 1952.

(9) Lepancer, *The Mystical Life of Jesus Christ*. Yuzu Asaph is mentioned in *Kamal-ud-Din* (962), *Tarikh-i-Kashmir* of Mulla Nadri (1454), *Waqiat-i-Kashmir* of Deedamari (1729), *Ahliyan-i-Paras* (1909), and *Farhang-i-Asfia* (1908).

(10) *Al-Quran*, Al-Maidah, 5:46.

(11) *Quran*, Al Nisa, 4, 157–158. For a translation and commentary see Ali, Maulana Muhammad, translation and commentary, *The Holy Quran – Arabic Text*, Lahore, 1951, pp230–232.

(12) *Al Quran*, Al-Imran, 3:54. "Exalt thee" signifies elevation in honour and not bodily ascent to heaven. See also: *Jesus in the Quran*, G Parrinder, London, 1965.

(13) The Fatwah of Shaikh Mohammed Shaltoot, the Weekly *Al Risalah*, Cairo, Egypt. Vol 10, No 462, p515. "A letter was received by the Senate of the Great Al-Azhar University of Cairo from Abdul Karim of the Middle East, which contained the inquiry: 1. Is Jesus alive or dead according to the *Holy Quran* and *Hadis*?; 2. what is the position of a Muslim who believes that Jesus is not alive?; 3. What will be the position of a Muslim who disbelieves in Jesus' Second Coming? The issue was referred by the Senate to the Rector and Senior Professor, Shaikh Muhammad Shaltut, who gave the following verdict: "The word *tawaffa* is used in so many places in the *Holy Quran* in the sense of death. The word *tawaffaitani* means natural death. The actual meaning of the verse is that Allah caused Jesus to die, and exalted him and sanctified him from the charges of his enemies. They did not kill or crucify him, but the mater was made dubious to them".

17

Rozabal

The Tomb of Yuzu Asaph

The research work of Mirza Ghulam Ahmad not only mentioned the tomb of Jesus but also gave a long list of sources in Persian and Arabic which deal with the life of Jesus in the East. The first thing which I did was to visit the tomb of Yuzu Asaph at Rozabal, in Srinagar, Kashmir. At that time I was the Director of Archaeology in Jammu and Kashmir State, and I could not only visit this monument but could also execute repairs.

Soon I learned that the tomb was held in great esteem by Muslims and it was impossible for me to think of any kind of major investigation or excavation – nobody would allow me to open this tomb for examination. I visited it a number of times and collected very valuable information about it. I also made a discovery which gladdened my heart and convinced me that I was on the right track.

The tomb of Yuzu Asaph is known as *Rozabal* or 'the sacred tomb in Kashmir'. It is situated in Anzimar, Khanyar Srinagar, the summer capital of Kashmir. The people believe that a prophet, Yuzu Asaph, came to the valley of Kashmir, two thousand years ago, from Egypt. He preached the same parables as Jesus, and he was a prophet of 'the People of the Book', the followers of Abraham, Moses and Jesus.

The legends about Yuzu Asaph in Kashmir come from Persia, Afghanistan and Kashmir: a prophet by the name of Yuzu Asaph came to the valley and was buried in this tomb. I had a chance to

173

The tomb of Yuza Asaph at Rozabal *(Lino Cremon)*

find this information in many printed books and manuscripts, housed in the Oriental Research Library, Srinagar. My further research into these manuscripts brought rich dividends and it came to light that there are also manuscripts in Sanskrit which mention Jesus. All these manuscripts will be quoted extensively in subsequent pages.

As Director of State Archaeology, I was interested to know more about this tomb. I met the caretakers and inquired about the legal standing of this property. I met Sahibzada Ghulum Mohi-ud-din, an elderly person who introduced himself as the custodian of this tomb. He showed me a legal document pertaining to it.

There is a striking feature of the ancient buildings in the valley of Kashmir. In most cases, the entrance to these edifices is towards the east. In the case of graves, while Jews lay their dead in an east-west direction, Muslims lay them in a north-south direction. Another general feature of the ancient buildings in Kashmir is that these were made of stone, until bricks were introduced in the

174

medieval period. The present building does not belong to the ancient period and has been constructed on top of an ancient structure.

The present structure is made mainly of bricks and wood, a rectangular building placed on an ancient structure which lies on a mound of earth. It has an entrance-chamber attached to the eastern side of the main building, with a door facing the north and an inner door facing the west. The walls of this building have three windows on the north and south sides, five windows on the west, and four windows on the east walls. All of the windows are made of wood, with latticework depicting a wooden cross in the centre. The main entrance, also made of wood, shows a cross in the middle.

Inside the hall of the building is the outer rectangular sepulchre, made of wood, decorated with latticework panels on all four sides. *(see plate 11)* This wooden sepulchre has two glass windows, one in the south side, for entering the inner sarcophagus, and another in the corner of the east side, for looking in at a stone slab showing foot prints of Yuzu Asaph. Another slab is fixed on the floor, in the corner of the sepulchre on the south side.

Inside the wooden sepulchre there is the main wooden sarcophagus, decorated with flowery designs on the south and north side. This wooden sarcophagus is covered with a sacred shroud. Nobody is allowed to enter the wooden sepulchre. The same restrictions apply to the wooden sarcophagus inside this sepulchre. In view of my official position and my friendly relations with the caretakers, I was permitted to go inside the wooden sarcophagus.

It was during my visits that I found the sacred footprint stone, bearing wound marks. I also found one rectangular stone slab in the south corner, maybe a signpost for a grave, or a relic. But the most interesting find was a wooden cross and a chiselled stone post about two feet high. Inside this wooden sarcophagus, there was an artificial grave of smaller dimension towards the south side. All these relics were photographed by me.

Let me now describe the plinth and the underground style of this building. During the course of my researches, I went inside the wooden sarcophagus: it appeared to me that I was standing on the

The wooden cross in front of the wooden sarcophagus
in the tomb of Yuza Asaph

176

roof of another building, which was hollow and beneath my feet. After much thinking I started the examination of the outer sides of this building, to see whether there could be an edifice under the present structure. It transpired that beneath the present foundation walls, there are stone walls of chiselled stones, which testify that the underground stone structure is ancient.

There are references in ancient works that many people would visit this tomb to seek blessings. Many decades back Kashmiri works speak of a door to the inner crypt, from which it was said one could once smell musk[1]. This stone door, not visible now, was made of decorated chiselled slabs. Fortunately, we have a photograph of its upper part, made by Khwaja Nazir Ahmad, who conducted and published his research work on the subject[2].

My study shows that the stone walls, which are underground at present, formed the walls of the ancient edifice, which contains the sacred relics of Yuzu Asaph. Now the access to the inner chambers is not visible and has sunk under the debris. Towards the east we find a rising mound of earth on which private houses have been built. There used to be graves of two kinds previously, some in the north-south direction and some in the east-west direction, pointing to their Jewish and Muslim origin. But now, all graves have been remodelled on the north-south direction so as to show that these belong to Muslims only. But there are photographs of the graves, taken two decades back, which show the distinct marks of the Jewish graves.

The question of trial excavations came to my mind several times and in this connection I had many discussions with the caretaker and the managing committee, but none agreed to expose this sacred site for these experiments. The net result of the investigations has been that the tomb has remained closed to any kind of scientific investigations.

The Decree of 1194 AH

The custodian of the tomb showed me a legal document pertaining to it. It is a decree dated 1194 AH (1766 AD) granted by the Grand Mufti of Kashmir. It is a genuine document duly sealed and authenticated. I will give its translation:

Decree dated 1149 AH (= 1766 AD) by the Grand Mufti of Kashmir
authenticating the tomb of Yuzu Asaph, who came to Kashmir in the reign of
Raja Gopadatta (49 AD)

*The seal of the Justice of Islam, Mulla Fazil, 1194 in the High Court
of Justice, the Department of Learning and Piety of the Kingdom of
Kashmir.*

Present: *Rehman Khan, son of Amir Khan, submits that since
ancient times many kings, nobles, ministers and the multitude visit this
holy tomb of Yuzu Asaph, the prophet of Allah, and make offerings in
cash and kind.*

Claim: *"I claim that I am the only and absolute claimant, entitled
to receive the offerings, and no one else has any right whatsoever on
these offerings. I pray that a writ of injunction be granted and all others
restrained from interfering with these rights."*

Verdict: *Now this High Court, after due consideration of the
evidence concludes as under:*

*It has been established that during the reign of Raja Gopadatta,
who had built and repaired many temples, including the Throne of
Solomon on the Solomon Hill, Yuzu Asaph came to the valley of
Kashmir. Prince by descent, he was pious and saintly and had given up*

178

earthly pursuits. He spent all his time in prayers and meditation.

The people of Kashmir, having become idolators after the great flood of Noah, sent Yuzu Asaph as prophet for the people. This great prophet proclaimed the oneness of God. When he breathed his last, he was buried in this tomb, which is known as Rozabal. In the year 871 AH, Syed Nasir-ud-din, a descendant of Hazrat Imama Mosa Raza, was buried beside the grave of Yuzu Asaph.

Order: *Since the shrine is visited by numerous devotees and since the applicant Rehman Kahn is the hereditary custodian of this shrine, it is ordered that he is entitled to receive all offerings, and none else has any right to claim these offerings.*

Given under our hand, 11th Jamad-Ulsani, 1184, signed and sealed: Milla Fazil, Mohammad Azam, Hafiz Ahsan Ullah, Khizar Mohamad, Faquir Baba, Abdul Shakoor, Mohamad Akbar, Raza Akbar Atta.

The above document provided me with certain new pointers. It mentions repair of the Throne of Solomon, which is known as *Takhat-i-Sulaiman*, usually considered a Hindu temple, sitting on a hill overlooking the Dal lake in Srinagar. Later I found that this temple had been repaired, and we have archaeological evidence of this. A study of the history of Kashmir revealed that Raja Gopadatta ruled over Kashmir during 49-109 AD. It was evident that Yuzu Asaph had come to Kashmir in the middle of the first century AD. Now the issue which remained to be taken up as about the identity of Yuzu Asaph. Was he Jesus Christ in disguise?

Footprints of Jesus Christ

It was in 1975 that I happened to visit the tomb of Yuzu Asaph along with a colleague of mine, Professor Ghulam Mohi-ud-din. We quietly entered the wooden sarcophagus through a side window. To my amazement, I found one wooden cross, which I photographed. I also found a stone in a corner carved out with a niche to keep a lamp. In another corner was a stone slab fixed in the floor, covered with mud.

We cleaned it, and to our astonishment the slab had foot impressions with traces of raised wound marks. I took several

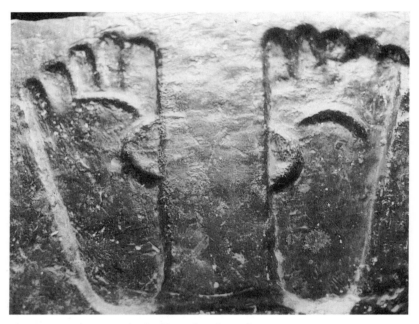

Feet imprinted in stone in the Yuzu Asaph tomb.
Discovered by F. M. Hassnain and Mohi–ud–din *(Nisar Hassnein)*

photographs of this slab. Next day I took Mr Bhan, curator of the
state museum, with me, and he prepared a plaster cast of the slab.
The result was marvellous. It was clear that whoever had chiselled
this impression had seen Yuzu Asaph with these wound marks.
Jesus had been put on the cross with nails struck in his feet. Both
Yuzu Asaph and Jesus had one thing in common: wound marks on
their feet.

It took me many months to examine and study the stone slab
bearing foot-impressions. The stone slab is permanently fixed in
the corner of the sarcophagus and the stone slab is polished like
glass. Its colour is black and shining. The carving had been extraordinary, because on the one hand, raised wound marks were
depicted, and secondly, two pads inside the soles of the feet were
also shown. It came to light, many years after, that these pads were
a clear proof of the genuineness of these feet impressions.

A German scholar[3], who had come to critically examine these
foot-impressions, informed me that these pads had a special sig-

180

nificance in relation to Jesus. During his travels he could have put pads under his soles so that the raised wounds would not irritate his feet. This extraordinary depiction of raised soles showed that the carver was genuine and his carving of the feet-wounds was real and genuine. He saw that there were wounds which had swollen the feet and deformed them. As such, he shows deformed feet, one foot a little different from the other.

Secondly, in one foot there is a little cavity or hole, which showed that one nail was struck on both feet, placed over one another. All this was explained to me by the German scholar who had come to study this stone slab. He congratulated me for this discovery.

In the meantime, I received a letter from Kurt Berna of Ludwigsburg, Germany, asking me to send to him exact photo-copies the stone slab. He is scientist who first invited attention of the world scholars towards the facila impressions of Jesus Christ on the Turin Shroud. Kurt Berna had even approached the Vatican and insisted on a scientific study of this Shroud, because he claimed that Jesus Christ was not dead when he was wrapped in this linen. He was kind to send me a copy of his report on the stone slab. Let me quote:

In this case, while it is very interesting to find the nail-wound reproduction of the left foot near the toes, the nail-wound repro-duction of the right foot is exactly at the place where the classic view said it should be. This means, this man has been crucified with the left foot over the right foot and only one nail was going through the feet.

These are not necessarily the real foot-prints of the man in the tomb. Yet the imprint-maker gave prominence to the signs that the man underneath the tomb-stone had been crucified, and he did have such signs at these places on the soles of the feet, distinguish-ing marks!

Fact: a crucified man is in the tomb, but if we look on the Holy Shroud of Christ at Turin, we find that the left foot was nailed over the right foot on the cross, because the left knee inside the shroud was more bowed and stiff than the right leg. A further indication that the man from the Turin Shroud and the person under the Srinagar tomb are the same![4]

This letter from Kurt Berna, the investigator of the Turin Shroud, was interesting, since it, for the first time, connected Yuzu Asaph of Rozabal, Kashmir with the Holy Shroud of Jesus Christ preserved in the Cathedral of Turin, Italy!

Barlaam and Josaphat

The tomb of Yuzu Asaph in Kashmir attracted the attention of Christian missionary scholars who were not ready to accept that Jesus lay buried in Kashmir. In 1895 two books were published giving the story of *Barlaam and Josaphat*[5]. It was claimed that Yuzu Asaph was being confused with *Josaphat*, who was said to be no other person than the Buddha, according to the books.

This story is a remnant of a Nestorian fable which told that Josaphat was the only son of an Indian king named Abenner. At his birth the astrologers had predicted that he would become a Christian. His father did not like this son to become a Christian, so he kept Josaphat in a palace, surrounded in luxury. One day Josaphat gained permission from his father to go out of the palace. The sight of a sick and blind man made the prince sad. Then he met *Barlaam*, a Christian who told him about Christ, his crucifixion and resurrection. Josaphat accepted Christianity and was baptised by Barlaam. After that, Josaphat preached Christianity in India – incidentally burning Buddhist and Hindu temples. Finally Josaphat came to Kashmir and died there[6].

The legend, on the face of it, looks like a fraud invented to create confusion about the tomb of Yuzu Asaph in Kashmir. It is also to be noted that the story comes from India, and was publicised by the Christian missionaries when they found they were confronted with the tomb of Yuzu Asaph in Kashmir.

The London Conference, 1978

An international conference was held in London, the subject being *Deliverance of Jesus from the Cross*. This international conference was convened by the Ahmadiyya Muslim organisation in London. By then, I had established myself as a researcher on the lost years of Jesus. So the organisers invited me to speak, and the subject of my lecture was the tomb of Yuzu Asaph.

At the outset, the organisers of the conference declared that it was not their aim to bring any religion or religious doctrine into contempt. Their only purpose was to seek truth, to clear Jesus, a righteous prophet of God, of the calumny of having suffered an accursed death, and to re-established his complete innocence. The Jews claimed that they had brought about the death of Jesus on the cross and that, therefore, he had become accursed in accordance with the pronouncement in *Deuteronomy*, 21, 23, where it is clearly stated:

> *When a man is convicted of a capital offence and is put to death, you shall hang him on a gibbet; but his body shall not remain on the gibbet overnight; you shall bury it on the same day, for a hanged man is offensive in the sight of God.*

While quoting the above verses, it came to light that the publishers of the Bible have changed two words: *gibbet* and *offensive*, at some time. In old versions, the word *cross* has been changed to *gibbet*, or *tree*, and the word *accursed* has been changed to *offensive*. Those who revised the verses of the Bible to suit their purpose knew that in the Old Testament, a hanged person is an accursed person. Hence they resorted to interpolation of words. Yet according to the Jewish tradition, a hanged person is an accursed person, most offensive to God. Jews could not accept a Messiah who had suffered his death on a gibbet, a tree or a cross.

This conference was a great success and roused tremendous interest among Christians and Muslims who deputed observers to the conference. The British Council of Churches asked for talks with the organisers, and for a sharing of thoughts on Jesus. However, the Council reaffirmed:

> *In the history of the crucifixion and death of Jesus, which is attested by the four Gospels, and by the unanimous testimony of early Christian tradition, we recognise that the death of Jesus on the cross may seem a scandal and an affront to divine justice, but we believe that in the*

death of Jesus on the cross we see the love of God which suffers on behalf of others, and which does not forgive without a cost[7].

After the conference the head of the Ahmadiyya Muslims declared that 'the recognition by the British Council of Churches that the death of Jesus on the cross may seem a scandal, and an affront to divine justice, is a welcome announcement. This raises the hope that if the reality of these questions is expounded to our Christian brethren with love and true understanding, they will modify their questionable tenets'.

This international conference was held in London for three days, and 1500 delegates from many countries of the world participated in its deliberations. It was evident that the accursed death of Jesus on the cross was a scandalous affair and required to be demolished in order to free Jesus from this stigma. Secondly, it was now necessary to make serious explorations into the lost years of Jesus. The verbatim record of this conference provided me with much hope and encouragement and I continued my researches with vigour.

---

(1) Ghulam Nabi Khanyari, *Wajeez-ut-Tawarikh*, (Persian) Vol II, Folio 279, Oriental Research Manuscript Library, Univ of Kashmir, Srinagar. See also: *Qabr-i-Masih* by Mufti Muhammad Sadiq, Qadian, 1936, p50.

(2) *Jesus in Heaven on Earth*, the Woking Muslim Mission and Literary Trust, Lahore, Pakistan, 1952. Nazir Ahmad has extensively elaborated source material contained in *Masih Hindustan Mein* by Mirza Ghulam Ahmad, and *Qabr-i-Masih* by Mufti Muhammad Sadiq, Qadian, 1936. Born in 1872, Mufti Sadiq spent his childhood learning Arabic, Persian and English, becoming a schoolteacher, and later graduating in English and Hebrew. In 1901 he became headmaster of the high school in Qadian. In 1914 he started work as an Ahmadiyya Muslim missionary in India. In 1917 he went to London for missionary work, and then went to America to establish the Ahmadiyya Muslim Mission and mosque in Chicago. He returned to India in 1923. In order to conduct researches on Jesus and Thomas, Mufti Muhammad Sadiq visited Kashmir in 1925 and completed his research in three years. His work entitled *Qabr-i-Masih*, or *The Grave of Jesus*, was published in 1936. It is a beacon-light for future research scholars on this subject. He has given excerpts from 29 foreign authors, to show that they all believed that the Kashmiris are among the Lost Tribes of Israel. He has visited 18 archaeological sites and found graves with Hebrew inscriptions. He has also provided a bibliography

of works on Thomas and Syrian Christians in S India.

(3) Gunter Hoffmann, Esoteriker Schriftpsykologe, Harzweg 32, D-3012 Langenhagen, Germany. He came to Kashmir in 1983 and we visited the tomb of Yuzu Asaph to examine the footprints of Jesus.

(4) Letter to me dated July 6, 1978 from Hans Naber, *aka* Kurt Berna, *aka* Reban John, D-7140 Ludwigsburg, Germany. He also endorsed copies of this letter to Mumtaz Ahmad Faruqui, in Islamabad, Pakistan, Andreas Faber-Kaiser in Barcelona, and Franz Sachse, D-5400 Koblenz-Arzheim, Germany.

(5) Jacobs, Joseph, *Barlaam & Josaphat*, London, 1896; Budge, Wallis, *Barlam and Yewasef*, Cambridge, 1923; Lang, David Marshal, *The Wisdom of Balahar*, New York, 1957. Shaikh Abdul Qadir, author of *The Qumran Scrolls* (Urdu) remarks on the story of Barlaam and Josaphat as a pure Buddhist legend confusing Yuzu Asaph with the coming Bodhisattva and 'gatherer of the flock of the true faith', who after his extensive travels in India, settled in Kashmir and died there. Johan Forsström, author of *King of the Jews*, remarks that this legend is an attempt to confuse posterity about Jesus and his tomb in Kashmir. See also: Saffdar Ali, *Kisa Yuzua-saf-v-Hakim Blohar* (Urdu).

(6) Macdonald, *The Story of Barlaam and Josaphat*, Calcutta, 1895; Jacobs, Joseph, *Barlaam and Josaphat*, London, 1895.

(7) *Truth about Crucifixion*, the London Mosque, Gressenhall Road, London, 1978. Transcripts from the International Conference on *Deliverance of Jesus from the Cross*, held at the Commonwealth Inst, Kensington, London, 2-4 June, 1978.

18

Back in Kashmir

The Dispersion of the Jewish Tribes

Dispersion of the Jewish tribes started with the destruction of Samaria in about 721 BC by the Assyrian Sargon II. It was accelerated by the eighteen–month siege and destruction of Jerusalem by the Babylonian Nebuchadnezzar II in 587 BC, leading to the Babylonian Captivity, lasting 48 years. From that year, they went on migrating and settled in far off lands – as far apart as Yemen and Ethiopia, Wales, Armenia and Ukraine. Eastwards from Israel these people settled in Bamiyan, Bokhara, Samarkand, Khorasan, Kashgar and Kashmir.

Some of their remnants reached as far as western China[1]. Many of the present-day tribes in Afghanistan are descendants of Jewish tribes: several ethnological studies have revealed that the overwhelming population among the Pathans living in Bamiyan, Kabul, Hazara and Kashmir are descendants of the lost tribes of Israel[2]. As centuries passed these Jewish tribes variously adapted their religion to Buddhism, Shivaism and Islam, due to political upheavals and religious persecution. Despite these drastic changes,, several segments of the people till call themselves *Bani Israel*, or the Children of Israel[3].

We find Jesus in Taxila in the year 49 AD. Gondapharos passed away in the next year, and soon after Kadphises, the Kushana king, annexed Taxila. After this, Jesus probably migrated towards Kashmir. But why Kashmir? Was it practical circumstances of the time, or was there a more particular reason? He was the Messiah of the

Gondpharos, King of Taxilla, as a Christian conqueror,
1st century AD *(Archeol. Survey of India)*

Israelites, and he had declared in clear words that he was sent to
serve the lost sheep in the house of Israel[4].

The valley of Kashmir was occupied by various tribes during
its 5,000 year history. Among the prominent tribes to have come
to Kashmir are the Nagas, Pishachi, Gandhara, Tungana and
Khash. The last named tribe is no other than the historical Kassites
from Mesopotamia. Cush or Kash was the overlord of this Semite
tribe, and these people, during their march towards the East,
founded many settlements which included their name: Kashan in
Iran, Kashgar in central Asia and Kashtawar and Kashmir in north
India. Speaking about Kashmir, Bernier writes in 1644[5]:

*There are many marks of Judaism to be found in the country. On
entering the kingdom, the people in the frontier villages struck me as
resembling Jews.*

Al Beruni, who was deputed by Sultan Mahmud Ghazni to Kash-

mir in the thirteenth century, is definite on the subject when he
reports[6]:

> The Kashmiris are particularly anxious about the natural defences of
> their country. They keep vigil and hold on the passes and routes leading
> into it. In ancient times, they used to allow one or two foreign families
> to enter their country, particularly Jews.

The above would show that during the ancient period there existed
some Jewish colonies in the valley of Kashmir. It is possible that
this may have tempted Jesus to move to this valley in about 55 AD.
He had himself declared that his mission was to gather all the
scattered tribes of Israel into one fold[7]:

> I am the good shepherd and know my sheep. And other sheep I have,
> which are not of this fold, them also I must bring and there shall be one
> fold and one shepherd.

Jesus wanted to seek and save his people, and for this reason he
chose to go to India. People obviously were receptive to him, as is
shown by pre-Islamic traditions of naming people and places. Both
in the past and the present, people named their children Issa, and
various names and words have emerged also, including Yusu-
Marg, the Meadow of Yuzu, Yusu-Maidan, a table-land in the Pir
Panchal mountain range, Yusu-Nag, a particular spring, Yusu-Gam,
a village, Yusu-Raja, a person's name, Yusu-Varman, the name of a
Kashmiri king, Issa-Vihara, the monastery of Issa, and Ishbar, a
sacred site on the banks of Dal Lake.

As my researches proceeded, I obtained definite historical
writings speaking of the visit of Jesus to Kashmir during the reign
of the Kashmiri king, Shalivahana. I obtained this information
from one of the most ancient Sanskrit manuscripts of the former
Maharaja of Kashmir. I had to establish the historicity of king
Shalivahana, and also the authenticity of the Sanskrit manuscript,
Bhavishya Maha Purana. I will speak about the king first.

After the departure of Alexander the Great from north India in
about 327 BC, the Greeks established various kingdoms in the
region, in Chitral, Gilgit, Kabul, Hazara and Kashmir. As Director

of State Archeology in Kashmir, I located a few hundred coins of these Greek rulers, about half a dozen from those who had ruled Kashmir. I wrote about these rulers in one my published works[8].

One of the Greek kings of north India was Kadphises, who made himself master of the region in about 60 AD. His viceroy, named Kanishka, subjugated the valley of Kashmir in about 73 AD. It was at this period that Shalivahana emerges on the scene as the Hindu champion of Brahmin rule against the Greeks. He succeeded in driving the Greek viceroy from the valley of Kashmir, though but temporarily. In order to commemorate his victory, he introduced a new era after his name, which is known as the Shalivahana Era. It was introduced on 1st Baisakh, 3179, corresponding to 14th March 78 AD. The history of King Shalivahana having been established, I started my investigations on the Sanskrit manuscript, entitled *Bhavishya Maha Purana*.

Bhavishya Maha Purana

This work, written in the Sharda alphabet of ancient Kashmir, is written on brick bark papyrus. It was compiled by Sutta in 3191, Laukika Era, which corresponds to 115 AD. This rare manuscript came into the possession of the Maharaja of Kashmir, who sent it to the Oriental Research Institute, Poona, India, for study and research. It was published in 1910 in Bombay, India[9].

Amongst other things, it mentions the existence of the followers of Moses in India. The *Bhavishya Maha Purana* is a book of events, information and prophecies started by devotees of the solar cult which existed in the third century BC. The present manuscript by Sutta is copy of the previous writings, and continuation from it. Sutta did this work around 115 AD, and he has given an interesting account of Jesus. He writes that the king of the Sakas (Scythians or *Yueh-Chi*) met a saint who had come from a foreign land, describing himself as the Son of God, and born of a girl.

Sutta records that Shalivahana ruled over Kashmir in about 78 AD. The same year he left for the south to make more conquests, and never returned to his kingdom again. Sutta records that at Wyien, an ancient site near Pampur, Kashmir, famous for its three mineral springs, the king of the Sakas met a saintly person, fair in

The Bhavishya-Maha-Purana; 115 AD. This ancient Sanskrit ms mentions the visit of "Issa Mashiha, the Son of God, born of a virgin" in Kashmir complexion, wearing a long white robe. When the king inquired about the saint, he replied:

> Know me as Ishvara Putaram, or 'Son of God', and Kanya Garbam or 'Born of a Virgin'.

I had the whole paragraph translated into English by a team of Kashmir University professors. The translation was interesting and thought-provoking:

> During this period, Shalivahana, grandson of Vikrama-Ditya, laid hold on the kingdom of his father. He defeated the invincible Sakas [Scythians], and fought off the hordes from Cheen [China], Balhika [Bactria], Kamrupa [Parthia], Tatari [Mongolia], Roma [Rome – more probably Greece] and Khura [Khorasan].
>
> He took possession of their treasures, and those who deserved punishment were punished. He also demarcated the border between the Aryans and the Mleechas [Amlekites], fixing Sindhu [river Indus] as the boundary between the two peoples.
>
> During this period, the king of the Sakas came to Himatunga [Himalaya]. In the mountain area, Wyien the king saw a dignified person of white complexion wearing a long white robe. Astonished to see this foreigner, he asked, Who are you? The dignified person replied in a pleasant manner:
>
> Know me as Ishvara Putaram, or 'Son of God', Kanaya Garbam, or 'Born of a Virgin'. Being given to truth and penances, I preach the truth to the Amlekites.
>
> After hearing this, the king was astonished. He asked: Which religion do you preach? The dignified person replied:
>
> O King, I hail from a land far away, where there is no truth, and evil knows no limits. I appeared in the country of the Amlekites. And I suffered at their hands.
>
> I appeared as Isha Masih or Jesus Messiah. I received the Messiahood or Christhood.
>
> I said unto them, "Remove all mental and bodily impurities. Recite the revealed prayer. Pray truthfully in the right manner. Obey the Law. Remember the name of our Lord God. Meditate upon him

whose abode is in the centre of the sun."

When I appeared in the Amlekite country, I taught love, truth and purity of heart. I asked human beings to serve the Lord. But I suffered at the hands of the wicked and the guilty.

In truth, O King, all power rests with the Lord, who is in the centre of the sun. And the elements, and the cosmos, and the sun, and the God, are forever. Perfect, pure and blissful, God is always in my heart. Thus my name has been established as Isha Masih.

After having heard the pious words from the lips of this distinguished person, I felt peaceful, made obeisance to him and returned[10].

As Shalivahana vanished from history in the year 78 AD, it is probable that the above incident occurred before that date. I am not certain whether the king was Shalivahana or another person acting as the king of the Scythians. The present edition of the *Bhavishya Maha Purana* was published from a manuscript supplied by the Maharaja Pratap Singh of Jammu and Kashmir state. As such the authenticity of the manuscript cannot be doubted.

Having found a reference to Jesus in a Sanskrit work, I felt tempted to make a search for other such manuscripts housed in the research libraries in Kashmir. I made a discovery that our ancient history in Sanskrit had the whole story of crucifixion and resurrection as well.

The Rajatarangini of Kalhana

The *Rajatarangini*, in Sanskrit, was compiled by Kalhana in about 1148 AD, and is the oldest available history of Kashmir. It was translated from Sanskrit into English by Aurel Stein in 1900 under the patronage of the then British Government of India[11]. Kalhana states that a great saint by the name of *Issana* lived at Issabar, on the bank of Dal Lake in Kashmir. He had many disciples and the chief among them was Samdimati, the prince of the Aryans. This disciple was so great that in every house they said: *To Samdimati shall belong the kingdom!*

The wicked approached the king and roused his hatred against Samdimati, who was put on the cross. When Issana heard about this incident, he reached the spot, and smelt a heavenly perfume of incense, and on the third night, "Samdimati rose from deep sleep covered with holy ointments. He had resurrected from death, and wore a magnificent dress." Before I examine the whole story, let me give a summary translation of the verses as given in the *Rajatarangini*:

> *At that time, there spread a mysterious report which declared "To Samdimati shall belong the kingdom". Thereupon, the king threw him into prison. There he pined, with his legs tormented. The king thought that the only way to frustrate the decree of fate was to kill the prisoner. If foolish people prepare a device to work off a coming event, one may be sure that fate opens new avenues.*
>
> *Samdimati was put on the cross under orders of the king. Issana, the great guru, heard the sad news and reached the site. He found Samdimati reduced to a skeleton on the cross. "Woe, that I see you today in this misery!" He then drew forth the bone which the cross had pierced throughout.*
>
> *He carried away the skeleton, and on its forehead he read: "He will have a poor life, suffer imprisonment, death on the cross, and still thereafter will he have a throne." Fate is the embodiment of all miracles. He smelt a heavenly perfume in the middle of the night. He saw the skeleton being fitted with all its limbs by yogins. Covered with holy ointments, Samdimati rose from deep sleep. Samdimati resurrected wearing a magnificent dress and bowed before his guru, Issana.*[12]

The above account is curious because it is the only recorded incident of crucifixion in the long history of Kashmir. This account, recorded by Kalhana in about 1148 AD, proves that in the early twelfth century, there existed a faded impression of a person having been put on the cross by the king. Kalhana, the most famous historian of India, was Hindu, and during his period Islam had not entered the valley of Kashmir, and he was not aware of Muslims. He had no knowledge of Christianity. But he says that his history is based on earlier manuscripts which were available to him. This shows that the above incident of crucifixion and subsequent resurrection had been recorded by earlier historians of Kashmir.

It is significant that the period of the crucifixion of Jesus in Palestine and the crucifixion of Samdimati in Kashmir is roughly the same. The only confusion is that in the Kashmiri version Issana has been mentioned as the teacher of Samdimati. What are the similarities between Jesus and Samdimati?

A close examination of both incidents reveals that both were ordered to be put on the cross by the king. At the same time both are accused of sedition against the government. Both are covered with perfumes and ointments. Both of them resurrect after crucifixion. The main conclusion which I can draw from the above account is that the story of crucifixion *was* known to the Kashmiri people about two thousand years ago. Someone prior to the twelfth century must have recorded a faded account of the incident. Whether or not it is an accurate record of real events, the very existence of this story is significant, indicating cultural contact and influence.

The end of Christianity in Kashmir

Christian communities survived in Persia, Afghanistan and Kashmir until the third century, according to my researches. These Christians were called *Nasara* and *Kristani*. Several crosses had been found by Christian missionaries on graves lying in the valleys of north India[13], though they surmised them to be the graves of Nestorians. I have not been able to locate where these crosses have gone. However, some interesting information has come to light:

> *The Nasara had forty priests who were well-read in the Talmud, the Torah, the Bible and the Apocalypse of Abraham. They would sit in the royal court and give verdict on cases referred to them by the Raja of Kashmir. After the advent of the Holy Prophet of Islam, these priests came to know that in their own scriptures, the Holy Prophet had been mentioned. In order to inquire into this matter, they deputed a mission under the leadership of Ganum Hindi to Balakh in Central Asia for advice and consultation with the chief priest. But Ganum Hindi saw that the region had accepted the truth of Islam. After some time he returned to Kashmir, and the remaining Nasara and Kristani converted and became Muslims. After this, they collectively joined the fold of Islam[14].*

This conversion will have taken place some time after the time of the Prophet, after the year 570. However, while this information is scanty, it indicates the existence of a small group of Christians in Kashmir, who collectively converted, and thus lost their separate identity, somewhere between 570 and 962, the date of the death of Shaikh-us-Sadiq, who recorded this information. All trace of the Kristani in Kashmir was wiped out, except for the tomb of Yuzu Asaph at Rozabal, Kashmir.

The Muslims of Issa

I have, however, found out about a community calling themselves the *Muslims of Issa*, living in Afghanistan:

> *The followers of Issa, son of Mariam, generally call themselves Muslims, and inhabit a number of villages scattered throughout the western area of Afghanistan whose centre is Herat. I have heard of them several times, but considered that they were probably the people who had been converted by the European missionaries from eastern Persia, or that they were a relic of the time when Herat had been a flourishing bishopric of the Nestorians, before the Arabs conquered Persia in the seventh and eighth centuries. But, from their own accounts, and from what I could observe, they seem to have come from a much older source. There must be about a thousand of these Christians. Their chief is Abba Yahiya, who can recite the succession of teachers through nearly sixty generations, to Issa, son of Mariam of Nasara, the Kashmiri[15].*

It is a puzzle that Burke speaks of *Issa of Nasara, the Kashmiri.* It implies that he came from Kashmir to teach them, and that they thought of him as Kashmiri or arrived from Kashmir. It was by chance that I located *Mujuzat-i-Masih*, edited by Farooq Argalli, which makes mention of *Issa, son of Mariam*, who preached Islam and not Christianity. Here are some interesting passages:

> *When Issa was young, revelations from Allah came to him through Jabreel. He asked people to shed kufur [see footnote following]. The Beni Israel stood, one and all, against him. He performed many miracles, and many became Muslims by making the invocation 'La-illa-ha-illul-la Issa Roh Allah', meaning that 'there is no God but Allah, and Jesus is the*

*spirit of Allah'. Once Issa went on a long journey along with his mother,
and she died due to fatigue. After her burial, he went to the city and called
people towards Allah. The kafir became his enemies, and employed a
yuhudi named Shiyuh to kill him. When the kafirs surrounded Issa's
house, Shiyuh went in but could not find Issa there, because Allah had
taken Issa up to heaven. When Shiyuh came out, his face had transfigured. The kafirs got hold of him, thinking that he was Issa, and they
killed him. Allah had protected Issa*[16].

Now I will quote from Burke:

*The followers of Issa, son of Mariam, call themselves Muslims. Once a
week, they join a ritual meal in which bread and wine are taken as
symbolic of the grosser and finer nutritions, which are the experiences of
attainment of nearness to Allah. They are convinced too that the day
would come when the world would discover the truth about Jesus*[17].

This line of work requires more research, and my wish is that
scholars would join me in uncovering the truth about this matter.

(1) Lord, Rev J H, *The Jews in India and the Far East*, SPCK, Bombay, 1907;
Frayzel, Solomon, *A History of the Jews*, Mentor, New York, 1947 & 1968, p639;
Benjamin, Yehoshua, *Mystery of the Lost Tribes*, New Delhi, 1989, p35. "A brief
history of Chinese Jews mentions that the earliest Jewish settlement in China was
during the first two centuries. It is not known as to why the Jews had to settle in
this far-off land. Perhaps one explanation can be that the Lost Tribes had already
reached Kashmir".
(2) Holditch, Thomas, *The Gates of India*, Macmillan, London, 1910, p50; Wolff,
Joseph, *Account of a Mission to Bokhara in the years 1843-45*, Parker, London, 1845;
Qureshi, Aziz Ahmad, *Asrar-Kashir* (Urdu), Srinagar, 1964; Sadiq, Mufti
Muhammad, *Qabr-i-Masih* (Urdu), Qadian, 1936; Bernier, Francois, *Travels in
the Mughal Empire*, tr Irving Black, London, 1891; Vigne, G T, *Travels in
Kashmir, Ladak and Iskardu*, London, 1842.
(3) Bryce, James, and Johnson, Keith, *Comprehensive Dictionary of Geography*,
Collins, London, 1880, p25; Benjamin, Yehoshua, *Mystery of the Lost Tribes*,
pp30–32.
(4) *Matthew*, 15, 24. Here Jesus proclaims the purpose of his advent in these
terms: "I am not sent but unto the lost sheep of the house of Israel". It is for this
reason that Caiaphas, the high priest, told Mary and others that Jesus had not
come "for that nation only", but for the main purpose that "he should also
gather together those children of God that were scattered abroad" (*John*, 11, 52).

It is for this reason that Jesus commanded his disciples "to go to the lost sheep of the house of Israel" (*Matthew*, 10, 6).

(5) Bernier, Francois, *Travels in the Mughal Empire*, Archibald Constable tr, OUP, London, 1891 & 1914, p75. The travels pertain to the period 1656–68.

(6) Al Beruni, *Kitab-al Hind*, or *India*, tr Edward Sachau, London 1888, vol 1, p206.

(7) *John*, 10, 14–16.

(8) Hassnain, F M, *Hindu Kashmir*, Light & Life Pubs, New Delhi, 1977, pp18–20.

(9) *Bhavishya Mahapurana*, (Sanskrit manuscript in Sharda alphabets), Oriental research Library, Univ of Kashmir, Srinagar; *Bhavishya Maha Purana* (Hindi), tr Vidyavaridi Shiv Nath Shastri, Venkateshvaria Press, Bombay, 1917; *Bhavishya Maha Purana*, tr & comm in Hindi, Oriental Research Inst, Poona, 1910.

(10) *Bhavishya Maha Purana*, v 17–32, manuscript, and separate printed edition, ch 3, sec 2, Shaloke 9–31, Oriental Manuscript Library, Srinagar, Kashmir.

(11) Stein, M A, tr, *Kalhana's Rajatarangini*, 2 vols, London, 1900, reprints New Delhi, 1961 & 1979.

(12) Stein, tr, *Rajatarangini*, book 11, 65–171. "An interesting feature is that in *Rajatarangini of Kalhana*, we have a description of a man of God who wrought miracles similar to those of Jesus. His name is said to be *Isana*. In point of time, he is said to belong to the first century AD. It seems very probable indeed that the life-events and episodes attributed to Isana are the life and events of Issa, otherwise Jesus" – *Truth about the Crucifixion*, p140.

(13) Bull, School of Oriental Studies, London, 9, 1938, p502; Francke, A H, *Sitzungsber der Berliner Akad Phil His, Kl*, 1925; Barkat Ullah, Rev, *Tarikh-i-Kalisa* or *History of the Churches in India*, (Urdu), Lahore, p120, 157.

(14) *Asool-i-Kafi*, (Arabic), Kitab-al-Hijat, p334; Shara, *Asool-i-Kafi*, (Urdu), vol III, p304; Shaikh-us-Sadiq, *Kamal-ud-Din*, p243; Sadiq, Mufti Muhammad, *Qabr-i-Masih*, p43–46.

(15) Burke, O M, *Among the Dervishes*, London, 1973, p12.

(16) Farooq Argalli, ed, *Mujuzat-i-Masih* or *Miracles of the Messiah*, (Urdu), Rattan & Co, Delhi, p26. The word *kufur* means disbelief, and *kafir* signifies a disbeliever.

(17) Burke, O M, *Among the Dervishes*, p13. "When Nadir Shah was marching to the conquest of India (1737), arrived at Peshawar, the chief of the tribe of the *Yoosoofzyes* presented him with a Bible written in Hebrew, and several articles that had been used in their ancient worship" – Ferrier, *History of the Afghans*, tr from French by John Murray, London, 1858.

19

The Writings of
the Mullas

Persian records of Yuzu Asaph in Kashmir
On researching further, I learned that Jesus had been mentioned by
a Persian historian also. My attention was drawn towards Mulla
Nadiri and his *Tarikh-i-Kashmir*. The manuscript was in the possession of the son of the chief caretaker of Rozabal, a friend of
mine, Sahibzada Basharat Salim. He avoided the issue for years,
but I came to know why he felt reservation over showing the
manuscript to me. At that time, I never knew Sahibzada Basharat
Salim claimed descent from Yuzu Asaph. In 1976 he informed
Andreas Faber Kaiser that Yuzu Asaph, on his arrival in Kashmir,
had married a Kashmiri shepherdess named Miran, and that he was
a descendant[1].

I have found only one reference to this issue of Jesus' marriage, *Nigariatan-i-Kashmir* by Zahur-ul-Hassan. On Jesus' arrival
in Kashmir, the Hindu king offered to place a number of women at
his service, but he declined this offer, saying he would have only
one maid servant. I surmised that Jesus maybe had children with
this lady, and that maybe Sahibzada Basharat Salim is justified to
claim descent from them. He, being a Muslim, cannot declare this
openly, for fear of Muslims who could give him a lot of trouble.
For this reason he would not show me the manuscript of the
history written by Mulla Nadiri, nor documents relating to his
family background. However, to foreigners he still confides that
he is a descendant of Yuzu Asaph[2]. But while in search of Mulla
Nadiri's manuscript I had been dragged into another controversy:

198

Tarikh-i-Kashmir: the first history of Kashmir (1420 AD) by Mulla Nadri, describes Jesus as an apostle of God sent to minister to the Kashmiri people

did Jesus marry, in Palestine or Kashmir?

A study of Persian works on the history of Kashmir and Iran reveals much useful information about the Lost Tribes of Israel, their settlements and assimilation among Eastern people, and also about Jesus of Nazareth. Among Muslims, Jesus is known as *Issa* or *Yusu* and one has to look for these names in these works. *Rauz-us-Safa* by Mir Mohammad, written in 1417, deals with the journey of Jesus from Jerusalem to Nisibis. Another Persian work, *Kamal-ud-Din*, by Shaikh Said us Sadiq (912 AD) tells of the visit of Thomas to Kashmir. The most important information in this work concerns the teachings and prayers of Jesus Christ in Persia.

The work by Mulla Nadiri, written in 1420, deals with the ministry of Jesus in Kashmir. He says that Yuzu Asaph came to Kashmir from Palestine. I will now translate the relevant passage:

Raja Ach ascended the throne and ruled for 60 years. He founded the town of Achabal in Kotiar, Kashmir. After his death, his son Gopa-

nanda ruled the country, under the name of Gopadatta. During his reign many temples were built and repaired. At that time the dome of the temple on the top of Solomon hill had cracked. He asked one of his ministers, named Sulaiman, who had come from Persia, to repair the cracked dome of the temple. On this, the local Hindus raised objections saying that as Sulaiman was an infidel and followed another religion, he had no right to repair the sacred temple of the Hindus.

During this very period, Hazrat Yuzu Asaph arrived from the Holy Land, Bait ul Maquaddas, to the Holy Valley, Wadi a Aqddas, and proclaimed his ministry. He absorbed himself in prayers day and night, and having attained an elevated position in virtue and piety, he declared to the people of Kashmir that he was the messenger of God. He called upon the people to follow the words of God, and many believed in him. Thereupon, Raja Gopadatta referred the objections of Hindus to him for his decision. It was under his orders that Sulaiman, whom the local Hindus named Sandiman, completed the repairs of the cracked dome of the temple, in the year 54. Sulaiman also had engraved the following inscriptions on the stones leading to the stairs of the temple: "During this period Yuzu Asaph declared his Ministry. He was Yusu, the Prophet of the Children of Israel".

In a work by a Hindu it is said that this Prophet was in reality Hazrat Issa, the Soul of God – on whom be peace and salutations. He had assumed the name of Yuzu Asaph during his life in the valley. The real knowledge is with Allah. After his demise, Hazrat Issa, on whom be peace and salutations, was laid to rest in the tomb in the locality of Anzimar. It is also said that the rays of prophethood used to emanate from the tomb of this Prophet. Raja Gopadatta passed away after having ruled for 60 years and 2 months[3].

It took me a few months to completely analyse the value of the information given by Mulla Nadiri. I drew the following conclusions:

a) Yuzu Asaph is Issa of the Muslims and Jesus of the Christians;

b) Yuzu Asaph came from Palestine to Kashmir during the reign of Raja Gopadatta (79-109 AD);

Takhat-i-Sulaiman, The Throne of Solomon, a temple on the Sankarachariya Hill at Srinagar, commemorates the visit of Solomon to Kashmir *(Frank Sache)*

c) Yuzu, Prophet of the Children of Israel, proclaimed his ministry in Kashmir in the year 54 AD;

d) Sulaiman had this inscribed on the stones of the stairs leading to the sacred temple on the hill of Solomon.

Takhat Sulaiman

The last result attracted my attention because of my archaeological interest. On the top of a hillock near the Dal Lake in Srinagar, we have the edifice known to Kashmiri Muslims as *Takhat Sulaiman* or the Throne of Solomon. At the time of the Hindu Maharaja, the edifice was renamed *Sankarachariya*, from 1848 on. I inspected the temple several times but found no inscription there. However, there were some scattered traces of a mosque nearby. Only at a short distance from the temple there were some graves hidden in the green grass. I found, in a travel account by Vigne[4], mention that these were the graves of Hebrew artisans employed by Sulaiman in repairing this temple. I also found that Mirza Haider Malik

201

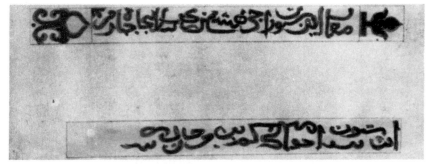

The Takhat-i-Sulaiman inscription says "The mason of this pillar is Bhisti Zargar Year 54."

Chaudura (16th century) mentions four inscriptions instead of two:

> *The mason of this pillar is Bhisti Zargar, Year 54. Khwaja Rukun son of Mirjan erected this pillar.During this period Yuzu Asaph declared his ministry. He was Yusu, the Prophet of the Children of Israel*[5].

Major H H Cole, in his archaeological treatise *Illustrations of Ancient Buildings in Kashmir*, gives a photograph of two inscriptions. But he remarks that there are also two mutilated inscriptions in each side of the two flank walls encasing the stairs. Their characters are in Persian[6].

Mulla Nadiri has mentioned that Sulaiman, entrusted with the repairs of this temple, had come from Persia. This explains why these inscriptions are in Persian. Secondly, the names of the two chief masons show that they were the Jews from Persia. All four inscriptions have been recorded by other Kashmiri historians[7], slightly altered according to the choice of the authors. However, mention of Year 54 is significant, inasmuch as it gives a date to Jesus' arrival and the beginning of his ministry in Kashmir.

Note that since Islam did not exist during the reign of Gopadatta (79–109 AD), connecting the year 54 with the Muslim Hijra Era is absurd. During that period, the Laukika Era was exclusively used in Kashmir. As this era started in 3076 BC, the 54th year mentioned in the inscription would come to either 22 BC or 78 AD (since Laukika Year 1 is 3076 BC, 3054 would be 22 BC, and 3154 would be 78 AD.) As it was not possible for Jesus Christ to have travelled to Kashmir in 22 BC, I take the year 78 AD to be the correct date of his arrival.

Corroborations

Shaikh-us-Sadiq Ali Mohammed, the great writer of Khorasan, composed his monumental work in Persian before his death in 912 AD. He was the first Muslim scholar to make mention of the two journeys of Yuzu Asaph in the East. He stated that Yuzu Asaph died in Kashmir, and that Thomas was present at the time of his death. In this work, sayings and parables of Yuzu Asaph are given, quoted below, which tally with those given in the Gospels.

Mulla Nadiri completed his work *Tarikh-i-Kashmir* before 1416, clearly mentioning that Jesus Christ came from Palestine and declared his ministry in Kashmir. He also gave the definite date of this as the Year 54 (78 AD). He also located the site of the tomb of Yuzu Asaph.

In his classic work in seven volumes, called *Rauzat-us-Safa*, Mir Mohammed Khwand wrote about the journey of Jesus from Jerusalem, through Nisibis, mentioning no more because Jesus then apparently "set the seal of silence on his lips".

Khwaja Mohammed Azam Deedamari, in his *Waqiat-i-Kashmir* of 1729, mentions Hazrat Yuzu Asaph, a prophet who came to Kashmir in ancient times from a distant land. He said that Yuzu Asaph had invited the people of Kashmir to repent and lead a life of devotion and prayers. He was the Prophet of Allah to the people of Kashmir. His tomb in Anzimar he reported to be full of grace and blessings.

The decree granted in favour of the keeper of the tomb by the Grand Mufti of Kashmir in 1766 mentions Yuzu Asaph as a messenger of God to the people of Kashmir. It mentions that Yuzu Asaph proclaimed his ministry during the reign of Gopadatta, in about 78 AD.

In research work entitled *Masih Hindustan Mein*, compiled in 1899, published in 1908, Mirza Ghulam Ahmad declared that Jesus Christ did not die on the cross but escaped to India in quest of the lost tribes of Israel. He made Kashmir his home and there he died. His tomb had been traced and found in Kashmir.

The Sermons of Yuzu Asaph

Some scanty but significant information is available about the
sermons of Jesus Christ in Kashmir. I compared these with his
teaching in the New Testament. To my surprise, I found many
parallels. Here are some examples:

> *Listen! I say unto thee words of wisdom and truth, so that ye may be
> able to make a distinction between right and wrong. Indeed this is the
> duty of those to whom the words of God come! I say unto thee that
> whosoever discards righteousness shall not enter heaven*[8].
>
> *Seek ye the kingdom of heaven, rather than that of the world. Woe
> unto the seekers of the world, for they shall perish. Verily, I say unto
> thee: death keeps no calendar. When the hour comes even the birds have
> no power over their enemies, save ye with faith.*
>
> *I say unto thee: so long as there is light ye may travel, yet keep
> your good deeds secret, lest these be for show only. Blessed are they
> [that do so], for they know that they shall be treated in the same way*[9].

These passages are remarkably similar in content to many in the
Bible. For comparison, I will quote another sermon attributed to
Jesus, recorded by oriental scholars:

> *My food is fasting, my natural condition is fear, my dress is a sack made
> from wool. My hearth is the sun in winter, my light in the night is the
> moon, my conveyance is my feet, my food the berries of the forest.
> When I go to sleep, I have nothing with me, and when I rise, I rise
> empty-handed. None is richer than me on this earth.*
>
> *Concentrate your thoughts upon God, and lead a detached life. If
> you aspire to meet God, concentrate upon Him.*
>
> *I say unto thee: shun worldly desires, give up anger and keep your
> heart pure. If you employ all energy to attain your aim with clear
> thoughts, even a thorn may be turned into a rose garland*[10].

We know from the Bible that Jesus taught in striking parables.
One of the best known of these is the parable of the sower of seeds:

> *Listen! A sower went out to sow. And as he sowed, some seed fell along
> the path, and the birds came and devoured it. Other seed fell on rocky*

ground, where it had not much soil, and immediately it sprang up, since it had no depth of soil, and when the sun rose it was scorched, and since it had no depth of root, it withered away. Other seed fell among thorns, and the thorns grew up and choked it, and it yielded no grain. And other seeds fell into good soil and brought forth grain, growing up and increasing and yielding thirtyfold and sixtyfold and a hundredfold. And he said: He who has ears to hear, let him hear[11].

It appears that Jesus taught this very parable in the East too, in a slightly different form. Shaikh-us-Saddiq records the following teaching:

By the sower is meant the wise person. By the seeds is meant his words of wisdom! The seeds picked up by the birds means those who do not understand. The seeds on the stony ground mean words of wisdom not heeded. The seeds that fall on thorns means those who do not heed. By the seeds which fall on good ground means those who understand, obey and follow[12].

The question arises as to whether his words had impact on the people. From time to time, the valley has witnessed inroads and migrations from all sides, and Kashmiris have been ruthlessly killed and assimilated by the invaders. There have been religious conversions, and people have changed their religions to save themselves. There have been Buddhists, Shaivites and Hindus at various times, and at present most are followers of Islam. Thus their culture appears mixed, an amalgam of many traditions and civilisations. They still retain Jewish traits from so many centuries ago. They retain some moral teachings of the Buddha. and some Buddhist customs and traditions such as reverence of relics and binding of thread at shrines. I feel that the teachings of Jesus in his new personality as Yuzu Asaph did have some effect on Buddhists. I will take up this issue next.

---

(1) Faber-Kaiser, Andreas, *Jesus died in Kashmir*, London, 1978, p93. A portion of the letter sent by Sahibzada Basharat Saleem to Andreas Faber-Kaiser, and reproduced in the above work reads as follows: "Finally, as regards your query, I would gladly tell you that the pious shepherdess married by Yuzu

Asaf was named *Marjan*, who was brought up amidst the enchanting and captivating scenic locales of heavenly and wild mountainous ranges of Pahalgam in Kashmir".

(2) For example, Forsström, Johan, *The King of the Jews*, p164.Is there anything to indicate that Jesus married before or after crucifixion? The Gospels are silent on the subject except some camouflaged references to Martha and her sister Mary who is also surnamed Magdalene. Despite periodical changes made by redactors, we can still find that Martha had only one sister, named Mary (*John*, 11), and demons were cast out of her body by Jesus (*Luke*, 10) and anointed his feet (*John*, 12). This Mary would accompany Jesus during his ministry and travels, without any guardian. The authors of *Holy Blood and Holy Grail* (London, 1982) have concluded that the wife of Jesus arrived in France along with her child in 36 AD. They settled down in a Jewish community in Marseilles. All this pertains to the pre-crucifixion period – see Forsström, Johan, *King of the Jews*, p164. In his letter dated August 8, 1985, Sahibzada Basharat Saleem informs the author: "By descent, as you might have read, I am a Palestinian, and my Holy Ancestor travelled from Jerusalem to Kashmir... Also, significantly, many foreign film-makers, notably from Germany, France and USA, have produced a number of films on me and my family. The chief mission of my life being to see goodwill and peace prevail on earth, I will always guide you with blessings and unrestricted tolerance. This is the gospel of truth. Lord be with you".See also: Zahur-ul-Hassan Nizami, *Nigaristan-i-Kashmir*, (Urdu), Hyderabad, 1941.

(3) Mulla Nadiri, *Tarikh i Kashmir*, Folio 69.

(4) Vigne, G T, *Travels in Kashmir, Ladakh and Iskardo*, 2 vols, Henry Colburn, London, 1842, pp395-397; and *A Personal Narrative of a visit to Ghuzni, Kabul and Afghanistan*, London, 1843; Wolff, Joseph, *A Narrative of a Mission to Bokhara 1843-1845*, London, 1846. *Takhat Sulaiman* or the Throne of Solomon is a commemorative edifice constructed in memory of Solomon's visit to Kashmir. It is curious that ancient Ethiopia was called Kush, and Solomon's consort, the Queen of Sheba, had a son, Menelik, by him. According to another legend, it was Menelik who brought Jewish artisans from Turkestan for repair of this historic edifice. In Kashmiri, there is a famous song which celebrates Solomon's visit to the valley – *Qabr-i-Masih*, by Mufti Muhammad Sadiq, p21.

(5) Mulla Nadiri, *Tarikh-i-Kashmir*, folio 35; Mirza Haider Malik Chaudura, *Tarikh-i-Kashmir*, (Persian), Muhammadi Press, Lahore, folio 12; Khanyari, Mufti Ghulam Nabi, *Wajeez-ut-Tawarikh* (Persian), Oriental Manuscript Library, Univ of Kashmir, Srinagar, vol 1, folio 54; Sadiq, Mufti Muhammad, *Qabr-i-Masih* (Urdu), p21; Khwaja, Nazir Ahmad, *Jesus in Heaven on Earth*, p370; *Truth about the Crucifixion*, p143.

(6) Cole, Major H H, *The Illustration of Ancient Buildings in Kashmir*, W H Allen, London, 1869, p8.

(7) Such as Mulla Nadiri, Mirza Haider Malik Chaudura, Mufti Ghulam Nabi Khanyari and Pirzada Ghulam Hassan Khuyami, historians of Kashmir,

whose Persian works are preserved at the Oriental Manuscript Library, University of Kashmir, the Archives Reference Library, the Cultural Academy Library, and SPS Public Library, all in Srinagar, Kashmir.

(8) Shaikh al-Said-us-Saddiq, *Kamal-ud-Din*, p359.

(9) Shaikh al-Said-us-Sadiq, *Kamal-ud-Din*, p359.

(10) Williams, Rushbrook, ed, *Sufi Studies: East and West*, Octagon Press, 1973, p202.

(11) *Mark*, 4, 3-8.

(12) Shaikh al-Said-us-Saddiq, *Kamal-ud-Din*, p327.

20

Buddhism and Christianity

During his first journey to India, Jesus had lived with Buddhists for six years. According to the Buddhist scrolls at Hemis, "the Buddha had elected him to spread his holy word. As such, he had become a perfect expositor of the sacred scriptures[1]. The following information recorded by Meer Izzut-Oolah, the early nineteenth century Islamic traveller, is full of interest:

Every Tibetan makes one of his sons a Lama – the one who has forsaken the world. Both male and female Lamas remain unmarried like priests and nuns, and are the spiritual guides to the people. They do not worship the idols kept in their monasteries, which they declare are merely representations of departed saints. Some of these figures are said to represent a certain prophet, who is living alive in the heavens, which would appear to point to Jesus Christ.

The Tibetans consider their scriptures to be inspired, and contain many moral precepts and exhortations to worship God, to fulfil promises, speak the truth and abandon what is evil. It is commanded that if any man takes away your sheet, you give him your cloak also. Again, if anyone strikes you on one cheek, you tell him to strike the other cheek also. Many of their observations are similar to those of Christians.

Their great feast is held at the time when the sun enters Capricorn, corresponding with Christmas. Another similar custom is to swear in the name of Trinity, which they term as 'Kunchok Sum' or 'Gods Three'. In the infliction on themselves of heavy penances also, the Buddhist monks resemble the Christian priests. The Tibetans assert that their original scripture was in a language now become unintelligible to them and has been translated to them. I was informed that some portions of the Bible had been revealed to the Tibetans[2].

I do not know who borrowed from whom. But I am struck by the extraordinary similarity between doctrine, traditions and rituals of Buddhism and the Catholic Church. Even their ranks in monastic orders resemble each other. Both Buddhists and Roman Catholic monks take vows of celibacy, poverty, chastity and obedience. It is amazing that both Buddhists and Catholics make suffrage (intercessory prayers), alms, prayers and offerings on a similar model. This similarity is so striking that one scholar made the observation that "Buddhism is the Christianity of the East and as such is in better conservation than is Christianity, the Buddhism of the West"[3].

It would be ungrateful on my part if I did not mention that it was the research treatise written by Mirza Ghulam Ahmad which impelled me to take up researches pertaining to Buddhist sources on the life and works of Jesus Christ. In his treatise, the learned scholar has given thought-provoking ideas about similarity between Christianity and Buddhism. He has pointed out that both Jesus and the Buddha were tempted by the Devil. The mode of teaching in parables is the same with both of them. Their titles are similar, their teachings are similar and even some of their parables are the same. Both make the same claim: "I am the Light and the Way"[4].

In search of Buddhist scrolls

Hippolytus, who was the Bishop of Rome in about 220 AD mentions a Judaeo-Christian scripture in the land of the Seres in Parthia. During this period, the name Seres denoted a region which produced silk and existed in the north of India. According to their tradition the holy book of Revelation had fallen from the heavens for *Elxai*, who was the incarnation of God on this earth. His sect believed in successive incarnations of heavenly power. I would guess that somewhere there is a connection between Elxai and his scripture, and the Buddhist lamas, and their information on Jesus.

It is interesting to note that early Christians in the West knew of the Eastern books on Christianity in the beginning of the third century AD.

The Ebionites cherished similar beliefs to those upheld by Buddhists. The Ebionites are the early Judaeo-Christians, who believed in the celestial mission of Jesus, but regarded him as an ordinary man born of Joseph and Mary. They followed James the Just, who was the head of the church at Jerusalem. As such, they denounced Paul and his teachings. They observed the Law of Moses, for which they were declared heretics. Their Gospel, which was earlier known as the *Gospel according to the Hebrews*, was modified, altered and revised in the form of the *Gospel according to Matthew*.

They believe in the reincarnation of the coming Christ, like the Buddhist belief in the coming Buddha, which makes clear that we have traces of parallelism in the doctrines of both the communities. For this reason many scholars feel there is an urgent need to make a search of documents and scrolls about Jesus Christ in north India, Tibet and Central Asia. Unfortunately, most of these relics have been stolen by the Western scholars, archaeologists and orientalists. But there may be still some scrolls lying buried underground or in huge collections of works in the Buddhist monasteries of Ladakh, Tibet and Central Asia.

I went to Ladakh a number of times to make a search. It was Nicolas Notovitch who had found the Buddhist scrolls in Ladakh. These scrolls can be divided into three sections; the first dealing with the reincarnation of Jesus, the second with his travels to India and the third deals with his ministry in Palestine. Publication of these scrolls by Notovitch, first in French and then in English, created a row among Christians of his time. Some denied the existence of such scrolls, stating that these were fictitious. But some believed that the scrolls were real and there was a need to find documents about the missing years in the life of Jesus. As the issue touched the very foundations of Christian dogma, the Church accelerated its efforts to dispatch agents into India, Tibet and other countries "to trace, buy, confiscate and steal ancient documents referring *inter alia* to Jesus' life in India and death in Kashmir"[5].

Shortly before the pilgrims departed, the librarian, carrying ancient mss
approached Mrs Caspari on the roof of the gompa and said;
"These books say your Jesus was here." *(Summit Univ. Press)*

Notovitch had found these Scrolls in 1887 in Hemis *gompa* in
Ladakh. In 1922, Swami Abhedananda succeeded in finding another version, slightly different from that found by Notovitch. He
published an account of his journey, along with a portion of the
text of the scroll he found at Hemis in his Bengali book *Kashmir-
o-Tibbate*[6].

The Chief Lama had made a serious allegation to Nicholas
Notovitch around 1810 that many Muslims would like to possess
these scrolls – which is very significant.[7] But why Muslims should
try to get them is not clear. Maybe the Church employed these
Muslims agents. I have read about one such attempt made by the
Church to depute a neo-Christian Ahmad Shah to Ladakh in 1894,
for this very sinister purpose. He wrote a book, *Four Years in Tibet*,
in which he tried "to refute the finding of Nicolas Notovitch"[8].

Despite my efforts, I could not find these Scrolls. I think that
due to their fear of the British, the masters of India up to 1947, the
Lamas may have concealed these Scrolls in the underground cells,

211

Monks at Hemis come out to greet the Caspari party in 1939 *(Summit Univ. Press)*

which they call the 'Black Treasure'.

In 1939, Elizabeth Caspari visited Hemis monastery. To her surprise, the Lama showed her some scrolls saying: "These books say your Jesus was here". She and her companions looked at these parchments in awe[9].

My search persuaded me that almost all documents about Jesus have found their way into the hands of neo-Christians in Ladakh, or the Church authorities. With much effort and persuasion, I located a Tibetan translation made in 1802 from an ancient Chinese manuscript, *The History of Religion and Doctrines – the Glass Mirror*. This was an ancient Chinese manuscript translated into Tibetan by Le-zan Chhes-kyi Nima in 1802, called *Grugtha Thamschand kyi Khuna dan Dod-Thsul Ston-pe Legs Shad Shel-gyi Melong*[10].

> *Yesu, the teacher and founder of the religion, who was born miraculously, proclaimed himself the Saviour of the World. He commanded his disciples to observe the ten vows, among which includes prohibition of manslaughter and attainment of eternal joy through good deeds. He preached that evil actions plunge one into hell, where there is eternal torment and misery. A sin committed in a state of consciousness cannot be condoned or pardoned. This is one of the virtuous results emerging out of the teachings of the Buddha. His doctrines did not spread extensively, but survived only in Asia, for a long period. The above information is derived from the Chinese treatises on religions and doctrines.*

I found this manuscript in the care of S S Gergan, who has a rich collection of Chinese, Tibetan and Ladakhi documents, scrolls and manuscripts. His father, Rev Gergan, was the first Ladakhi Christian priest, who translated the New Testament into Ladakhi. It is natural that being a Christian, he worked with zeal in his missionary work, and may have obtained many documents relating to the traces of Christianity in Ladakh and Tibet[11].

We are told by the same author that it was a certain Babaad who performed the burial rites of Yuzu Asaph in the Jewish tradition. Who was this Babaad? It is interesting to find that *Babaad*, in Arabic, means 'twins who suck milk from the same

The Glass Mirror – an ancient Chinese History of Religions (translated into Tibetan entitled Grub-tha-Thamas-Chad) mentions "Yesu" and his teachings in Asia

mother'. According to Jewish tradition, a corpse had to remain on a shelf until its decomposition, so that the bones could be stored in a wooden or stone chest. I was not able to find any details about this. The only information available was that the dead body of Yuzu Asaph was laid in sepulchre according to the Jewish tradition. A cave-type sepulchre was made by cutting through a huge mound of earth.

Early Christian relics

It is interesting to note that early Christian relics and tombs have been located in the north-western regions of India. Relics and tombs have also been found in Ladakh, Gilgit, Afghanistan, Baluchistan, Tibet and Central Asia.

In Ladakh, at Tangste, there are big stone boulders on which are carved crosses. An inscription in Aramaic says that Churn, a native of Samarkand, traversed a few hundred marches to reach this site. Further, the name Yusu is also engraved near the crosses

214

found in northern India in archaeological excavations[12]. These relics demonstrate the existence of Judaeo-Christian settlements in the region in ancient times. But the Church has refuted this claim by saying that the relics pertain to Nestorian Christians of the early fifth century[13].

However, it is significant that the Aramaic language was not flourishing in the fifth century. These relics and tombs pertain to very early period of Christianity. When the Archaeological Survey of India located these Judaeo-Christian relics, its Director, a Christian, gave the following explanation:

> At Hindan, on the right bank of the river Hab, near Las Bela in Sind, is an extensive cemetery, containing nearly one hundred sepulchres, ornamented with sandstone slabs. Constructed with layers of carved slabs, these sepulchres give the general appearance of slender pyramids.
>
> A peculiar feature of the ornamented slabs is that some slabs carry crude representations of the Cross. In some slabs, the design shows a human figure with outstretched arms, mounted on an ass with a representation of a crucifix. Some slabs show a knight-in-arms, riding on a horse. Another slab shows a small cross on the face of the horseman. Another un-Islamic feature of these sepulchres is the peculiar form of their burial, which is Syrian as well as Roman[14].

It is significant that these tombs with crosses and a crucified human being date back to the first century. All the signs carved on them demonstrate that these graves belong to early Christians who may have migrated to or settled in Hindan, Sindh. The *Report of the Archaeological Survey of India* has made an important observation regarding the two kinds of burials, without any explanation. It is mentioned only that the peculiar form of their burial is Syrian as well as Roman, and it is un-Islamic.

It is also significant that many slabs exhibit lotus flowers and inscriptions in Arabic also. This suggests that in later periods these Christians had to change their religion. They may have become Buddhists, as indicated by the lotus flowers. The Arabic inscriptions prove that ultimately, they embraced Islam. It is also significant that these early Christians came from Rome and Syria.

In the valley of Kashmir, I found graves oriented in the east-west direction, contrary to the Islamic tradition. Also in Kashmir, beside the usual form of graves we do have another form known as *Mosai*, or 'to the style of Moses'. In the early days of Islam, the Muslims used to pray facing the Temple of Jerusalem. Later the Prophet ordered that the Muslims were to face the Holy House of God in Mecca in Arabia. The followers of Judaism built their graves in the east-west direction, but later when they became Muslims they changed to the north-south direction.

Among the Christian relics, I was fascinated by a Kushana seal of the first century, preserved in the British Museum, London. It shows a Scythian dignitary on the horse, holding a cross in his hand. It is interesting to note that the designatory is 'RA' on the seal, and RA means Raja, the title adopted by the Indo-Scythians. Holding of the cross in the hand implies that the figure is Christian of the first century. His cap and bridle is Central Asian. This demonstrates that during the first century Christianity did exist in Central Asia.

A review of Christian sources

Among early Christian writings, the New Testament Gospels are the primary source of information about Jesus. We are told about his genealogy, birth and migration to Egypt. These events cover four years of his life. There is then a gap of eight years, when, at the age of twelve, Jesus visits the Temple in Jerusalem. After this, his life becomes an empty mystery for about seventeen years. We are informed that he began a mission at the age of thirty and gathered many followers. At the insistence of Jewish priests, the Roman governor ordered Jesus to be crucified. He was put on the cross by four Roman soldiers but was taken down at the behest of Joseph of Arimathaea. He rose from the dead and lived with his followers for forty days.

The New Testament is not our only source of information about the life of Jesus. However, filling in the story from a number of texts is not easy. For example, the Gnostics' version of the crucifixion differs in important ways from that in the New Testament Gospels. In the manuscripts found at Nag Hammadi in

Egypt, we are informed that:

> *I did not succumb to them as they had planned. I did not die in reality but in appearance, and it was another who drank the gall and the vinegar. It was another, Simon, who bore the cross on his shoulder. It was another upon whom they placed the crown of thorns. I was laughing at their ignorance*[15].

It is evident that there are many contradictory reports about the life of Jesus, and we would be foolish to consider only a small range of the available sources. We would be unwise, too, to rely heavily on the discrimination of the Church, which clearly has theological and perhaps other rather more dubious interests which may be quite at odds with open-minded historical investigation.

Within 20-25 years after the departure of Jesus Christ, devotees began to collect fragmentary records of his words and deeds[16]. Paul's epistle falls within this period. Peter's version of the events in the life of Jesus was probably written slightly later. *Matthew* recorded the life and teachings of Jesus Christ, originally in the Hebrew dialect[17], but this original version is no longer available to us, and we have only a slightly later, Greek version of this first Gospel. We can safely presume that the original *Gospel according to Matthew* was written earlier then 85 AD and maybe even before 70 AD. The *Gospel of Mark* is commonly dated before 70 AD. Probable dates for compilation of the authorised Gospels have been given as: *Mark*, 60-70 AD; *Matthew*, 85 AD (or earlier); *Luke*, 90-95 AD; and *John*, 110 AD.

Luke clearly states that his compilation is based on earlier writings. He states:

> *For as much as many have taken in hand, to set forth in order a declaration of those things which are most surely believed among us, even as they delivered them unto us, which from the beginning, were eyewitnesses, and ministers of the word, it seems good to me also, having had perfect understanding of all things from the very first, to write unto thee in order, most excellent Theophilus, that thou mightest know certainty of those things, wherein thou hast been instructed*[18].

From the above, two things are clear: that many authors had undertaken to construct the life of Jesus, and that many of them derived information from the narratives of previous authors. Unfortunately, the writings of most of these earlier authors have been destroyed by the Church. Luke may have consulted the *Gospel of Mark* as well as the Gospels of other Apostles which are not available to us now.

The authorship of the *Gospel according to John* is under dispute. This Gospel has similar style and teachings to some of the Essene writings from the Dead Sea Scrolls. According to the Essenes, John the Baptist belonged to their Order, and many who were to become disciples of Jesus were first disciples of John. The *Gospel of John* provides interesting information about the first disciples, the women of Samaria, the healing of Paul, details of the crucifixion, the second coming of Jesus and meeting his disciples, and the final sermon he gave before parting from them. It tells of Joseph of Arimathaea, Nicodemus and others (who we know from the Essenes to have been members of the Order) being involved in trying to save Jesus from crucifixion.

Even if one takes only the New Testament as a source for the historical Jesus, the task is far from easy.

Texts rejected by the Church

The search for the historical Jesus has resulted in the discovery of many early Christian writings, despite the attempts of the Church to destroy evidence which contradicts its teachings. There are many other Gospels which have been either repudiated by the Church as 'unauthentic' (though it is doubtful that any of these decisions were based on historical criteria of authenticity), or they have been rejected outright as 'heretical' – such as the *Apocryphal Gospels*, which contain a great deal of information about Jesus' life and teachings.

About fifty Apocryphal Gospels have been discovered so far. Most of these works were destroyed under various decrees of the Church, but some copies have survived and seen the light of day. Tradition has handed down a list of twenty-six Apocryphal Gospels, seven Acts and ten Epistles, all used during the early days of

Christianity. Some of these original writings now exist in name only, and of some we have only a few fragments.

Tation, the famous Syriac scholar of Edessa, compiled a volume containing five Gospels in the second century AD, which became known as *The Five Gospels of Tation*. After thorough research into Greek and Hebrew sources, he compiled his Bible, which remained in vogue for hundreds of years among followers of the Syrian Church. With the coming to power of the Roman Church, the Bible compiled by Tation was ordered to be destroyed. It seems that all copies were collected and burned.

According to Tation, Mary and Jesus did not belong to the line of David. It also appears that Tation had mentioned that after resurrection, Jesus did meet his disciples, and especially his mother Mary, several times, and that he was a living being.

Fifty Apocryphal works discovered so far have been denied official patronage because they do not conform to the revised doctrines formulated by the Church. The most important Apocryphal Gospels of which we have copies still are the following: the *Gospel of the Hebrews*, the *Gospel of the Egyptians*, the *Gospel of Nicodemus*, the *Gospel of Thomas*, the *Gospel of James*, the *Gospel of Barnabas*, the *Gospel of Peter*, the *Gospel of the Ebionites* and the *Gospel of Philip*.

The *Gospel of the Hebrews* was originally written in Aramaic and then translated into Greek and Latin. It gives prominence to James, the brother of Jesus. The *Gospel of James* provides information about the childhood of Jesus. The *Gospel of Barnabus* was compiled by Joses, a Levite surnamed Barnabas, meaning the son of consolation. Barnabus describes himself as an apostle of Jesus Christ and says that he was directed by the Lord to record the life and works of Jesus. Barnabas worked together with Paul in preaching about the message of Jesus. He was an uncle to Mark and a companion to Paul, who travelled throughout Palestine preaching from his Gospel. As a missionary to Antioch, he accompanied Paul several times but parted from due to differences. Barnabus was stoned to death by the Jews at Slamis in Cyprus.

The *Gospel of Barnabas* was accepted as a canonical gospel in the churches of Alexandria until 325 AD, when the Nicene Council ordered that all copies of this Gospel be destroyed and anyone in possession of a copy be put to death. The result was that this Gospel was almost lost to posterity. The *Gospel of Barnabas* was banned in 382 AD by decree of the Western Churches. However, a manuscript seems to have existed in the private library of Pope Damascus. In the fifth century, a copy, apparently written in Barnabas' own hand, was found lying on his breast in a tomb in Cyprus. This manuscript found its way into the Library of Pope Sixtus V (1500-1590). It is believed that the manuscript was obtained from the private library of the Pope by an Italian priest, Fra Marino, and made accessible to the public by him.

The *Gospel of Thomas* and the *Gospel of Philip* are known as the Coptic Gospels because they are in Coptic and were discovered at Al-Hammadi in Egypt. They throw a great deal of light on the hidden life of Jesus. It is evident from these Gospels that the early Christians did not believe that Jesus died on the cross. They believed that he arose and remained in hiding with his disciples, eventually dying in a natural way.

The *Acts of Thomas*, or *Acta Thomae*, written by Leucius in the beginning of the second century AD, is based on letters written by Thomas from India, and was translated into German by Max Donet and published in Leipzig in 1883. The *Gospel according to Thomas*, dated about the third century, was discovered in 1947 from Luxor in Egypt[19]. It was translated from Greek into Russian in the 13th century.

It was Thomas who introduced Christianity to the south of India around 52 AD. He built many churches but suffered martyrdom in 72 AD and was buried at Mylapore, where the San Thome Cathedral Basilica stands at present. The Syrian Christians of Malabar, India, claim that Thomas was their founder. There is some evidence that Thomas may too have been an Essene.

This Gospel was proscribed by the Roman Catholic Church, probably because it denies the virgin birth of Jesus Christ. It was denounced as heretical by a Decree of Gelasius in 495 AD. The Gospel, among other things, provides information about a meeting between Jesus and Thomas at Taxila, long after the crucifixion.

It seems that most of these 'heretical' gospels were unacceptable to the church because in one way or another they portrayed Jesus as a human being. For instance, the *Gospel of James* informs us about the marriage of Mary with Joseph. In the *Gospel of the Ebionites*, Jesus is believed to have been born in a normal way, as a son of Joseph and Mary. Similarly, another Gospel says:

> *My brother, I wish to tell you about a most wonderful thing; sometimes when I wanted to touch him, I could feel a solid material body, but at other occasions, his being was immaterial as if it had not existed at all*[20].

The reasons for the banning of the *Gospel of Philip* are obvious, for it informs us that Jesus migrated towards the East with his mother and with Mary Magdalene, who appears in this Gospel as Jesus' consort.

The Church, in various councils and decrees, accepted and rejected the different Gospels, the net result of such suppression being that we are now deprived of much useful and authentic source material on the earthly life of Jesus. What is needed is that the New Testament be rearranged, with all available Gospels, Acts and Epistles included in it. Otherwise, this censorship will lead to disillusion amongst followers of the Church.

The Dead Sea Scrolls

In 1947, a number of manuscripts were discovered in a cave at Wadi Qumran, near the Dead Sea. In 1949, fragments of the Old Testament were recovered from the same cave. In 1952, a considerable number of fragments and coins were discovered in the caves of Wadi Murabbaat. These manuscripts, popularly known as the *Dead Sea Scrolls*, are the compilations of Essenes, whose community, Khirbet Qumran, was destroyed by the Romans in around 70 AD.

The Scrolls were written before the birth of Jesus. The *First Enoch* was written around 170-164 BC, and the *Testament of the Twelve Patriarchs* was compiled around 109-107 BC. During Jesus' lifetime all these scrolls, including the *Psalms of Solomon*, the *Testament of God* and the *Book of Jubilees* were available for study. In fact, the Sermon on the Mount, now included in the New Testament, was known to Jesus, for he had already read it!

---

(1) Notovitch, Nicolas, *The Life of St Issa*, IV, 1-8. The statement that Jesus became a perfect expositor of the Buddhist scriptures is thought-provoking and needs thorough research. Kanishka (78-103 AD) convened the Fourth Buddhist Council in Kashmir, for settlement of differences between various Buddhist sects. The final decisions of the Council were engraved on copper plates and deposited in a stupa (Hassnain, *Buddhist Kashmir*, New Delhi, 1973, pp21-22). Kanishka was so impressed with the progress of the Council that he handed over the administration of Kashmir to the Buddhist priests and monks. Was it Jesus who had propounded the idea of a priestly kingdom? Did he also take part in the Council? No final answer can come until these copper plates are excavated. However, it is proper to point out that Jesus himself had once declared: "All people are alike the servants of our Father-God are kings and priests" – Levi, *The Aquarian Gospel*, p74. Had not Jesus made an unsuccessful attempt to establish such a kingdom of priests in Palestine? Is it a simple coincidence that after this Council, the Mahayana iconography depicts statues showing their palms with round marks, symbolically depicting wounds of crucifixion?

(2) Meer Izzut-oolah, *Travels in Central Asia, 1812*, tr Henderson, Calcutta, 1872, p13.

(3) Williams, Sir Monier, *The Mystery of the Ages*, London, 1887, p541; Rhys Davids, T W, *Indian Buddhism*, London, 1891: "The *Chakka-Vatti* Buddha was to the early Buddhists what the Messiah *Logos* was to the early Christians. In both cases, the two ideas overlap one another, run into one another, supplement one another".

(4) Mirza Ghulam Ahmad, *Masih Hindustan Mein* (Urdu), p128. "It is indeed curious to find the name of the Messiah in a Buddhist work, though the name comes in quite accidentally" – Takakusu, J Ting, *A Record of the Buddhist Religion*, Oxford, 1896, p223.

(5) Forsström, Johan, *The King of the Jews*, p187; Hopkirk, Peter, *Foreign Devils on the Silk Road*, Oxford, 1980.

(6) Ghose, Ashutosh, *Swami Abhedananda*, Ramakrishna Vedanta Math, Calcutta, 1967.

(7) Roerich, Nicolai, *Altai Himalaya*, pp89-90; Roerich, Nicolai, *Heart of Asia*, New York, 1929; Prophet, Elizabeth Clare, *The Lost Years of Jesus*, California, 1984; Meer Izzut-oolah, *Travels in Central Asia*, Calcutta, 1872.

(8) *The Museum*, New Series, Newark Museum Association, vol 24, no 2&3, 1972, p51. "Ahmad lived in Leh, Ladakh, from 1894-97, practising medicine. He wanted to refute the find by Notovitch, a Russian, of a hitherto unknown manuscript of a Tibetan version of the life of Christ between the ages of 12 and 30".

(9) Prophet, E C, *The Lost Years of Jesus*, p317.

(10) John Hill, an Australian anthropologist, got this Tibetan document,

translated for me by a team of scholars at the Library of Tibetan Works & Archives, Dharamsala, India, in November 1979.

(11) Mr S S Gergan is the author of a monumental work in Tibetan on the history and culture of Ladakh, published by him under the title of *Ladags-rGyal-rabs Chimmed*. He took many Tibetan manuscripts and documents to Germany for editing and transliteration, where he worked as the chief researcher in a German university for some years.

(12) Bull, *School of Oriental Studies*, London, vol IX, part 3, plate V, 9, 1938, pp502–503; Gropp, G, *Archaologishe Funde aus Khotan, Chinas, Ostturkestan*, Bremen, 1974, p367; *Jammu & Kashmir Research Biannual*, vol II, no 1, 1978, p7; Francke, A H, *History of Ladakh*, ed Gergan & Hassnain, Sterling, New Delhi, 1977. The Cross signifies crucifixion. As such, existence of these crosses in Iran (*Barrasshiba-ye-Tarikhi*, Historical Studies, vol 7, no 3, 1942), in Ladakh (*op cit*), in Kashmir and Afghanistan and N India (Barkatullah, *op cit*), in China (Tucci, *Trans-Himalaya*, p39), signifies that there existed Christian colonies in these countries during ancient times.

(13) Barkatullah, *Tarikh-i-Kalisa* or *History of the Indian Churches*, Lahore, p157. The Nestorians were followers of Nestorius, a Christian bishop and patriarch at Antioch and Edessa in Syria. According to his doctrines "the source of the divine nature is God, while human nature originated from Mary. As such, Mary is not the mother of God, but is the mother of a human being, and that Messiah who appeared among the people is the embodiment of love – a link between God and his son. This human Messiah is not a God but a sign of God and His Glory" – *Tarikh-ul-Ummat-al-Qabtia*, by Yaqub Nakhla Rafila, quoted in *Masihat*, Lucknow, 1976, p123. Nestorius was condemned by the Councils of Nicaea (325) and Ephesus (431), and exiled. His followers, the Nestorians, emigrated to Persia, and later eastwards to India, Central Asia and China. See: Fossier, Robert, ed, *The Cambridge Illustrated History of the Middle Ages*, CUP, 1989.

(14) *Report of the Archaeological Survey of India*, 1912–1914, pp213–216.

(15) Quoted from *The Second Treatise of the Great Seth*, by Johan Forsström in *The King of the Jews*, p10. See also: Toynbee, Arnold, *The Crucible of Christianity*, London, 1969; *The Lost Books of the Bible*, New York, 1944.

(16) Schonfield, Hugh, *The Passover Plot*, pp220–233; Stevens, George Barker, *The Teaching of Jesus*, p21.

(17) Eusebius of Caesarea, *Historica Ecclesiastica*, III, p39.

(18) *Luke*, 1, 1–4.

(19) Keller, Werner, *The Bible in History*, p407.

(20) Quoted from *The New Testament Apocrypha*, vol 2, p225, in Johan Forsström's *The King of the Jews*, p12.

21

Yuzu's passing on

Like his birth, the demise of Yuzu Asaph is shrouded in mystery. While the Gospels make him die on the cross in his early 30s, the oriental works make him pass away at a ripe old age.

It is interesting to find that reliable reports of the sayings of the Prophet of Islam assign an age of 125 years to Hazrat Issa, or Jesus[1]. The account given by Shaikh-us-Sadiq about the demise of Yuzu Asaph in Kashmir is full of important information. He records:

> At the approach of death, he sent for his disciple Babaad. He made his last will and gave directions about carrying on his mission of peace. He gave directions about preparation of the sepulchre for him, at the very place where he breathed his last. He then stretched his legs towards the west and kept his head towards the east and passed away[2].

The inner chambers of the sepulchre were covered with stone walls and a door was provided for entrance. Master craftsmen engraved the stone frame of the door with its beautiful design. It is recorded in old works that many people would visit this tomb with the aim of seeking blessings. There was a hole in the western wall of the tomb, out of which the aroma of musk used to emanate[3].

An unknown carver, who had served Yuzu Asaph for many years, carved out the feet impressions of the master on a black stone slab. He gave prominence to the fact that the feet had been pierced. He showed the nail wound on the right foot in full, in

224

order to show that at the time of crucifixion, the left foot had been placed over the right foot and then nailed. He also made a round hole in one foot, and in the other foot he carved out a raised wound. A few wooden and stone crosses were placed near the sarcophagus.

As the centuries passed the stone walls slipped down into the earth, and after some time, one could only see the upper portion of the carved stone door. It has now disappeared. Fortunately, we have a photograph by an archaeologist, which shows the upper portion of the carved stone door, drowned in earth.

A poem on the tomb, recorded in the versified Persian *History of Kashmir*, entitled, *Bagh-i-Sulaiman* or 'The Garden of Solomon', by the Kashmiri poet Saad–Bllah was so interesting that I translated it into English:

> *This is the renowned Tomb! Sepulchre of the Prophet, so illuminating!*
> *Whosoever bows before it, receives inner light, solace and contentment.*
> *As in the tradition, there was a prince, so accomplished, pious and*
> *great, Who received the Kingdom of God; He was faithful to the Lord*
> *God, who ordained him to be the Prophet! Thus he became the guide to*
> *the people living in the blessed valley of Kashmir. This is the renowned*
> *Tomb of that Prophet who is known by the name of Yuzu Asaph.*[4]

It was a sheer coincidence that I was drawn into researching the missing years in the life of Jesus Christ. It appears to me that the time has now come to ask the people of the West to join hands in the rediscovery of the historical Jesus. It is an irony that while Western scholars have undertaken and accomplished great projects to study the ancient civilisations of the East, they have made little intentional effort to study the vital matters concerning Christianity itself. It is for this reason that the real contents and meaning of the scattered works such as the Buddhist scrolls, the Dead Sea Scrolls, *Bhavishiya Maha Purana*, the Gospel of Barnabas and other Gospels, and the writings of the Essenes have all remained an unrevealed secret of Christianity. I submit the results of my own work for the unbiased consideration of all people interested in the life of Jesus and the roots of Christian cultures, in the hope that this contribution be useful for future researchers in uncovering the truth around this important matter.

---

(1) Hazrat Mirza Ghulam Ahmad, *Masih Hindustan Mein*, p98. Abdul Salam Madsen, translator of the *Holy Quran* into Danish, quotes from the *Hadis* or the sayings of the Holy Prophet of Islam:"1. If Moses and Jesus had been alive, they would have had no choice but to follow me (*Kathir*, vol II, p245);2. Verily, Jesus, son of Mary, lived for 120 years, and I see myself as only entering upon the beginnings of the sixties (*Kanz-al-Aimal*, pt 6, p120);3. During his spiritual ascent to heaven, the Holy Prophet saw Jesus together with John in the second heaven (*Bukhari*, pt 2, chapter on *Miraj*)."While Mirza Ghulam Ahmad had fixed 125 years as the age of Jesus according to *Hadis*, Abdul Salam Madsen quotes the relevant *Hadis* where it is mentioned that Jesus lived for 120 years. See *Truth about the Crucifixion*, p115.

(2) Shaikh-us-Sadiq, *Kamal-ud-Din*, p358. It is interesting that the name of the disciple is given as Babaad, which in Arabic means the twins who suck milk from a common mother. It is the equivalent to the Greek *Didymus*, by which surname John speaks of Thomas (*John*, 20, 24).

(3) Ghulam Nabi Khanyari, *Wajeez-ut-Tawarikh*, vol II, Folio 279.

(4) Saad-Ullah, *Bagh-i-Sulaiman*, (Persian), as quoted in *Qabr-i-Masih*, p48. MS to be found at the Oriental Research Library, Srinagar. See also: Sadiq, Mufti Muhammad, *Qabr-i-Masih*, and Zahoor-ul-Hassan, *Nigaristan-i-Kashmir*.

Bibliography

GENERAL SOURCES

Ahmad, Ghulam, *Jesus in India*, Ahmadiyya Muslim Foreign Missions Dept, Rabwah, Pakistan, 1962;

Allegro, J M, *The Dead Sea Scrolls and the Christian Myth*, Newton Abbot, UK, 1979;

Faber-Kaiser, A, *Jesus Died in Kashmir*, Sphere, London, 1977;

Graves, R, & Podro, J, *The Nazarene Gospel Restored*, London, 1953;

Kersten, Holger, *Jesus Lived in India*, Element, Shaftesbury UK, 1986;

Khwaja, Nazir Ahmad, *Jesus in Heaven and Earth*, Azeez Manzil, Lahore, 1952;

Prophet, Elisabeth Clare, *The Lost Years of Jesus*, Summit Lighthouse Press, Malibu, USA, 1984;

Wilson, Ian, *The Authenticity of the Shroud of Turin*, Doubleday, London, 1987.

FURTHER REFERENCES FOR RESEARCH PURPOSES

Pagan sources

Josephus, Flavius, *The Jewish Wars*, tr W Whiston, London, 1872;

Josephus, Flavius, *Antiquities of the Jews: A History of the Jewish Wars and Life of Flavius Josephus, Written by Himself*, tr W Whiston, London, 1872;

Josephus, Flavius, *Antiquities of the Jews*, ed Loeb, London & Cambridge MA, 1924ff; *Historia Antiqua Judaico* or *Antiquities of the Jews*, by Flavius Josephus, edited by Loeb, London & Cambridge MA, 1924ff;

Josephus, Flavius, *The Wars of the Jews*, T Nelson & Sons, London, 1873;

Josephus, Flavius, *The Jewish Wars*, tr G A Williamson, Penguin, Harmondsworth, 1978;

Philo, Judaeus, *Works*, ed Loeb, Loeb Classical Lib, Heinemann, London, and Harvard Univ Press, Cambridge MA, 1960;

Philo, Judaeus, *Every Good Man is Free*, tr F H Colson, London & Cambridge MA, 1962, 1967;

Pliny the Elder, *Natural History*, tr H Rackham & W H S Jones, 10 vols, London, 1938-42;

Pliny the Elder, *Natural History*, Loeb Classical Library, Heinemann, London, and Harvard Univ Press, Cambridge MA, 1969;

Pliny the Younger, *Letter to the Emperor Trajan*, ed Loeb, Loeb Classical Library, Harvard Univ Press, Cambridge MA, 1964.

Jewish Sources

Albright, W F, *Archaeology and the Religion of Israel*, Hopkins, Baltimore, 1953;

Authorised Jewish Prayer Book, Eyre & Spottiswoode, London, 1916;

Black, A, *The Prophets of Israel*, Edinburgh, 1882;

Charles, R H, tr, *The Book of Enoch*, 2 vols, Clarendon Press, Oxford, 1893, 1912;

Charles, R H, tr, *Testament of the Twelve Patriarchs*, A & C Black, London, 1908;

Driver, S R, *Introduction to the Literature of the Old Testament*, 1892;

Encyclopaedia Judaica, Jerusalem, 1971;

Greenlees, Duncan, *The Gospel of Israel*, Adhyar, Madras, 1955;

Haupt, P, ed, *Sacred Books of the Old Testament in Hebrew*, New York, 1898;

Moore, G F, *Judaism in the First Century of the Christian Era*, Cambridge, 1930, Vol 1, p20.

Ryle and James, ed, *The Psalms of Solomon*, Cambridge UK, 1891;
The Talmud, Standard Edition, Macmillan, London, 1938.

Bani Israel
Barakat, Ahmad, *Muhammad and the Jews*, Vikas, New Delhi, 1979;
Bruhi, J H, *The Lost Ten Tribes*, London, 1893;
Barber, Izekiel, *The Beni Israel of India*, Washington DC, 1981;
Bell, A W, *Tribes of Afghanistan*, London, 1897;
Bellew, H W, *Are the Afghans Israelites?*, Simla, India, 1880;
Benjamin, Yehoshua, *Mystery of the Lost Tribes*, New Delhi, 1989;
Khan, Roshan, *Tazkirah* (History of the Afghans), (Urdu), Karachi, 1982;
Kehimkar, Haeem Samuel, *Bani Israel in India*, Tel Aviv, 1937;
Lord, Rev J H, *The Jews in India and the Far East*, SPCK, Bombay, 1907;
Margolis, Max, & Marx, Alexander, *A History of the Jewish People*, Temple Books,
     Massachusetts, 1969 & 1978;
Mir Izzut-oolah, *Travels in Central Asia*, tr Henderson, Foreign Dept Press, Calcutta,
     1872;
Mohammad, Yasin, *Mysteries of Kashmir*, Srinagar, 1972;
Moore, George, *The Lost Tribes*, Longman Green, London, 1861;
Moore, George, *Judaism in the First Century of the Christian Era*, Cambridge UK, 1930;
Qureshi, Aziz Ahmad, *Asrar-i-Kashir* (Urdu), Srinagar, 1964;
Rose, George, *The Afghans and the Ten Tribes*, London, 1852;
Wolf, Joseph, *Researches and Missionary Labours among the Jews and Mohammedans and
     other Sects*, London, 1835;
Wolf, Joseph, *Mission to Bokhara*, 2 vols, London, 1845;

Apocrypha
The Ante-Nicene Christian Library, 25 vols, T & T Clark, Edinburgh, 1869;
Andrews, A, ed, *Apocryphal Books of the Old and New Testament*, Theological
     Translation Library, London, 1906;
Bonnet, Max, tr, *Acta Thomae*, Leipzig, 1883;
Charles, R H, tr, *The Old Testament Apocrypha and Pseudepigrapha*, 2 vols, Clarendon
     Press, Oxford, 1913;
Charles, R H, *Religious Development between the Old and the New Testament*, Henry Holt,
     1913;
Cureton, *Ancient Syriac Documents*, 24 vols, London, 1864;
Gartner, Bertil, *The Theology of the Gospel of Thomas*, ;
Gospel of the Hebrews, Edenite Soc Inc, Imlaystown NJ, 1972;
Hennecke, E, and Schneemelcher, W, *New Testament Apocrypha*, Philadelphia, 1963–66;
James, Montague, *The Apocryphal New Testament*, Oxford, 1924, 1953;
Klijn, A F J, tr, *The Acts of Thomas*, E J Brill, Leiden, 1962;
Lost Books of the Bible, World Publishing Co, New York, 1944;
Pagels, Elaine, *The Gnostic Gospels*, New York, 1979;
Pratten, tr, *Syrian Documents attributed to the First Three Centuries*, Ante-Nicene Christian
     Library, vol XX, Edinburgh, 1871;
Ragg, Lonsdale and Laura, tr, *The Gospel of Barnabas*, Oxford Univ Press, 1907;
Robinson, Forbes, *The Coptic Apocryphal Gospels*, Methuen & Co, London, 1902;
Robinson, James M, ed, *The Nag Hammadi Library*, New York, E J Brill, Leiden, 1977;
Schonfield, Hugh, *The Authentic New Testament*, London, 1956;
Swete, H B, ed, *The Gospel of Peter*, Macmillan, London, 1893;
Walker, Alexander, tr, *Acts of Barnabas*, Ante-Nicene Christian Library, Vol XVI, T &

T Clark, Edinburgh, 1970;

Wilson, R M, ed, *The Gospel of Philip*, London, 1962;

Wright, W, *Apocryphal Acts of the Apostles*, Soc for Publ of Oriental Texts, London, 1871, vol II;

Barnabas Ki Anjeel, (Urdu), Markazi Maktaba Islami, Delhi, 1982;

Anjeel-i-Barnabas, (Arabic), Al-Minar Press, Cairo, 1908.

Christology and Theology

Ahmad, Mirza Ghulam, *Jesus in India*, Ahmadiyya Muslim Mission, Qadian, India, 1944;

Ahmad, Mirza Ghulam, *Massih Hindustan Mein*, (Urdu), Qadian, 1908;

Bock, Janet, *The Jesus Mystery*, Aura Books, Los Angeles, 1980;

Bornkamm, G, tr, *Jesus of Nazareth*, Hodder & Stoughton, London, 1956;

Bultmann, Rudolf, *Primitive Christianity and its Contemporary Setting*, tr R H Fuller, Collins, Glasgow, 1960;

Cadoux, C J, *The Life of Christ*, Pelican, London, 1948;

The Crucifixion by an Eye-Witness, Indo-American Book Co, Chicago, 1907;

Dummelow, Rev J R, *Commentary on the Holy Bible*, Macmillan, London, 1917;

Faber-Kaiser, Andreas, *Jesus Died in Kashmir*, Gordon & Cremonesi, London, 1977;

Faruqi, Mumtaz Ahmad, *The Crumbling of the Cross*, Lahore, 1973;

Ferrar, Dean F W, *The Life of Christ*, Cassell, Peter & Galpin, London, 1874;

Forsström, Johan, *The King of the Jews*, Nugedoga, Sri Lanka, and East West Books, Hango, Finland, 1987;

Fuller, R H, *The Foundations of New Testament Christology*, Collins, London, 1965;

Goeckel, Helmut, *Die Messias-Legitimation Jesu*, Liber Verlag, Mainz, 1982;

Graves, Robert, *The Nazarene Gospel Retold*, Cassell, London, 1953;

Gregory, A, *The Canon and Text of the New Testament*, New York, 1907;

Hastings, J, *Dictionary of the Bible*, T & T Clark, Edinburgh, 1904;

Hastings, J, *Dictionary of the Apostolic Church*, T & T Clark, Edinburgh, 1918;

Hastings, J, *Dictionary of Christ and the Gospels*, T & T Clark, Edinburgh, 1908;

Holy Bible, King James Version, reference ed. with Concordance, New York, London;

Kamal-ud-Din, Khwaja, *The Sources of Christianity*, MMI Trust, Woking UK, 1924;

Kashmiri, Aziz, *Christ in Kashmir*, Roshni Pubs, Srinagar, 1984;

Keller, Werner, *The Bible as History*, Hodder & Stoughton, London, 1956;

Kersten, Holger, *Jesus Lived in India*, Element, Shaftesbury, UK, 1986;

Levi (H Dowling), *The Aquarian Gospel of Jesus the Christ*, De Vorss, Marina del Ray CA, 1972;

Lewis, Spencer H, *Mystical Life of Jesus*, AMORC, San Jose CA, 1929;

The Life of Christ, Rev Edn, Mazdaznan Elector Corp, Los Angeles, 1960, reprinted by Stockton Doty Press, Whittier, California, 1969;

Muggeridge, Malcolm, *Jesus, the Man who Lives*, Collins, London, 1975;

Muses, G A, ed, *The Septuagint Bible*, Falcon's Wing Press, Colorado, 1954;

Nazir Ahmad, Khwaja, *Jesus in Heaven on Earth*, Azeez Manzil, Lahore, 1973, first published by Muslim Mission and Literary Trust, Woking, UK, 1952;

Notovitch, Nicolas, *The Unknown Life of Christ*, Rand McNally, Chicago, 1894 & Hutchinson, London, 1895;

Peake, A S J, *Commentary on the Bible*, London, 1920;

Peloubet's Select Notes on the International Lessons, Boston, 1918;

Prophet, Elizabeth Clare, *The Lost Years of Jesus*, Summit Univ Press, Malibu, USA, 1984;

Robinson, J M, *New Quest for the Historical Jesus*, London, 1959;

Sadiq, Mufti Muhammad, *Qabr-i-Masih* (Urdu), Talif-o-Ishait, Qadian, 1936;

Shams, J D, *Where Did Jesus Die?*, Baker & Witt, London, 1945;
Schweitzer, A, *Quest for the Historical Jesus*, London, 1945;
Stroud, William, *On the Physical Cause of Death of Christ*, London, 1965;
Talmud Immanuel, Freie Interessengemeinschaft, Switzerland, 1974;
Wehrli-Frey, *Jesat Nassar*, 2 vols, Drei Eichen Verlag, Munich, 1965;
Wilson, Ian, *The Turin Shroud*, Penguin, Harmondsworth, 1978;
Yosuf, Chalpi, *Mashihat*, (Urdu), Majlis Tehqiqat, Lucknow, 1976.

The Shroud

Berna, Kurt, *Jesus ist Nicht am Kreuz Gestorben*, Hans Naber, Stuttgart, 1957;
Berna, Kurt, *Christ did not Perish on the Cross*, Expositions Press, New York, 1975;
Berna, Kurt, *Das Linnen*, Stuttgart, 1957;
Forsyth, William H, *The Entombment of Christ*, Cambridge UK, 1970;
National Geographic, vol 157, no 6, Washington DC, June 1980;
Reban, John (Kurt Berna), *Inquest of Jesus Christ*, London, 1967;
Rinaldi, Peter M, *Is It The Lord?*, New York, 1972;
Segal, J B, *Edessa, the Blessed City*, Oxford, 1970;
Vignon, Paul, *The Shroud of Christ*, London, 1902;
Wilcox, R K, *Shroud*, Macmillan, New York, 1977;
Wilson, Ian, *The Turin Shroud*, Penguin, Harmondsworth, 1978.

Anthropology & Archaeology

Al Beruni, *Kitab-al-Hind, India*, from Arabic, tr Edward Sachau, 2 vols, Trubner, London, 1888. Reprint: S Chand & Co, Delhi, 1964;
Aziz-us-Samad, Ulfat, *Great Religions of the World*, Lahore, 1976;
Bowle, John, ed, *Concise Encyclopaedia of World History*, Hutchinson, London, 1958;
Chakraberti, C, *Classical Studies in Ancient Races and Myths*, Puja Publications, New Delhi, 1979;
Cole, Major H H, *The Illustration of Ancient Buildings in Kashmir*, W H Allen, London, 1869;
Cole, Sonia, *Races of Man*, British Museum, London, 1965;
Kak, Ram Chandra, *Ancient Monuments of Kashmir*, London, 1933;
Kellet, E E, *Short History of Religions*, Pelican, Harmondsworth, 1972;
Khwand, Mir Muhammad, *Rauzat-us-Safa* (Persian), 7 vols, translated in *The Garden of Purity*, tr E Rehatsek, 5 vols, Royal Asiatic Soc, London, 1892;
Marshall, John, and others, *Taxila*, 3 vols, Cambridge, 1951;
Rapson, Prof E J, *Ancient India*, CUP, Cambridge, UK, 1911;
Roerich, Nicolai, *Altai Himalaya*, New York, 1929;
Roerich, Nicolai, *The Heart of Asia*, New York, 1929;
Smith, Arthur Vincent, *The Early History of India*, Clarendon Press, Oxford, 1904;
Smith, Sir George Adam, *Historical Geography of the Holy Land*, Hodder, London, 1894;

Dead Sea Scrolls

Allegro, John, *The Dead Sea Scrolls: a Reappraisal*, Penguin, Middlesex, 1964;
Allegro, John, *Dead Sea Scrolls: The Mystery Revealed*, New York, 1981;
Allegro, John, *The People of the Dead Sea Scrolls*, Routledge, London, 1959;
Allegro, John, *The Dead Sea Scrolls and Christian Myth*, Abacus, London, 1981;
Barthelemy, D, & Milik, J T, *Discoveries in the Judaean Desert*, Oxford Univ Press, 1955;
Brownlee, W H, *The Dead Sea Manual of Discipline*, BASOR, New York, 1951;
Brownlee, W H, *The Meaning of the Qumran Scrolls for the Bible*, New York, 1964;
Burrows, M, *The Dead Sea Scrolls*, Viking Press, London, 1956;

Burrows, M, *More Light on the Dead Sea Scrolls*, London, 1958;
Davies, Powell, *The Meaning of the Dead Sea Scrolls*, Mentor Books, New York, 1956;
Dupont-Sommer, A, *The Dead Sea Scrolls*, New York, 1956;
Schonfield, Hugh, *The Secret of the Dead Sea Scrolls*, New York, 1960;
Vermes, G, *The Dead Sea Scrolls in English*, Pelican, Middlesex, 1962;
Wilson, Edmund, *Scrolls from the Dead Sea*, Oxford, 1955;
Yadin, Y, *The Ben Sira Scroll from Masada*, Jerusalem, 1965.

Christians of St Thomas in India

Brown, L W, *The Indian Christians of St Thomas*, Cambridge, 1956;
Buchanan, Claudius, *Christian Researches in Asia*, Cambridge, 1811, Ogle, Edinburgh, 1912;
Geddes, M, *History of the Christian Church of Malabar*, Walford, London, 1894;
Farquhar, J N, *The Apostle Thomas in North India*, Manchester, 1926;
Keay, F E, *History of the Syrian Church in India*, Madras, 1938;
Matthew, P V, *Acta Indica*, Cochin, 1986;
Medlycott, A E, *India and the Apostle Thomas*, London, 1905;
Menacherry, George, ed, *The St Thomas Christian Encyclopaedia of India*, Madras, 1973;
Milne, Rae, *Syrian Church in India*, Edinburgh, 1892;
Mingana, A, *Early Spread of Christianity in India*, Manchester, 1926;
Plattner, F A, *Christian India*, Vanguard Press, New York, 1957;
Raulin, *Historia Ecclesiae Malabartica*, Rome, 1745.

Essenes

Cannon, Dolores, *Jesus and the Essenes*, Gateway Books, Bath, 1992;
Dupont-Sommer, *The Jewish Sect of Qumran and the Essenes*, Macmillan, 1956;
Szekely, Edmond Bordeaux, *The Essene Code of Life*, San Diego, 1977;
Szekely, E B, tr, *The Gospel of the Essenes*, C W Daniel, Saffron Walden UK, 1978;
Szekely, E B, *The Gospel of Peace of Jesus Christ by the Disciple John*, C W Daniel, London, 1937 & 1973;
Szekely, E B, *The Teachings of the Essenes from Enoch to the Dead Sea Scrolls*, C W Daniel, London, 1978;
Szekely, E B, *The Essene Jesus*, San Diego CA, 1977;
Szekely, Edmond Bordeaux, *The Essene Humane Gospel of Jesus*, Santa Monica, 1978;
Szekely, E B, *The Essene Teachings of Zarathrustra*, 1973;
Kosmala, H, *Hebraer, Essener, Christen*, Leiden, 1959;
Larson, Martin A, *The Essene Heritage*, New York, 1967.

Islamic

al-Bukhari, Imam, *Al-Jami-al-Sahih*, 3 vols, Cairo;
al-Jajjaj, Muslim bin, *Al-Sahih*, 18 vols, Cairo;
Al-Sahih of Muslim, 2 vols, Ghulam Ali & Sons, Lahore, 1962;
Bashir-ud-Din, Mahmood Ahmad, *Introduction to the Study of the Holy Quran*, London, 1949;
Mohammed Ali, Maulana, tr, *The Holy Quran*, Ahmaddiyya Anjuman, Lahore, 1951;
Mohammad Ali, Maulana, *A Manual of Hadis*, Lahore, 1949;
Ibn-i-Jarir-at-Tibri; *Tafsir*, 30 volumes, Kubr-ul-Mara Press, Cairo, 1921;
Sale, George, *The Koran*, London, 1939;
Yusuf Ali, Abdullah, tr, *Holy Quran*, Lahore, 1961.

ORIENTAL MANUSCRIPTS AND WORKS
Arabic
Ibn-i-Hazam, *Almallal-o-Alnahal*, Cairo;

Ibn-i-Tamima, Shaikh-ul-Islam, *Al-Jawab-al-Sahi-Liman-Badil-Din-al-Masih*, 4 vols;

Mohammad Abdul, Shaikh, *Al-Islam-al-Nasrania*, Cairo;

Shahrastani, Mohammad ibn Abdul Karim, *Kitab al-Milal wa al-Nihal*, Soc for Publ Oriental Texts, London, 1842.

Persian
Abdul Qadir, *Hashmat-i-Kashmir*, Persian MS no 42, f7, Royal Asiatic Soc of Bengal, Calcutta;

Khwaja Muhammad Azam Deedamari, *Tarikh-i-Azami* (in Persian), Muhammadi Press, Lahore, 1747;

Khwand, Mir Muhammad, *Rauzat-us-Safa* (Persian), 7 vols, translated in *The Garden of Purity*, tr E Rehatsek, 5 vols, Royal Asiatic Soc, London, 1892;

Mustafa, Agha, *Ahwal-i-Ahalian-i-Paras* (Persian), Teheran, 1909;

Said-us-Saddiq, Al Shaikh, *Kamal-ud-Din*, Sayyid-us-Sanad Press, Iran, 1881.
Translated into German by H Muller, Heidelberg Univ, Germany, 1901.

Dehlvi, Syed Ahmad, *Farhang-i-Asafiyah*, Persian dictionary, Hyderabad, 1908.

Urdu
Ahmad, Mirza Ghulam, *Jesus in India*, Ahmadiyya Muslim Mission, Qadian, 1944;

Ahmed, Mirza Ghulam, *Massih Hindustan Mein*, Qadian, 1908;

Argali, Farooq, ed, *Mujazat-i-Masih* (*Miracles of Jesus*), Delhi;

Qadir, Abdul Shaikh, *Ashab-i-Kahf-kay-Sahijay* (*The Scriptures of the Cave-Dwellers*), Lahore, 1960;

Sadiq, Mufti Muhammad, *Qabr-i-Masih* (*The Grave of Jesus*), Talif-o-Ishait, Qadian, 1936;

Shams Tabriz Khan, tr, *Masihat* (*Christianity*), Lucknow, 1976.

Sanskrit
Bhavishya Mahapurana, MS, Oriental research Library, Univ of Kashmir, Srinagar;

Kumari, Ved, tr, *Nila-Mata-Purana*, Cultural Academy, Jammu, 1968;

Shastri, Vidyavaridi Shiv Nath, tr, *Bhavishya Maha Purana* (Hindi), Venkateshvaria Press, Bombay, 1917;

Bhavishya Maha Purana, tr & comm in Hindi, Oriental Research Inst, Poona, 1910;

Stein, M A, tr, *Kalhana's Rajatarangini*, 2 vols, Constable, London, 1900, reprints New Delhi, 1961 & 1979.

Tibetan
Le-zan Chhes-kyi Nima, *Grub-tha Thams-chand kyi Khuna dan Dod-Thsul Ston-pe Legs Shad Shel-gyi Melong*, (Tibetan, translated from Chinese), or *The History of Religions and Doctrines - The Glass Mirror*, in the collection of S S Gergan, Srinagar, Kashmir.

Bengali
Abhedananda, Swami, *Kashmir O Tibbate*, Ramakrishna Vedanta Math, Calcutta, 1927;

Ghose, Ashutosh, *Swami Abhedananda - the Patriot Saint*, Ramakrishna Vedanta Math, Calcutta, 1967.

Chronology

100	Apollodutus king of Gandhara.	40	Thomas meets Gondapharos at Taxila. Jesus in Parthia. Death of Mary Magdalene at Kashgar?
100	Compilations of the Dead Sea Scrolls.		
73	Herod the Great king of Judaea.	49	Jesus and Thomas meet at Taxila. Gopadatta rules Kashmir.
70	Maues king of Gandhara.		
63	Pompey of Rome storms Jerusalem.	50	Downfall of Gondapharos: Yueh-Chi invasion from Bactria. Death of Mother Mary.
37	Herod of Idumaea king of Judaea [?].		
27	Octavian becomes Augustus, Roman emperor (to 14 AD).	52	Thomas reaches Malabar
		55	Kadphises, Kushana king, unites N India, annexes Gandhara & Taxila.
6	Birth of Jesus of Nazareth		
5	Jesus adopted by Essenes.		
4	Jesus taken to Egypt.	60	Yuzu Asaph arrives in Kashmir.
AD 4	Herod Agrippa, Jewish ruler under Romans.		
		60-70	Compilation of Gospel of Mark.
6	Census carried out by Quirinius for Romans.		
		70	Pliny's Historica Naturalis, noting the Essenes. Destruction of Jerusalem by Titus.
7	Jesus leaves parental house, journeys to the East.		
14	Tiberius Caesar, emperor of Rome.		
20	Return of Jesus to to West, probable journeys to Greece and Britain.	78	Shalivahana meets Jesus, then leaves Kashmir.
		85	Compilation of Gospel of Matthew.
21	Gondapharos, king of Gandhara.	87	Kanishka founds Kushana empire, convenes Fourth Buddhist Council in Kashmir.
28	Jesus returns to Palestine.		
33	Baptism of Jesus by John.		
34	John the Baptist murdered.	90-95	Compilation of Gospel of Luke.
35	Ministry of Jesus.		
36	Crucifixion of Jesus.	100	Abdagases, king of Gandhara.
37	Holy Shroud taken to Edessa. Caligula, emperor of Rome.	109	Reputed death of Jesus in Kashmir.
		110	Official time of compilation of the Gospel of John.

115 Sutta compiles Bhavishya Maha Purana.

163 Bones and relics of Thomas carried from Madras to Edessa, Syria.

175 Migration of Christians from the West to NW India.

189 Demetrius deputes Pantaenius to India to preach Christianity.

300 Eusebius writes about the Essenes.

368 Epiphanius, Bishop of Salamis, collates the Acta Thomae.

375 Eusebius divides New Testament into authentic, disputed and spurious parts.

382 Gospel of James and Gospel of Barnabus condemned.

397 Third Council of Carthage (Augustine) settles final Canon of the New Testament.

405 Gospel of James and Gospel of Barnabus proscribed and destroyed.

422 Rab Ashi compiles the Jewish Talmud.

478 Gospel of Barnabus rediscovered in a tomb in Cyprus.

495 Acta Thomae proscribed.

496 Gospels of James and Barnabus declared heretical (Decree of Galasous).

525 Holy Shroud found at Edessa.

570 Birth of Muhammad, the Prophet of Islam.

614 Damascus and Jerusalem sacked by Persians. Holy Cross carried away.

622 Hijra Islamic Era starts.

754 Dionysus Exignus, a Scythian monk, introduces the Christian Era dating system.

800 Amalgamation of Church and State in Rome (Charlemagne).

960 Al Shaikh Al-Said-us-Sadiq completes Ikmal-ud-Din, on Jesus' India journeys.

1010 Butchery of Jews in France.

1096 Massacres of Jews in Germany. First Crusade.

1099 Crusader storming of Jerusalem. Crusader states in Jerusalem, Edessa, Antioch.

1147 Second Holy War for Jerusalem (response to Second Crusade).

1148 Kalhana compiles Rajatarangini, history of Kashmir (Kashmiri crucifixion).

1187 Recapture of Jerusalem from Crusaders by Sultan Saladin.

1290 Jews expelled from England.

1236 Cardinal Hugo de S Caro reorganises New Testament.

1306 Holy Shroud relocated to France.

1357 Holy Shroud first exposed to devotees.

1417　Mir Muhammad's Rauzat-us-Safa mentions Jesus in Nisibis, Persia.

1420　Mulla Nadri completes Tarikh-i-Kashmir.

1451　Nasir-ud-Din buried beside Jesus' tomb in Kashmir.

1455　Gutenberg's printed Bible.

1514　New Testament in Greek printed.

1521　Martin Luther excommunicated: beginning of Reformation.

1523　Talmud printed in Holland.

1534　Founding of the Jesuit Order (Counter-Reformation).

1578　Holy Shroud taken to Italy.

1616　James I's Authorised Bible appears.

1694　Holy Shroud moved to Royal Chapel at Turin.

1729　Azam's *Waqiat-i-Kashmir* notes Yuzu Asaph's tomb

1741　Badi-ud-Din Abul Qasim notes one of Apostles is buried at Yuzu Asaph's tomb.

1766　Decree in favour of custodian of Yuzu Asaph's tomb, by Grand Mufti of Kashmir.

1787　Full rights given to Jews in USA.

1803　A Wrede writes Account of St Thomas' Christians in Malabar.

1820　Abdul Qadir, in *Hashmat-i-Kashmir*, calls Kashmiris descendants of Jews.

1823　Thilla publishes *Acta Thomae.*

1861　Moore's *Lost Tribes* traces Jews in Afghanistan and Kashmir.

1870　*Acts of Barnabus* published in English.

1871　*Acta Thomae* published in English by W Wright.

1872　Meer Izzut-Oolah's *Travels in Central Asia*, mentions Jesus in Ladakh.

1873　*The Crucifixion by an Eye-Witness* surfaces in USA, proscribed and burnt.

1890　Notovitch's *Life of Saint Issa*, based on his findings in Ladakh.

1891　Moore's *Ethnography of Afghanistan*. Mir Khwand's *Rauzat-us-Safa* publ in English.

1893　*Gospel of Peter* published by H B Swete.

1894　Notovitch's *The Unknown Life of Jesus* published.

1898　Holy Shroud first photographed. Threatened demolition of Yuzu Asaph's tomb.

1904　Zionist Movement for establishment of Israel.

1907　*The Crucifixion by an Eye-Witness* published.

1908　Mirza Ghulam Ahmad publishes *Massih Hindustan Mein*. Levi's *Aquarian Gospel.*

1910　*Bhavishya Maha Purana* published.

1916– Marshall's excavations at
  18   Taxila reveal first century
       Christian relics.
1920   Docker's *If Jesus Did Not
       Die on the Cross: A Study in
       Evidence.*
1930– Nazi persecution and
  44   murder of Jews in Germany
       and Europe.
1936   Mufti Mohammed Sadiq
       publishes *Qabr-i-Masih*, on
       Yuzu Asaph's tomb.
1945   J D Shams publishes *Did
       Jesus Die?*. Discovery of
       Nag Hammadi texts.
1947   First discovery of the Dead
       Sea Scrolls. Establishment
       of state of Israel.
1949   Fragments of Old
       Testament brought to
       Jerusalem from Qumran.
1950   Tomb of Mary at Murree
       repaired.
1952   Qumran: new fragments.
       Nazir Ahmad's *Jesus in
       Heaven on Earth* published
1953   Robert Graves' *The
       Nazarene Gospel Restored.*
1956   Millar Burrows translates
       *Dead Sea Scrolls; Copper
       Scrolls deciphered.*
1956   A Powell Davis' *The
       Meaning of the Dead Sea
       Scrolls.*
1957   Kurt Berna's *Jesus Nicht am
       Kreuz Gestorben* and *Das
       Linnen* (on Turin Shroud).
1964   Aziz Ahmad's *Asrar-
       i-Kashmir.*
1969   Turin Shroud exposed to
       scientific investigation.

1973   Mumtaz Ahmad Farooqi's
       The Crumbling of the Cross.
1975   Discovery of slab with
       Jesus' foot-marks, by F M
       Hassnain & Ghulam Mohi-
       ud-Din.
1976   Andreas Faber-Kaiser's
       Jesus Died in Kashmir.
1977   *Die Messias – Legitimation
       Jesu* published by Helmut
       Goeckel.
1977   Turin Shroud studied by
       NASA scientists.
1978   Turin Shroud draws
       500,000 visitors. Ian
       Wilson's *Turin Shroud*
       published. International
       Conference on The
       Deliverance of Jesus from
       the Cross, London.
1980   Janet L Bock's *The Jesus
       Mystery.*
1982   Diego Rubio Barrera's
       Jesucristo.
1983   Holger Kersten's *Jesus Lebte
       in Indien* published.
1984   E C Prophet's *Lost Years of
       Jesus*, drawing together
       many testimonies.
1987   Johan Forsström's *King of
       the Jews.*
1991   Baigent and Leigh's *The
       Dead Sea Scrolls Deception.*
1992   Barbara Thiering's *Jesus the
       Man*, on Essene Biblical
       ciphers.
1993   Publication of many
       hitherto unpublished Dead
       Sea Scrolls.

Jeffrey Gale : delt. Dec. 1991.

"Rozabal Restored : Tomb of the Prophet & Healer St. Isa."
SRINAGAR, INDIA.

ROZABAL RESTORED: Tomb of the Prophet and Healer St. Issa. This sketch by a British architect Jeffrey Gale proposes an international appeal to restore this historic shrine. It is badly designed and in a very dilapidated condition, there being no local funding available. He says that his restoration would cost at least $60,000. All enquiries to him at 3 Alpha Terrace, Totnes, Devon TQ9 5PT. UK. (Tel:★49.803.867.826)

Index

Prof. Fida M. Hasnain MA, LLB, D.Arch. D.Indol

Prof Hassnain was born in 1924 in Srinagar, Kashmir. His parents were school teachers, his father having fought with the British Indian forces in the Boer War in 1902. Fida Hassnain graduated from the University of Punjab, and the Muslim University, Aligar, and became a barrister. With the Partition of India he lost confidence in the law and after a bout of social work and his own creative studies, he became a lecturer at SP College, Srinagar. He later gained the chair of History and Research. In 1954, he became Director of the Kashmir State Archives, of Archeological Research and Museums, continuing until his retirement in 1983.

Prof Hassnain is active in the World Reconciliation of Faiths movement and in the international yoga field.

In spite of the continuing and tragic civil strife in Srinagar, he maintains his home in that poignant city.

Now that you've read A SEARCH FOR THE HISTORICAL JESUS, you might be interested in other Gateway books which re-examine or question the doctrines and beliefs we feel restrain the forward evolution of our society.

Our culture seems to be disintegrating, if you believe that its orthodox values are unquestionable. But if you believe that there are more wonderful, inclusive, inter-connecting and cosmic realities to be discovered, then you may indeed participate in a transformation of our human societies that has never happened before, as far as we know. This is what some call a "quantum rise in consciousness"; at least it is an opportunity to wake up from a long slumber. It is truly a gift to be witness to these changes! Gateway Books are pioneers of affordable books likely to expand your realities.

If you want to know more what the Bible doesn't tell us about Jesus, read:

JESUS AND THE ESSENES: Fresh Insights into Christ's Ministry and the Dead Sea Scrolls, by Dolores Cannon.
A 'far memory' recall of a tutor at the Essene monastery at Qumran, who believed he taught Jesus as a boy and followed his ministry right up to the crucifixion.

THEY WALKED WITH JESUS: Past Experiences with Christ, by Dolores Cannon.
Two women, a teacher and a healer, movingly describe what it was like to be around Jesus, and how others responded to him. There is fascinating background material on the conditions of Palestinian society at that time.

ALTERNATIVE SCIENCE:
THE VORTEX – KEY TO FUTURE SCIENCE, by David Ash & Peter Hewitt.
This book merges physics and metaphysics, matter and energy in a study of the vortex, first researched by Lord Kelvin. Particularly useful for understanding how different realities interpenetrate.

LIVING ENERGIES – Victor Schauberger's Insights into Nature's Laws, by Callum Coats.
If you feel that modern science is manipulative and has lost its way, and that we need to rediscover how to work closely with Nature, then this inspiring book will excite you!

WHEN THE EARTH NEARLY DIED: Compelling Evidence of a World Cataclysm 11,500 Years Ago, by Derek Allan & Bernard Delair.
Two scientists present convincing evidence from many disciplines of how nearly our species was destroyed by a major disaster in the Solar System. Cataclysmic thinking is coming back into vogue, and millennial anxieties make this a timely study.

YOUR HOME CAN MAKE YOU ILL: How to counteract harmful electrical and earth energies, by David Cowan & Rodney Girdlestone.
This new book will make you aware that the Earth is alive, and that we need to be more aware of how its energies can affect us. The man-made energies that have developed exponentially this century clearly having alarming consequences for our health, in spite of governmental and scientific reassurances.

THE COSMIC FACTOR:
THE ONLY PLANET OF CHOICE: Essential Briefings from Deep Space, compiled by Phyllis V Schlemmer & Palden Jenkins.
This riveting document is acknowledged as a truly significant book of our times. It presents a cosmic view of Earth, and concerns the past, present and future of humanity. It has already expanded their view of reality for thousands all over the world.

COSMIC CONNECTIONS: Demonstrating the link between Extra-terrestrials and the Crop Circles, by Michael Hesemann.
The fear of the unknown has driven many rationalists (and the media) from studying the greatest mysteries of our times. Careful observation of events connected with these two phenomena has made the ET connection more obvious. This is the first book to relate these phenomena to one another.

VISITORS FROM SPACE: Concerning UFO Phenomena, ET contacts and Government Cover-up, by Richard Giles.
An introductory overview of serious research into UFOs, close encounters and government involvement. There is now a serious 'need-to-know' concerning governments, suppression of information, for not less than the future of our species is at stake.

A VISION OF THE AQUARIAN AGE: The Emerging Spiritual World-view, by Sir George Trevelyan.
This book is about the Second Renaissance in which we are setting out to explore the cosmos and reality. It is about the vision which is arising to meet the growing world crisis, and a new age of mystery, wonder and hope.

THE HUMAN CONDITION:

AVOIDING SOCIAL AND ECONOMIC DISASTER: The Politics of World Transformation, by Dr Rudolf Bahro.
Brilliantly analyses the world's committment to economic growth and consumption, its destructive effects, and how changes in our world view can come about. Bahro was a founder of the German Green Party and is one of the most creative visionaries in the new political economics.

HEAL THE WORLD: A do-it-yourself guide to Human & Planetary Transformation, by David Icke.
What can ordinary people do to heal the world? The notable 'truth teller' and world visionary who shows how our society is on a dangerously wrong track, gives practical pointers to what we need to do to change direction and save ourselves from extinction.

HOW TO BE HAPPY, by John Pepper.
The Dalai Lama said of this book: ". . . by paying as much attention to our inner development as to our external circumstances, we can lay the foundations sphere both ourselves and other to be happy."

WHO DIES? Conscious Living and Dying, by Stephen Levine
How to participate fully in life as a preparation for whatever may come next, be it sorrow or joy, loss or gain, death or a new wonderment at life. Stephen has worked with many dying and bereaved people, showing them positive ways forward. He has an enthusiastic following all over the world.

MOON OVER WATER: Meditation made clear, for beginners and initiates, by Jessica Macbeth.
Written with gentleness and humour, without dogma, it is packed with clear and practical insights and instruction on silent meditation, and has become a standard work on the subject.

There are many more books like these, and on healing and the human potential, on Gateway's list. Why not write today for a catalogue? It might be a passport for you to a new and transformed reality!